WORKTOWNERS AT BLACKPOOL

WORKTOWNERS AT BLACKPOOL

Mass-Observation and popular leisure
in the 1930s

Edited by
Gary Cross

Afterword by
John K. Walton

London and New York

First published 1990
by Routledge
11 New Fetter Lane, London EC4P 4EE

Simultaneously published in the USA and Canada
by Routledge
a division of Routledge, Chapman and Hall, Inc.
29 West 35th Street, New York, NY 10001

Typeset in 10/12 pt Palatino by
Colset Private Ltd, Singapore
Printed in Great Britain by
TJ Press (Padstow) Ltd, Padstow, Cornwall

British Library Cataloguing in Publication Data
Worktowners at Blackpool mass-observation and popular
leisure in the 1930s.
1. Lancashire. Blackpool. Social life, history
I. Cross, Gary
942.7'65

ISBN 0-415-04071-X

Library of Congress Cataloging in Publication Data
Worktowners at Blackpool: Mass-Observation and popular leisure in the 1930s:
edited by Gary Cross; afterword by John K. Walton.
p.   cm.
Includes bibliographical references.
ISBN 0-415-04071-X
1. Leisure—England—Blackpool (Lancashire)—History—20th
century.   2. Working class—England—Blackpool (Lancashire)-History—20th
century.   3. Mass-Observation.   I. Cross, Gary S.
GV76.E7B588   1990
917.53—dc20   89-49693

CONTENTS

CONTENTS

INTRODUCTION: MASS-OBSERVATION AND WORKTOWNERS AT PLAY

Gary Cross

In January 1937, a small band of young English people formed the research group, Mass-Observation. This collective of artists, students, non-academic social scientists, and workers undertook the ambitious and, to some, naive task of creating a 'new science of ourselves'. Combining an enthusiasm for close observation of ordinary life with a desire to present these facts to the public, Mass-Observation set out to overturn the academic world of social science. This group went in many directions. One of its most celebrated projects was the community study of Worktown (or Bolton), a cotton centre in West Lancashire, and of its 'outcropping', the seaside resort of Blackpool. While four volumes from this two-year study were to be published, only *The Pub and the People* ever saw print.[1]

Now that fifty years have past, the Mass-Observer's panoramas of Lancashire life in the Depression can be seen through the lens of historical perspective. Perhaps the most fascinating of these pictures are from the files of observations of Worktowners at play. Drawn from some three dozen draft chapters and reports from the Mass-Observation Archive at the University of Sussex, this book tries to preserve the flavour and method of the Mass-Observers while giving the texts clarity and focus. I view it as a document of twentieth-century social history, a sourcebook of the ordinary experience of leisure, and as an example of a unique and controversial anthropology of industrial life.

Mass-Observation was the brainchild of Charles Madge and Tom Harrisson. Both were dropouts from Cambridge, critical of the academic intelligentsia, and gifted journalists. Yet each gave the group a particular twist: Madge left Cambridge to become a correspondent for the *Daily Mirror* and joined a group of poets and documentary film makers in the writing of a collective surrealistic poem in 1935. Harrisson's interests differed: after quitting Cambridge, he became an amateur ornithologist and proved his organising skill by engaging hundreds in bird-watching trips. As he later pointed out, this was in many ways like his success in winning dozens to watch the people of Bolton. Forever restless, Harrisson soon was taking part in anthropological trips to Borneo, living among the cannibals of Malekula,

1

serving briefly as a consultant to Douglas Fairbanks in a film project in Tahiti, and writing a popular anthropology, *Savage Civilisation*, selected for the Left Book Club.[2]

Madge and Harrisson were brought together by a common interest in the popular response to the royal abdication of 1936; to them, this suggested the persistence of myth and superstition in Britain. Geoffrey Pike's call for an 'anthropological study' of Britain in the *New Statesman* brought Madge to announce the formation of Mass-Observation to undertake this task. Soon Harrisson joined.

From the beginning, Mass-Observation went in two quite different directions. First, Madge gathered an ever changing group of volunteer correspondents, recruited by notices published in magazines like *New Statesman*. This 'national panel' kept diaries and responded to a multiplicity of 'directives' – questions asked by the Mass-Observation office in London. The first effort led to *May the Twelfth*, a collection of one-day diaries kept on the day of the coronation of George VI.[3] Madge believed that these correspondents would provide the grist for a study of the 'collective unconscious of the ordinary men and women of the land'.[4] Second, Tom Harrisson organised a community study of Worktown (and Blackpool). As Harrisson put it, he went 'to study the cannibals of Britain'. Since mid-1936, Harrisson had been working at odd jobs and visiting the pubs in Bolton. In much the same way as he observed the Big Nambas, he lived among the 'natives' of Lancashire. By February 1937, six supporters joined Harrisson in Northtown (soon called Worktown).[5]

Both Madge and Harrisson drew upon a wide circle of associates for intellectual and financial support in the early years. They claimed assistance from such diverse luminaries as H. G. Wells, Bertrand Russell, the economist P. Sargant Florence, the BBC commentator and professor John Hilton, the psychologist T. H. Pear, the biologist Julian Huxley, and many others. Two Northern industrialists, Sir Thomas Barlow (whose daughter was an observer) and Sir Ernest Simon, provided funds. Mass-Observation obtained help also from the publisher, Victor Gollancz, who gave the group generous advances for Worktown books. A steady if transient supply of unemployed, largely Southern, and university-educated youth willingly took jobs or lived on subsistence pay as 'full-time observers' in Bolton. According to Mass-Observation, up to sixty were involved at one time or another in this project; and in addition to the five 'permanent' observers stationed in Blackpool for most of the fourteen months following August 1937 and field workers from Bolton who came to Blackpool for long weekends, about twenty-five university students descended on the resort town during holidays to observe.[6]

By November 1938, Harrisson had shifted his attention to London, and although Madge continued the Bolton project, the Worktown study was permanently abandoned shortly after the war began. In 1940, Madge and

Harrisson worked for the Ministry of Information doing a study of the impact of the Blitz on civilian morale. By 1941, Madge broke from Harrisson to join John Maynard Keynes in investigating consumption and saving patterns. In 1950, he joined the sociology faculty at Birmingham University.[7] Meanwhile, in 1941, Mass-Observation shifted from the Ministry of Information (which distrusted its non-quantitative survey techniques) and did research for the Advertising Service Guild, a consortium of seven agencies. During the war, M-O published books and booklets dealing with a wide assortment of home front issues from attitudes towards rationing and expectations of post-war holidays and social services to workplace behaviour in war factories and women's attitudes towards family planning.[8] Harrisson entered the military and in 1944 was sent behind Japanese lines in Borneo; H. D. Willcock largely took over the Mass-Observation office.

When Harrisson returned to England in 1946, he found radically new conditions. The techniques he used before the war no longer worked in the more pragmatic world of market research; moreover, the supply of cheap observers had dried up in the post-war boom. Soon Harrisson was back in Southeast Asia where he became a museum curator in Kuching, turning his attention to the study of paleontology, birds, turtles, and monkeys. In 1949, Mass-Observation became a limited company providing consulting services to advertisers and product developers. The war and 'cool careerism' (as Charles Madge wrote in 1961) turned M-O and its leaders from their idealism of the late 1930s to market research.[9]

Yet, in 1960, Tom Harrisson returned to England and gathered a group to write an update, *Britain Revisited* (1961). In 1970, with the founding of the Mass-Observation Archive at Sussex University, he returned to the manuscripts from the Worktown study (among other projects). This effort was cut short by his death in a car accident in Thailand in 1976.[10]

*

During the early years, Madge and Harrisson's approach was deceptively simple: 'M-O's job is to study real life; and the people it studies are people who can be interested immediately in the results, which often directly concern their everyday lives.' 'Real life' included everything from 'talking to sleeping, fighting to drinking, churches to brothels, jokes to crowd hysteria. To the sociologist everything is a social problem.' 'Our first concern', Madge and Harrisson wrote in 1937, 'is to collect data, not to interpret it.'[11]

The social survey or opinion poll was not enough. Harrisson favoured observation of people in their own time and space – in the routine of their work in the card-room of the mill or on the Promenade at Blackpool in those nine days per year when they were completely free from work. The Mass-Observers had a keen eye for the physical and cultural worlds of ordinary people; they had a passionate interest in how people behaved in their familiar surroundings of bars, churches, and dance halls. What people said in overheard conversations was as important as opinion polls, perhaps even more so. Like anthropologists, Mass-Observers collected cultural artefacts: the postcard sent home from Blackpool, the vacation brochure, candy rock, and the themes of popular music hall jokes and songs. Only these collages of facts could display 'real life'.[12]

Madge and Harrisson were natural journalists, publishing the results of their investigations in cheap pamphlets and popular articles. They were broadly part of the documentary movement, which from 1934 attempted through film, picture, and popular writing to present everyday life to the people themselves, unfiltered by the 'official media'.[13] In 1937, the Mass-Observers anticipated titles of articles such as 'What is on your Mantel-pieces?' and 'What do You Mean by Freedom?' Topics to be studied included: behaviour of people at war memorials, shouts and gestures of motorists, anthropology of football games, anti-semitism, distribution and significance of dirty jokes, and the private lives of midwives. The small book *Britain* (1939) is full of material of this type. Even later pamphlets like *Meet Yourself on Sunday* (1947) were good examples of this popular sociology.[14]

The methodological limits of this approach were often noted, even by friends: Bronislaw Malinowski admitted in 1938, 'they had started from the side of a rough and perhaps crude empiricism. They also did not encumber themselves with either . . . methodological scruple, conceptual precision or terminological consistency.'[15] Yet he was sure that the 'main idea' is '100 percent right'. The Mass-Observers granted 'social significance to ordinary life and the subjective experience'. They provided 'subjective data which form scientific analysis'. And the group succeeded in introducing anthropological ideas to the study of British culture.[16]

The historian, Angus Calder, may well be right that the group was largely ignorant of social theory and sociological method. This surely made their empiricism all the more natural to them. As early as 1937, Harrisson argued that the real social questions will emerge from the interaction of both the 'untrained observer' and the 'scientific expert'. This cooperative approach suggests an openness to new models but also masks theoretical uncertainty.[17]

Of course, Harrisson was indebted to some aspects of cultural anthropology (especially Malinowski's functionalism). Observers drew upon the qualitative approaches of the new sociology of communities. Harrisson corresponded with Robert Lynd and was influenced by the Lynds' *Middletown* and the Austrian group that observed the unemployed in Marienthal. He also took an interest in the social psychology of everyday life, especially as interpreted by O. A. Oeser: observers drew out meanings from fads, attitudes towards media stars, and popular religion.[18] Harrisson condemned such well-known models as the London and Liverpool social surveys of the 1930s.[19] These studies – following in the tradition of the Booth and Rowntree investigations of the turn of the century – were patronizing; their economic and social classifications were arid and lifeless.[20] The Mass-

Observers' passion for the subjective lives and environments of the common people was *their theory*.

This approach produced both the fresh insights and blind alleys of the autodidact. Angus Calder argues that 'the war saved M-O's methodological bacon' for it forced its leaders to focus their observations on specific issues and to direct their energies to practical problems.[21] This shift of direction also produced the climate for the group's transformation into a commercial public opinion service.

Yet there was another element to Mass-Observation – an undercurrent of political consciousness. In the crisis year of 1939, Harrisson and Madge warned: 'the democratic system has broken down in other countries, and may break down in our own. . . . The voicelessness of every man and the smallness of the group which controls fact-getting and fact-distributing' created an 'urgent situation'. By seeking to give the ordinary citizen a voice, M-O was making a political statement.[22]

This quest for the opinion and the audience of the everyman was, however, tempered by pessimism towards popular culture. The signs of barbarism in Nazi Germany had their analogies in the customs of the savage and in the 'familiar but no less curious [customs] which prevail at home'. An interest in the 'superstitions' of modern Britain led Harrisson to join Mass-Observation. He held that modern culture is an adaptation of 'old superstitions to new conditions'. The Mass-Observers found many instances of this principle in the popular attractions of Blackpool amusement parks. At the side-show stalls, they found the religious fatalism of the past directed towards 'modern science' in the fascination with the exhibition of a 'death ray' and faith in the 'miracle' of the fortune telling machine. Harrisson believed that these quasi-religious ideas and behaviours were manipulated by 'suggestion for commercial, political, or other reasons'.[23] Harrisson claimed that M-O did not want to 'pass a moral judgment on superstition but simply to examine and describe it'. Still this treatment of working-class culture as 'tribal life' was a rejection of the progressivist presumptions about modernity in industrial-urban culture.[24]

While this anthropological model assumes the survival of the irrational in modern culture, it did not go so far as to suggest that the masses were essentially primitives. As Stuart Laing argues, the word 'mass' in the name Mass-Observation did not imply (as it would in the 1950s) the homogeneity and passivity of the manipulated majority.[25] Part of the point of Mass-Observation was to inform the people of their 'superstitions' and thus, like in Freudian therapy, to enhance the possibility of reasoned decision to change behaviour. Moreover, beneath this theoretical overlay of cultural determinism, the observers at Blackpool and Bolton found workers who could laugh at the impresario's idea of collective fantasy. There was always an ambiguity.

*

The Worktown project was the most ambitious and perhaps the best example of the M-O method, spanning the years 1937 to 1940. John Sommerfield was director of field work at Bolton and largely responsible for *The Pub and the People*. Herbert Howarth played a similar role in Blackpool and was later an English professor at the University of Cairo. Other major observers were Bruce Watkin, Walter Hood (later a noted trades unionist), Brian Barefoot, Julian Trevelyan (painter), Humphrey Spender (photographer), Zita Crossman (journalist and wife of the Labour MP), Bill Naughton (coalman turned writer), Richard Glew (a Blackpool contact), Ralph Partner (later a *Times* correspondent in Moscow), Gertrude Wagner, and Woodrow Wyatt.[26]

Investigators in Bolton 'penetrated every part of local life'. As Harrisson wrote, 'at least three-quarters of the work was concentrated in *describing* what observers could see and hear without doing anything to alter the situation or affect the conversation'. M-O in Blackpool, however, made no effort to operate undercover and even sought publicity in the spirit of the holidays stunts that prevailed in this summer resort. Although observers took weekend trips to Blackpool as early as Easter 1937, by August 1937 M-O established an office on Shetland Road. As one observer wrote:

> The office was soon turned from a respectable front sitting room, into a cross between a drawing room with its charts and diagrams, pinned on the wall, and a novelty or gift shop and a toffee shop with its sweets in cellophane wrappers. Picture post-cards and trick novelties all over the mantelpiece; and the mantelpiece figures were decorated with a string of coral beads and a monkey on elastic. Blackpool Rock and a trick bottle of Bass completed the set. Newspaper and cuttings were scattered all over the table, chairs and floor.[27]

Observers fanned out in the whole range of boarding houses and hotels and went on a wide variety of missions. While sometimes they simply followed isolated individuals (like a pastor in the crowd in Blackpool), often with rather uninteresting results, gradually the study developed focus as the investigators gained knowledge of both towns. Observers also employed a vast array of creative, if not always fruitful, information gathering techniques – from analysing the contents of children's classroom essays to listing themes in ordinary conversations and music hall jokes to describing the crowd dynamics at Saturday night dances. Harrisson, who probably wrote most of the draft chapters, came up to Blackpool for long weekends. According to Walter Hood's memory (1972), Harrisson would read and write in bed, inspired by the continual replaying of George Formby's 'When I'm Cleaning Windows' on a hand-operated gramophone.[28]

Obviously these were not the projects of the dispassionate cultural anthropologist. They were part of a populist trend which attracted middle-class intellectuals to discover, with George Orwell, that 'race apart' – the working class of the industrial North. Not only *Road to Wigan Pier* but numerous less well-known works centred on the 'real life' of industrial workers. Participant-observation techniques, used by E. Wight Baake in his works concerning the unemployed, were similar to those used in the Worktown study. Perhaps also influential was Walter Greenwood's portrayal of the culture of the 'distressed areas' in the novel, *Love on the Dole*. Middle-class feelings of guilt and anxiety attracted some to these books and to Worktown – as the prosperous South slowly became aware of protracted industrial distress and unemployment in the old industrial centres of the North. Yet, like other investigators, Mass-Observers found workers who were not militant but fatalistic and isolated.[29]

Worktown was an ideal choice for study in that it expressed for many the essence of the grimy North. Against a growing nostalgia for the rural landscape, Bolton was the nadir of the ideal: 'Bolton', note William Gerharde, 'looked like the bottom of a pond with the water drained off. In here were the people who, if they could endure this, could endure anything.'[30] Between Manchester and Bolton, noted Priestley, was an 'ugliness that is so complete that it is almost exhilarating'.[31] The industrial Northern environment produced an honest proletariat, an inspiration for the soft, jaded Southerner. The act of observation expressed a complex of feelings – guilt, social concern, curiosity, and a search for the 'authentic' in the hardy North.

The Mass-Observers were particularly interested in culture, less labour or economic conditions. They focused on four broad themes: popular religion, the culture of popular politics, the culture of the pub, and finally the industrial holiday. It was in the pubs, the chapels, and the dreams and realities of the annual holiday that Worktowners really lived. And they expressed – through everyday encounters, seasonal rituals, and symbols – those 'superstitions' or values that dominated their lives.

*

Surely the key to the 'real life' of the Worktowner was the changing meaning of holiday leisure. The Mass-Observers chose this topic in a context of widespread interest in the potential and threat of mass leisure among social scientists, adult educators, and publicists in the 1930s.[32] In his *In Praise of Idleness*, Bertrand Russell looked forward to a time when instead of a leisure class, which 'produced a few Darwins and many fox hunters', 'ordinary men and women, having the opportunity of a happy life, will become more kindly and less inclined to view others with suspicion'. But for others, like Henry Durant, mass leisure in the age of commercialisation had more pessimistic implications: it produced a 'machinery of amusement [which] completes the industrial training of turning actors into spectators'.[33]

This ambiguity towards workers' leisure was reflected in the thoughts of

M-O investigators. For example, one observer wrote in 1938 about the Savoy Dance Hall at Deansgate:

> What strikes me most about this place, its people, is the spontaneous reality and genuineness of everything. All present are working-class people – nearly all are workers in the mills and factories. To them, this dance is temporary freedom from hard work and worries – 'Let's enjoy ourselves to-day for to-morrow we. . . . ' No class; no snobbery; no forced laughter – just reality.

Yet in a preface to a report on the 'usual detail' of a dance hall crowd in Bolton (January 1940), one young male observer found 'merely mechanical shuffling over a syncopated and cacophonous din'. Dance music was a ruling-class drug; it was a way to 'falsify normal human images'. He wished the audience would abandon the 'Blue Heaven' themes for 'more topical and penetrating subjects' and predicted that socialism would bring 'the gradual disappearance of jazz and "modern dancing" and the start of more steady and less hysterical amusement, with more intelligence to guide the development of bodily grace and musical satisfaction'.[34] These conflicting perceptions of working-class leisure run more subtly throughout the Worktown material.

While much literary concern with workers' leisure in the 1930s was rather paternalistic, focusing on problems of education and provisioning, a few writers were more open to workers' recreation as it was. Note Mass-Observer adviser John Hilton in his objective and amusing survey of working-class opinion in *Why I Go in For the Pools* (1935). This approach was echoed in M-O's *The Pub and the People* and prevails in this panorama of holiday play.[35]

The international movement for the paid holiday in the 1930s also stimulated interest in the leisure question. In the first summer (1937) of the Worktown study, Bolton textile workers were preparing to give testimony to a House of Commons Holiday with Pay Committee. James Whittaker, a BBC journalist and author of a well-known book about Lancashire, had offered in the *Bolton Evening News* a £5 prize for the reader who sent in the best statement on what they would like to do on holiday. The essays from 220 contestants provided an important source for M-O's Blackpool study. The major themes which dominated the holiday debate in Parliament and in the press were echoed in the Blackpool study – the problem of inadequate funding for a 'real holiday' (especially for the large family) and the congestion due to concentrated annual holidays in August.[36] A relatively weak Holiday with Pay Act was passed in 1938.[37]

In the 1930s, the holiday was a major domestic political issue. Moreover, leisure and its organisation were contested terrain for both the international right and the left. Leisure was not to be merely a privately experienced compensation for industrial work but rather a means to recover the lost values of family and community and to inculcate political ideals.

The Depression ironically produced a new interest in the relationship between work and leisure. Workers' leisure was a major theme in studies of the culture of the unemployed. As the traditional cycle of work and non-work time was disrupted by joblessness, sociologists found that accustomed leisure activities also declined. In a society where poverty was not general, economic scarcity meant loss of self-respect. Worktown observers found that wage earners defined themselves not as jobholders but as consumers; their ability to express themselves in funded free time was critical to their self-esteem. Not surprisingly observers found a passion for holiday saving clubs and carefree holiday spending.[38]

In the 1930s, the holiday had become a right of citizenship. Harold Laski and Clement Attlee even organised a committee to subsidise holidays for the jobless: the 'industrial refugees . . . need to get away from the misery and drabness of their everyday lives', their manifesto affirmed. And a growing awareness that mothers too needed time away from their domestic work was reflected in the Mass-Observers' sensitivity to the significance of holidays for Worktown women.[39] The central meaning of the holiday in the lives of Worktowners was expressed not only in the mad crush of fun-seekers at Blackpool but in the saving clubs and anticipations of mill families through-out the work year. The holiday expressed a democratic right as well as a compensation for the rigours of work.

As important was the question of the quality of the holiday. The seaside holiday had a special meaning in the on-going debate about mass leisure. The commercial seaside resort had grown with the democratisation of leisure time in the second half of the nineteenth century. And while many resorts succeeded in maintaining their exclusivity, Blackpool had become by the 1870s a popular centre, increasingly catering to the middle and working classes of nearby Lancashire towns. It was probably the most popular resort in Europe in the early twentieth century.[40]

At the same time, Nonconformist religious and socialist groups were repulsed by the mass commercial holiday. From the 1890s, they produced a movement of country ramblers and holiday campers in a cult of nature and fellowship. The seaside resort may have retained the loyalty of the masses but not the leftist elite. Priestley reflected this revulsion when he distin-guished between that section of the working class who 'does not care for mass entertainment and prefers to spend its leisure in quieter places, cycling and walking and playing games in the sun' and the 'less intelligent and enter-prising' who are 'patrons of the New Blackpool, which knows what to with the passive and the listless'. The attempt to bring the comradely ethic and contact with nature experienced in camping and group travel to the working classes was the promise of groups like the Holiday Fellowship and Workers' Travel Association. These organisations grew in the 1930s, despite their minimal impact on those attracted to Blackpool.[41] The dichotomy between the communion with nature and the commercial fleshpot ran through the Worktown surveys of holiday dreams and coloured observers' responses to Blackpool culture. For all of their vaunted objectivity, Worktown investigators were often repulsed by what they saw as the tacky commercialism of Blackpool. For them, Blackpool was a symbol of the modernised primitivism of the passive working class.

Yet M-O's study of leisure does let other images show through. Unlike other studies of mass culture in the period, observers reveal the time and space of popular leisure, its relationship to the work year, and its symbols and images.[42]

*

The Worktown/Blackpool project was never completed. This was not because it lacked coherence but because of the accidents of war and personality. On a number of occasions from 1942 to 1976, in between his other interests, Harrisson planned to complete the Worktown series with updated research. His *Britain Revisited* was a hurried effort to do this but failed to exploit seriously the Worktown or Blackpool material. What remains today from the study are a series of texts and reports. They do not offer a theory of industrial culture, but they reveal a unique, deeply textured image of the holiday and some of its meaning in Lancashire in the Depression.

Of course, the reader will find many gaps in the Worktown/Blackpool materials. These include: 1) the social scientist may be occasionally appalled by the lack of survey technique and quantitative sophistication. 2) Workers were generally seen as a homogeneous mass; the contemporary social scientist may be disappointed with the paucity of nuance in the analysis of class, age, and gender. Harrisson despised Gustav Le Bon's elitist analysis of the crowd, but observers seldom revealed Worktowners on holiday as individuals. Rather they were primarily seen as an aggregate acting, not perhaps according to the rules of the collective unconscious, but surely as a mass and often without much self-awareness. 3) The observers never really got on the 'inside' of the Worktowners personal lives. Little material on home life was gathered. The well-known privacy of the Lancashire working class was revealed in the failure of the observers to 'penetrate' this bastion of personal life.[43] 4) The dynamics of the work process and of labour relations were far less developed than the cultural side of the Worktowners' lives. This neglect of economic society surely limits the analytical power of the data. 5) Contrary to Harrisson's claim, observers were not 'unobserved'. Not only did public school accents give them away, but obvious class privileges and values shaped how they perceived and were seen by the Worktowners. One observer was hardly unobtrusive when he arrived at Blackpool in his Bentley while Worktowners took the train. And the views of both observers quoted above towards the dance hall – surely the central leisure activity in many

Worktowners' week – were a barrier to objectivity. 6) Finally the research is hampered by the lack of comparative and historical perspective. Harrisson was aware of this and tried to rectify it in his update study in *Britain Revisited* (1961). He found that beach behaviour had grown more informal but that surprisingly little had changed since the late 1930s. Still on the wider social canvas, popular attitudes towards the holiday were beginning to change even during the war. M-O reports on holiday expectations in the 1940s showed that the appeal of the crowded seaside was declining as young workers began at least to dream of long-distance travel and the charms of the holiday camp. John Walton suggests still other biases in his essay on the image and reality of Blackpool in this volume. Clearly the Worktown/Blackpool material is merely a snapshot – but one taken with a panoramic lens.

As Golby and Purdue have recently argued, popular leisure – in both the 'traditional' fairs and 'modern' Blackpools – shares more than a susceptibility to commercial exploitation: they both reveal a common anarchism, a refusal of these pleasure spots to take themselves seriously. Yet M-O's image of Worktowners and their holiday escape also suggests much about the evolution of mass commercial leisure and the significance of leisure to the labouring classes in a not atypical corner of the industrial world. The study also reveals as much about the observers and their quest for understanding a 'foreign people' in their midst. The Worktown project was filtered through the idealistic young minds of a generation of British intellectuals lodged between the Depression and the Second World War.[44]

In a period when historians are calling for 'thick descriptions' and when anthropologists and literary critics are embracing new theories of language, the Mass-Observers' details of beach behaviour and conversation and their descriptions of sideshow curiosities may appear to be more than 'crude empiricism'. Veteran Mass-Observer Julian Trevelyan wrote over thirty years ago: 'What became of all this material that cluttered up the rooms of Davenport Street, the little house in Bolton that became our centre? How could it possibly be used? We liked to think that it was forming a museum for some future generation of social historians.'[45] Welcome to the museum!

NOTES

1 Of course, Harrisson and others wrote popular magazine and newspaper articles drawing from the Blackpool material. Some of these are 'So This is Blackpool', *Picture Post*, 7 January 1939; Tom Harrisson's 'Industrial Spring', *New Writing*, n.s. 2, Spring 1939; and 'Blackpool Remembers', *Shelf Appeal*, October 1937.

2 The following summary of M-O history is dependent upon Angus Calder, 'Mass-Observation 1937–1949', in *Essays on the History of British Sociological Research*, Martin Bulmer, ed., Cambridge, 1985, pp. 121–36. For additional material on the founders of Mass-Observation and their circle, see T. Green, *The Adventurers: Four Profiles of Contemporary Travellers*, London, 1970; M.

Green, *Children of the Sun. A Narrative of 'Decadence' in England after 1918*, London, 1977, pp.26–36; and especially Tom Jeffrey, *Mass-Observation: A Short History*, Centre for Contemporary Cultural Studies, Occasional Paper no.33, Birmingham, 1978, and Nick Stanley, 'The Extra Dimension: A Study and Assessment of the Methods Employed by Mass-Observation in its First Period, 1937–1940', Ph.D. Dissertation, Birmingham Polytechnic, 1981.

3 Charles Madge and Herbert Jennings, *May the Twelfth: A Mass Observation Day Survey*, London, 1937.

4 Alan and Mary Tomlinson, 'Mass-Observation Surveys: Insights into Leisure and Culture', a paper for the Sports Council, SSRC, a Review for the Joint Panel on Leisure and Recreation Research, 1984, pp.1–2. This source lists relevant materials in the M-O Archive.

5 Mass-Observation, *The Pub and the People*, London, 1970, reprint of 1942 work, 1970 preface; Charles Madge and Tom Harrisson, *First Year's Work*, London, 1938, pp.7, 46; Green, *The Adventurers*, pp.97–118.

6 The landlady of the M-O office in Blackpool recalled forty-six observers in an undated report. There were doubtless others who dropped in and out of this highly informal fact-gathering group. Mass-Observation Archive, Worktown Papers, 48E 'Holiday Town' (a post-war report) and 'Mass-Observation in Blackpool'. See also Mass-Observation, *The Pub*, 1942 preface, pp.8 and 13, and Angus Calder and Dorothy Sheridan, *Speak for Yourself: A Mass-Observation Anthology, 1937–1949*, London, 1984, p.41.

7 Liz Stanley in her paper, 'Economics of Everyday Life: Mass-Observation and the 1930s' presented at the British Sociology Association, Edinburgh, 1988, stresses that Madge had become committed to more conventional economics research as early as November 1938, when he took over the Bolton office from Harrisson and began a study of consumption and savings, a project that won the blessing of J. M. Keynes and academic sociologists. See also Mass-Observation Archive, Topical Collection 69.

8 See Calder and Sheridan, *Speak for Yourself*, Chapters 3–6.

9 Tom Harrisson, *Britain Revisited*, London, 1961, Postscript by Madge, pp.275–81.

10 Calder, 'Mass-Observation 1937–1949', pp.121–2, and Green, *The Adventurers*, pp.140–56.

11 Mass-Observation, *The Pub*, p.12, and T. Harrisson, 'The Future of Sociology', *Pilot Papers*, vol.2, March 1947, p.10, cited in Tomlinson, 'Mass-Observation Surveys', p.2. Charles Madge and Tom Harrisson, *Mass-Observation*, London, 1937, p.34.

12 Mass-Observation, *The Pub*, pp.10–11.

13 Included in the documentary movement were Stefan Lorant, later founder of *Picture Post*, Humphrey Spender and Humphrey Jennings, leading members of the GPO Film Unit (both for a time Mass-Observers), as well as Stuart Legg and W. H. Auden. George Orwell, *Road to Wigan Pier*, London, 1937, and J. B. Priestley, *English Journey*, London, 1934, were perhaps the best-known expressions of this tendency. See Nick Stanley, 'Beyond Empiricism: Social Reportage via Artistic Means in the Mass-Observation Experiment, 1937–40', in M-O Archive for full discussion and bibliography.

14 Madge and Harrisson, *Mass-Observation*, p.40. Calder and Sheridan, *Speak for Yourself*, p.4; Charles Madge and Tom Harrisson, *Britain, A Mass Observation Study*, Penguin Special, London, 1939; and Mass-Observation, *Meet Yourself on Sunday*, London, 1947.

15 Malinowski cited in Mass-Observation, *The Pub*, pp.6–8. See also Malinowski's

comments in Madge and Harrisson, *First Year's Work*, pp. 83–121. Raymond Firth, 'An Anthropologist's View of Mass-Observation', *Sociological Review*, 31, 1939, rejects the presumption of M-O that science and random observation were compatible. T. H. Marshall in 'Is Mass Observation Moonshine?', *Highway*, December 1937, p. 48 (also in *Sociology at the Crossroads*, London, 1963, p. 16) remarked: 'Some of us still prefer to spend time over such gross and obvious things as law, justice, authority and citizenship instead of joining the merry hunt after the laws that determine whether men lean on the right or left side against the bar when drinking.' These problems were obvious in *May the Twelfth*, and even their *Britain* was really only good journalism. See also Calder, 'Mass-Observation', pp. 129–30, and Stanley 'Extra Dimension', Chapter 4.

16 Mass-Observation, *The Pub*, pp. 6–8. M-O was attacked in 1937 for overgeneralising (*Daily Mail*) and under-theorising (*Daily Worker*), for belabouring the obvious (*The Listener*), for formlessness, and for too great a preponderance of left-wing thought (*Times Literary Supplement*). See Madge and Harrisson, *Mass-Observation*, pp. 56–7, for details.

17 Harrisson said he found intellectual allies in a motley band of social investigators and reformists. He claimed as friends the Industrial Welfare Society, the National Institute of Industrial Psychology, the Peckham Health Centre, and the Institute of Social Research (Frankfurt), etc. – the leaders of many of which hardly shared the populist empirical views of the Mass-Observers. ibid.

18 Harrisson admits the influence of American sociology in *The Pub*, pp. 349–50. In addition to the Lynds, he notes Robert Park and E. W. Burgess of the University of Chicago, the community studies of Yale sociologists, the University of North Carolina Society Study Series, and the Payne Fund's Cinema Research. M. Johoda, P. Lazarsfeld, and H. Zeisel, *Die Arbeitslosen von Marienthal*, Leipzig, 1933, is in the same tradition. Note also O. A. Oeser, 'Methods and Assumptions of Field Work in Social Anthropology', *British Journal of Psychology*, vol. 27, 1937.

19 Madge and Harrisson, *Mass-Observation*, pp. 57–60, and M-O Archive, Worktown Papers, 46A. See also Tom Jeffrey, 'Origins and Development of Mass-Observation', paper for the Annual Conference of the Society for the Social History of Medicine, University of Liverpool, July 1980 (M-O Archive).

20 J. Llewellyn Smith, ed., *The New Survey of London Life and Leisure*, London, 1934, and D. Caradog Jones, ed., *The Social Survey of Merseyside*, Liverpool, 1934. Note also D. M Goodfellow, *Tyneside: The Social Facts*, Newcastle, 1940, and B. S. Rowntree, *Poverty and Progress*, London, 1941.

21 Calder, 'Mass-Observation', p. 130.

22 Madge and Harrisson, *Britain*, preface; Jeffrey, 'Origins', pp. 3–4, and Calder, 'Mass-Observation', p. 127. See especially Penny Summerfield, 'Mass-Observation: Social Research or Social Movement?', *Journal of Contemporary History*, vol. 20, 1985, pp. 439–52.

23 Like the members of the Frankfurt School, Mass-Observation was convinced that 'traditional art, science and philosophy was unable to address the meaning and consequences of these superstitions'. Madge and Harrisson, *Mass-Observation*, pp. 16–17.

24 Madge and Harrisson, *Mass-Observation*, pp. 10–12. See also Tom Harrisson, *Borneo Jungle*, London, 1938.

25 Stuart Laing, 'Presenting "Things as They Are": John Sommerfield's *May Day* and Mass-Observation', in *Class, Culture, and Social Change: A New View of the 1930s*, Frank Gloversmith, ed., Sussex, 1980, pp. 142–60.

26 M-O Archive, Worktown Papers, 48A and 'Former Mass-Observers File', Memo, Charles Madge to Tom Harrisson; Mass-Observation, *The Pub*, p. 8; and Green, *The Adventurers*, pp. 119–20.

27 M-O Archive, Worktown Papers, 48A.

28 Mass-Observation, *The Pub*, pp. 6–10; Calder and Sheridan, *Speak for Yourself*, p. 41; and M-O Archive, 'Former Mass-Observers File', Walter Hood's letter to Mrs Ree, 2 April 1972. See also in same file the 'Golf' interview of Hood.

29 Examples of this literature are E. Wight Baake, *The Unemployed Man*, London, 1933; Pilgrim Trust, *Men Without Work*, Cambridge, 1938; Carnegie Trust, *Disinherited Youth*, Edinburgh, 1943. For additional background see Stephen Constantine, *Social Conditions Britain 1918–1939*, London, 1983, and John Stevenson and C. Cook, *The Slump: Society and Politics during the Depression*, London, 1979, Chapter 1. For a broad background see Steven Jones, *Workers at Play: A Social and Economic History of Leisure, 1918–1939*, London, 1986.

30 William Gerharde, *The English Genius*, London, 1939, cited in Ian Jeffrey, *The British Landscape*, London, 1984, pp. 11–13.

31 Priestley, *English Journey*, pp. 263–65.

32 Some examples of this literature are E. B. Castle's survey of adult education in *The Coming of Leisure*, London, 1936, and the similar work, Lancelot Hogben, *Education for an Age of Plenty*, London, 1937; studies of unemployment and leisure include C. Northcott Greene, *Time to Spare*, London, 1933; L. R. Missen, *The Employment of Leisure*, Exeter, 1935; and especially Baake, *The Unemployed Man*. Finally one should note works like John Hammond, *The Growth of Common Enjoyment*, London, 1933, and Madeline Rooff, *Youth and Leisure*, Edinburgh, 1934.

33 Bertrand Russell, *In Praise of Idleness and Other Essays*, London, 1935, pp. 26–30, and Henry Durant, *The Problem of Leisure*, London, 1938, pp. 10–19.

34 M-O Archive, Worktown Project, W 42D.

35 John Hilton, *Why I Go in For the Pools*, London, 1935. Compare with the utilitarian approach of F. W. Ogilvie, *The Tourist Movement*, London, 1933, or the often patronising approaches of Smith, *New Survey of London Life*, vol. VI; Sidney Dark, *After Working Hours*, London, 1929; and Constance Harris, *The Use of Leisure in Bethnal Green*, London, 1927.

36 *Bolton Evening News* (20 September 1937); see Mass-Observation Archive for eleven 'File Reports' dealing with the holiday question between August 1940 and April 1949.

37 While this law only enabled statutory bodies to provide holidays with pay, debate over legislation stimulated the widespread extension of paid holidays through collective bargaining. The number of employees enjoying paid vacations increased from 1.5 million to 11 million in the 1930s. House of Commons, *Report on the Committee on Holidays with Pay*, London, April 1938, Cd. 5724, 1–30, and John Pimlott, *The Englishman's Holiday*, London, 1947, pp. 215–41.

38 Walter Greenwood, *Love on the Dole*, London, 1933, pp. 130–1, 171; William Boyd, *The Challenge of Leisure*, London, 1936, p. 50; Fernand Zweig, *Labour, Life, and Poverty*, London, 1951, pp. 43–4, 75–6. See also Gary Cross, 'Vacations for All: The Leisure Question in the Era of the Popular Front', *Journal of Contemporary History*, October 1989, and Paul Johnson, 'Credit and Thrift in the British Working Class, 1879–1939', in *The Working Class in Modern British History*, Jay Winter, ed., London, 1983, pp. 147–70.

39 'The National Committee to Provide Holiday for Unemployed Workers in Distressed Areas', London, 1938, in Trades Union Congress Archive, HD 5106. See also F. Zweig, *Women's Life and Labour*, London, 1952, 141–8.

40 Included in this rich literature are James Walvin, *Beside the Seaside*, London, 1978; Harriet Bridgeman and Elizabeth Drury, *Beside the Seaside*, London, 1977; Simon Adamson, *Seaside Piers*, London, 1977; the novel by J. L. Hodson, *Carnival at Blackport*, Manchester, 1938; B. Turner and S. Palmer, *The Blackpool Story*, Blackpool, 1976; John K. Walton, *The Blackpool Landlady: A Social History*, Manchester, 1978, and especially his *The English Seaside Resort: A Social History, 1750–1914*, London, 1984. Note also Harold Perkin, 'The Social Tone of Victorian Seaside Resorts in the North West', *Northern History*, vol. 11, 1975–6, pp. 180–94, and Sue Farant, 'London by the Sea: Resort Development on the South Coast of England, 1880–1939', *Journal of Contemporary History*, vol. 22, 1987, pp. 137–62.

41 Recent works on this movement are Jill Drower, *Good Clean Fun: The Story of Britain's First Holiday Camp*, London, 1983; Dennis Hardy, *Goodnight Campers! The History of the British Holiday Camp*, London, 1986; John Lowerson, 'Battles for the Countryside', in Gloversmith, *Class, Culture*, pp. 258–80; and Priestley, *English Journey*, pp. 267–8.

42 Madge and Harrisson, *Mass-Observation*, p. 4.

43 An attempt to reveal the private side of working-class life in this period is Phyllis Willmott, *Growing Up in a London Village: Family Life Between the Wars*, London, 1979.

44 J. M. Golby and A. W. Purdue, *The Civilisation of the Crowd*, London, 1984. Note Simmy Viinikka, 'The Summer Holiday as a Growth Industry and Literary Image in the 1930s', January 1979, unpublished paper in the M-O Archive.

45 Julian Trevelyan, *Indigo Days*, London, 1957.

EDITOR'S NOTE

A simple convention was followed in editing this material: where words or sentences are added for clarity or to facilitate transitions, I bracket them. When reports are quoted, I indent or place quotation marks around them and note where I edit out material with ellipses. All other material is edited from the 'texts'. Although there was no table of contents upon which to base the organisation of the study, I tried wherever possible to follow internal evidence as a guide for ordering the flow of the chapters. While some of the chapters are combined texts, unless bracketed, all titles are taken from the texts written by the Mass-Observation authors, principally Tom Harrisson.

Part 1

1

WORK

Blackpool is visited annually by 7,000,000 visitors who breathe the sea air and throng the 5,000 sideshows and joy-machines. They are greeted by the pierrots, the Sharma Yogis and the Five-Legged Cow, the Headless Woman, the Museum of Anatomy with the female Jesus and the pregnant male, Colonel Barker and his or her bride, the relics of Stiffkey, Professor Aubrey Winston Grey with his pool-winning Buddha, and the Revivalist Pastor, Four-Square Jefferies, under the Big Tent. Chinamen sell May's Vests and Sally's Whatnots in sugar sweet while the Sheikh machines tell fortunes against a background of T. E. Lawrence and the Sphinx.

This is the rich outcrop of industrialism, the bright mirror of how the workers spend their week of freedom from factory and mine. Powerful, often dominant in Blackpool culture is the Negroid, the Indian, the Oriental, and the Buddhist. These counteract the regular emphases of the rest of the year, spent in inland towns where the air is not so fresh, where many of the Blackpool shows would be unshowable.

One such town is Worktown, the town where we have been working on an intensive Mass-Observation survey for nearly two years. Blackpool and Worktown are essentially integrated. 95 per cent of Worktown's population have been there, 38 miles away – many more than have been to Manchester, which is nearer. So we have studied both Blackpool and Worktown, side by side, simultaneously, with headquarters and permanent personnel in each place. In this book we are going to give a picture of English civilisation which may at times seem un-English. In order to understand how Lancashire industrialism produced 'Europe's greatest seaside resort', we must understand how industrialism works in terms of all the ordinary people involved in it.

THE THREAD OF COTTON

Worktown's 170,000 people live on cotton; on cotton today it still manages to keep rates down, unemployment fairly well up, chimneys smoking many tons a year on to the slate roofs of 50,000 houses, mostly in continuous gardenless rows, 75 per cent with four rooms (14 per cent less), mainly

19

without baths and with exterior lavatories. The trees in the parks have black stems and the town offers only 1 acre of open space per 500 people. Of 65,000 people employed, over half work in branches of the cotton industry.[1]

Axis to the cotton industry is the spinning section of the cotton industry. Employing relatively few people, it is nevertheless the vital link in the thread of cotton. Most basic is the 'wheel-gate', the space between two spinning-mules, generally about 42 yards long, 6 yards wide. With their rows and rows of bobbins of white cotton, the lower platform of the mules continually moves out and draws the thread towards the centre of the alley-way, then moves back, with the whistle of thread and the bump of the wheels on the rails. That happens about 235 times an hour. In this alley-way, three men work: the 'spinner', the 'side-piecer', and the 'little-piecer'. All day long they walk up and down the alley-way, barefoot on the oily surface, stepping with precision without looking over the numerous rails, covering up to 20 miles a day with eyes trained on the whirling lines of cotton. The moment one breaks, you must 'piece it up', leaning over as the platform goes in towards the fixed part, and twisting quickly with thumb and first finger to rejoin the delicate broken ends of thread, with a cheap crude oil, spraying scrotal cancer down on your overalls . During these hours, life does seem to hang on a thread.

The spinner gets piece rates on a system of payment so complicated that only a few experts can really calculate it. He is the aristocrat of the mill workers, and his union has built a great hall, where most other unions and the Labour Party meet. It is bigger and more ornate than Conservative or Liberal headquarters. The piecers do, in effect, the same job as the spinner, though without the responsibility. Before the decline after 1920, the piecer was sure to get promoted to spinning. Now the alley between the mules is a dead-end: only about one in eight piecers have a chance of 'getting their wheels'. In consequence many piecers are now becoming middle-aged.

In 1937, the side-piecer and little-piecer, who are paid directly by the spinner, were receiving respectively 30 and 18 shillings per week. A married side-piecer would thus benefit economically by getting the sack. Recently these wages have been upped to just above the unemployed level. Yet most piecers have to pay dues to the spinners' unions, in which they have no vote and no delegated representation. These earnings seem absurdly low; but in Lancashire, the family is still the economic unit. The wife continues at work until her husband is promoted or until the care of the children becomes too burdensome. After a period of straightened means, the family budget improves: children go to work in the mill and family income increases as they grow older, since they remain at home until marriage and pay in their earnings to their mother, only receiving back a few shillings as pocket money.

Others work in weaving sheds which typically contain about 1,250 looms. The duty of the weaver is to watch for any breakages in the weft and to stop the loom and repair them when they occur. Under the old system, still widely in force, each weaver tended four looms, but would take on two more when assisted by a 'tenter' or juvenile learning the trade. The majority of the weavers are women; but the overlookers, who usually supervise about eighty looms each, are all male. The card-room, where girls work, prepares and cleans cotton for spinning; the noise is too great to enable speech, and card-room workers become skilful at lip reading.

The work [48 hours per week, including Saturday mornings] is exceedingly arduous. Eye strain especially affects ring-spinners [a more modern form of spinning which is gradually replacing the mules]. They are compelled to stand all day long in a narrow and confined space, with their eyes glued to the thread. [In the card-room, combers, if not careful, can get their hands trapped. Card tenters, brushing between machines, sometimes get caught by a moving belt or pulley.] The change from a humid atmosphere and the heat to the cold, bleak streets outside makes cotton operatives peculiarly subject to rheumatism and bronchial complaints, which are not improved by the smoke-laden air of the typical Lancashire town. Many mills are over a century old, so that the general amenities do not compare well with those of the most up-to-date factories. A diet of 'hot-pot', potato pie, meat pies, and fish and chips, bolted at breakfast or eaten in the heat and dust of the spinning room, is not conducive to good digestion.

Working for the first time in the cotton mills, three things impressed us most: 1) the way in which workers, some of them on the job twenty years, noticed the job and still felt the effects of heat, dust, and high humidity [of the mill]; 2) the constant focus on the clock or redlight in the trajectory of the day's work; and 3) the constant focus of interest on Friday in the trajectory of the week's work. [So let's take a look at that workday and week.] Most mill workers rush their breakfasts, or take a sandwich in paper and arrive some minutes early, while older men often arrive regularly twenty to thirty minutes ahead of time. Most walk to work but others get there by any of the tram lines which radiate on a complex loop from the town centre. The majority must be at work by 7:45.

Piecers made reports and kept diaries of their jobs. This one is representative of talk before and after work:

As we turned into our spinning-room, one spinner said, 'Oh, it's not so bad' (meaning the temperature of the room). Another spinner said: 'Aye, but wait till we've been running five minutes.' [The first spinner responded:] 'Yes they'll have to carry us out tonight!' [He] reached his pair of mules, shouted after looking at the thermometer, 'It is ninety degrees now.'

Dinner time, 12:15, as the engine stopped and everyone rushed out, a worker said, 'Is it warm enough?'

5:30 Coming out. A side-piecer says, 'It's like breathing fire in here.'

21

During the day the under-manager during his prowl round saw that the windows in our room were open about 1 inch. He complained to the spinners and made them close them.

[Another observer wrote]:

> In the mill the job is such that it demands constant attention. The machines need watching continually lest there is a hitch somewhere. Even when there is a pause when nothing needs doing and the tenters are resting on the machine, they are constantly glancing up and down the line. This is firstly, to see that all is well with them and, secondly to be on the look-out for the overlooker. . . . Most of the windows are of frosted glass. One or two are of plain glass, and give a view of the two factories opposite. . . . I often look out, but I have never yet seen anyone else looking out, even in the dinner-hour.

Frosted glass, in the weaving and doubling rooms, keeps the sun from affecting the cotton. Lest the threads should dry and snap, an atmosphere of tropical heat and humidity is maintained.

In all departments of the mill, the climax to the day is when the red bulb flashes for a second at one corner of the great room. Everyone waits, watches for that, clothed and ready to rush the swing doors and go out into the air. With a rush and scramble, workers stream out of the mill the moment the red light goes at 5:30. Flecked all over with pieces of cotton waste, they seem to have come from some internal snowstorm.[2] The route to and from work is so familiar that the only things in which people take an interest are the people ahead. 'They never look at the shop-windows as they pass in the evening,' wrote an observer who came to work in the card-room.

The average wage of weavers working four looms for 1937 in Worktown was 30/4 per week. Winders averaged 25/10, warpers 30/1. It is easy to see how, with low wages, the emphasis on payday becomes particular. Unquestionably in Worktown behaviour and mentality, Friday pay night is fundamental, with its consequent economic and leisure release for the weekend. A new girl in the card-room describes the end of the week:

> One of the men said,'another day gone and tomorrow's Friday when we get your Pennies from Heaven.' Mabel gets 22/11 a week without overtime. She said, 'We all queue up for [wages] outside the watch-house; there's an awful squash. The engine goes on running, but the machines can go to hell when it's pay-day.'

All through the year, the 42,000 spend their day in these tropics and follow this endless routine. From age 14, this is the life available for most Worktowners who cannot get to secondary schools or find better jobs.

[But there is more to the job than routine and weekly wages. While there is much tension between spinners and piecers,[3] there is also cooperation at work. For example, in the card-room:] 'Anyone seeing a card going wrong – overflowing or lap running out – will always leave her job to stop the card, even if not to put it right.' [And traditional 'footings' survive.]:

Footings are feasts of the whole of one department for some special occasion, e.g. the Jubilee and coronation and every Christmas. They are unofficial, but the management turn a blind eye so long as no alcohol is brought into the mill. They take place at the 3:30 rest pause, which means that little more work is done that day. They take place on a smaller scale when someone gets married, the bride or bridegroom 'footing' the bill.

[But surely most social intercourse occurs at the midday dinner hour even though this is muted, and seldom do they talk of work:]

At dinner time a large number of people go home. . . . There was a small dining room, but it was very little used. . . . On the whole, people sit in secluded corners in twos and threes. The majority of people who stayed in brought something to read – *Red Letter, Red Star Weekly, Peg's Paper, Home Chat*. Some of the copies going the round were of last August (now mid-November).

[But sometimes workers talk. Here is a report from the card-room concerning young women at dinnertime:]

Conversation centred round the present rather than the past or the future. It related mostly to such matters as dress; what's going on in Bolton, i.e. the cinemas, . . . Keep-Fit classes, young men (I suppose this has reference to the future, also); gossip about people in the mill and neighbours. There seemed to be little interest in external affairs, such as the Spanish war, but there was excitement about the four work-people chosen to attend the coronation, and particularly the textile weaver. A lot of the juniors are keen rounders players, so sport must be included. I never heard pools mentioned, nor saw a coupon. So I suppose that this is confined to the men.

[Only occasionally did this observer hear anything about work:]

Lil said, 'I'd like to do something, some sort of job – when you wouldn't know what would happen next. I think journalism must be about the best job – full of variety. Of course, it wouldn't be so nice when you had to make yourself write something and didn't feel like it. I expect I shall be glad tomorrow that I've got a routine job. I'm going to a dance tonight, and I shall be dead tomorrow.'

[WORKTOWN AND INDIA]

Worktown had been the centre of cotton's progress. It was the birthplace of the spinning-mule inventor, Samuel Crompton, and was incorporated in

23

1838 as a borough with a Unitarian as the first mayor and an all-Liberal Council. In 1847, working hours in Lancashire were limited to ten. Active in petitioning for this were the Worktowners, who were described by Marx in 1848 as 'the most radical in Europe'. They were in the forefront of the Chartist movement.

Yet by 1889, old Chartist Thomas Cooper revisited Worktown and heard, instead of men discussing the 'great doctrine of political justice',

> well-dressed working men talking, as they walk with their hands in their pockets, of 'Co-ops', and their shares in them, or of building societies. And you will see others, like idiots, leading small greyhound dogs, covered with cloth, on a string! They are about to race, and they are betting money as they go! And yonder comes another clamorous dozen of men, cursing and swearing and betting upon a few pigeons they are about to let fly! As for their betting on horses – like their masters – it is a perfect madness.

If Mr Cooper came to Worktown today he would not find anyone leading about small greyhound dogs, and very few betting on pigeons; instead they would be betting on the football pools or leading small motorcycles. The early Liberal tradition has turned Conservative. The percentage using their vote in municipal affairs has steadily fallen to 53. With the spinners in the forefront of union activity, wages and conditions have improved. Yet a quarter of the adults over 21 do not know who their M.P. is. The population is now shrinking rapidly. Faster than the decrease in population is the decline in church attendance, pub visits, voting, and the birthrate. All the traditional social activities are declining; and this decrease is not only numerical: many who still favour these occupations (drink, prayer, sex, vote, etc.) do so with observably less vigour and enthusiasm than thirty years ago.

The era of what seemed like inevitable progress is now over. In a world that now seems to nearly everyone to 'have gone crazy' and where all the older institutions seem impotent in the face of new powers, the individual increasingly believes only in himself. Immortality has been largely undermined as a hope for the future; and private life and its rhythms have grown enormously. Interest in theories of *your* future determined by the position of planets at the minute of your birth and the belief that man is part of an endless uncontrollable cyclic process have developed tremendously. We see this in the football pools, astrology columns of the mass-circulation papers, and the new evangelical Adventist sects which are the only churches fully thriving in Worktown.

The essential background to all this is the contracting market for Britain's basic cotton industry. The savings of tens of thousands of thrifty mill workers in company shares disappeared in the depression of 1921. New mass-production methods are resulting in more intense work, especially for women and young persons. Lower piece rate earnings, increased unemploy-

ment, and the substitution of cheap labour for skilled craftsmen are dimi-
nishing still further the prospects of the adult male worker. Ring-spinning is
spreading rapidly and the automatic loom is steadily gaining ground. Since it
is uneconomic to run automatic looms on single shifts, double shifts are
becoming more common. The East is pushing us out of traditional markets.
In the words of a recent employers' report: 'The loss of 85 per cent of the
Indian market is by far the most important single factor in the decline of
Lancashire trade. . . . The loss [since 1912 has] reduced whole towns from
prosperity to stagnation.'

The situation gives particular point to the hit-song of the famous
Lancastrian, George Formby, 'Hindu Howdo Hoodoo YouDo':

> Over there in India a Hindu resides
> Smoking his hokum all day
> bits of stick and bits of rope and fag-ends besides
> A wise man from the East Whitechapel way

The world, as the cotton worker sees it, is continually shrinking, and the
fortunate ones seem to be those who can escape beyond its bounds.
Increasingly it is difficult to get any young chap to go into the blind alley
between Crompton's mules; youths seek any alternative, however
transitory. Of spinners investigated, 72 per cent dislike the job that was once
the most valued in Worktown. Many have left the trade to become lodging-
house keepers in Blackpool or poultry farmers in the Fylde, while the less
fortunate become Corporation labourers or lorry drivers, or drift into the
sweated industries and munitions works of the South. Others keep on
working only to give their children an education which will enable them to
escape from the industry altogether. But for most workers there is no chance
of escape, and children still continue to go into the mills for lack of anything
else to do. The younger generation frankly take the view that they are 'going
to have a good time' rather than waste their time at night school, and for
their elders Littlewood's football pools hold far more hope of gain than
studying to qualify themselves for positions they will never attain.

'Looking forward', 'climbing the ladder of promotion', 'the test of time',
and 'making the world a better place to live in', have been vital to
Worktown's growth. These ideals seem threatened by an apathy not only for
cotton workers but also for the civilisation of poison gas and incendiary
bomb. It is only possible to be sure that I am alive. Little else seems as certain
as that in 1938.

Blackpool lends the most vivid colour to this personal view. Like the
cinema, the newspaper, and Littlewood, it attempts to form the largest
possible group of consumers, but does not attempt to establish any social
relationship between them; nor does it offer any direction for social activity
to influence their social environment. But Blackpool changes its own status
every year and it does not have to be changed by society. Blackpool's motto

is 'Progress'. [And Worktowners expect 'progress' in entertainment if not in work.]

In the holiday week, the Worktowner gets nine days away from work – a week with no red light and no need to get up any earlier than the manager. In that week, we should find much in the mind and habit of the Worktowner which cannot be expressed in his work or the limited hours of his play; yet the Worktowner is conditioned by the fact that he has been born and brought up in a town where you go on working even if you are paid less than unemployment benefit, even if you hate your job. Still we should remember that the phrase used for unemployment, the way a man will explain that he had been 'laid off for a few days', is 'I'm playing me'.

NOTES

1 Here are the 1931 census figures, and since then textile machinery – once the greatest business of the town – has further declined:

	Male	Female	Total
Manufacture of textile machinery	2,312	90	2,402
Cotton carding and spinning	10,108	10,183	20,291
Weaving	2,678	6,834	9,512
Thread	176	605	781
Other preparatory processes	2,970	1,939	4,909
Bleaching	2,154	756	2,910
Manufacturing of clothing	718	873	1,591
Total	21,116	21,280	42,396

Other main occupations were in engineering machinery (6,945), coal mining (1,887), food, drink, and tobacco (1,924), building (3,135). In other sections of enterprise over 10,000 were engaged in 'commerce and finance', including 532 hawkers and streetsellers, while of the 1,043 professionals, the largest group was in religion with 227.

2 Not all observers agreed with this assessment. One wrote:

there is not such a rush at 5:30 as there is at 12:15, when people have to get home, have lunch, and be back again in an hour, and I think that the rush is largely for trams. Moreover, if this horror of the mill, why do they turn up so early in the morning? Many of them used to arrive at 7:15 or 7:20 for 7:45 . . . . And it is quite compatible with an absence of disgust with the mill to be anxious to get home to cook your own and your husband's supper.

3 A proverbial story is of the tram conductor who saw a spinner leave his dinner on a hanky on the seat. Too late to recall him, the conductor opened it and found a slice of bread on which were five 'cowd slabs' – i.e. cold potato chips. Such meanness is associated with the spinner, and if you are ever in a shop where a woman comes in to buy watercress, it's likely she'll say 'give me some spinners beef, will yer.'

2

[THE ORDER OF TIME]

[The routine and wages of labour dominate Workdown culture. But the Mass-Observers focused on those hours after 5:30 and noon Saturday when Worktowners were free, within the constraints of time and money, to choose their own lives. *The Pub and the People* reveals the rich culture of mostly male evening leisure. This chapter, drawn from a number of reports and text fragments, will present more generally the meaning of leisure, the weekend, the changing seasons, and the centrality of the summer holiday in the lives of Worktowners.]

[AFTER HOURS]

[After work and tea, the workers' time is their own.] What happens next, in what is Worktown's leisure and recreation time, depends on how many nights it is after payday. From Monday to Thursday, this working man's evening is characteristic of the more dynamic group:

> I get *Worktown Evening News*. 6:00 A quiet read and smoke until 6:30, [when it's] off for a walk to visit a brother who has just got a new all Electric Radio. . . . Talk on family matters until 7:45. Began to mess about with the old battery set trying all manner of tricks with it until his wife said, 'clear the deck. We want supper.' So stayed and had supper (fish and chips, tea, bread, and butter.) Started home at 10:30, arriving at 11:00. Just had a drink of tea and off early to bed, 11:20.

[Observers found a more static pattern among those living in the traditional street dwelling.] The terraced house, 'two up and two down' of brick, contains two bedrooms, a scullery at the back which opens on to a small stone flagged yard, and a large living room just off the street. [Women spend a good deal of time keeping up appearances:] 'Despite the grime of the atmosphere, curtains are always spotlessly clean and the doorsteps, rubbed to a pure white or brilliant yellow with "donkey stone", are a joy to the eye. Woe betide the negligent housewife whose doorstep disgraces the street by falling below the general standard of cleanliness, and a really energetic women will go beyond her doorstep and holystone a strip of the paving flags in front.'

Let us look at the male employed worker in the street dwelling:

behaviour over long periods is much the same during leisure hours. For instance, in one street, one man will surely leave his home between 6:30 and 7:00 p.m. in the summer months and walk at a peculiarly leisurely gait to the Merchall park bowling green. He will just as surely stroll at the same speed around 9:00 p.m. to the Alexandria Hotel in Stewart St. for a pint or two and a game of dominoes.

Another neighbour can be depended upon to stand either at his home front door or at the street corner for long periods, during the fine weather, at evening . . . steadily puffing his pipe, sometimes for hours on end . . ., with an occasional nod to an acquaintance, but very seldom speaking.

The wives of these men appeared never to go out during week nights (except perhaps on Mondays, to the cinema), but the whole ritual of both the men and the women had a definiteness about it. . . . In the colder weather, much the same thing occured except that times for going-out were later and the immediate objective was the pub.

But spinners and other better-paid workers, being of an ambitious and energetic turn of mind, often live in larger street dwellings with an extension in the back. Many of them take on extra occupations outside mill hours. They are not great gardeners (except on council estates), and allotments arouse little enthusiasm; still the number of hen-coops in Worktown runs into many thousands. Some are keen teetotalers, while others see nothing wrong in convivial enjoyment at some hostelry or political club. But football and cricket are a common bond of interest which 'makes the whole world kin', while fishing, bowls, and choral singing claim numerous ardent devotees.

The interests of the post-war generation take a different direction. If they unshamedly prefer turning on the loudspeaker to learning to play on the piano, and spend more time on filling in 'Littlewood's' than in actually sitting in the grandstand at Burnden Park, their zest for cycling, hiking, and dancing appears almost unlimited.

The working-class wife's activities outside her own home are not very numerous. She does not 'go out' very much in the evening. A young mother described her evening like this:

I do all me washin for Tommy after tea, we generally get to bed about midnight, while baby's little, there's bottles an that. I do odd jobs, ave a look at th' *Bolton Evening News*. The baby goes to bed at seven o'clock. I've got to get im undressed and put to bed. I do all the mending on Thursday. It's very seldom I go out. Ernest (husband) never goes out. I've only been but three times since Thomas was born.

When the wife does gets out, even if just to the market, it is a means of social intercourse for her. There, people meet each other and listen to the talk of the barkers, particularly those selling herbs, cures, or dealing in magic. Many come in the afternoon but the market enjoys a hectic 'last hour' between 7:00 and 8:00. During that rush hour one day, women without children or husbands comprised 60 per cent of the crowd, groups including men 31 per cent, and units including children 8 per cent.

These markets are relics of the old trading fair, and it is on this spot that the big travelling fair comes during holiday week [for those unable to get away]. In the market we get an agglomeration of thousands of people densely packed together. This pressure of numbers in Blackpool is a major factor in determining the holiday-makers' 'carefree enjoyment'. In Worktown, the same 'atmosphere' is developed in the marketplace on Tuesday and on Thursday.

Here alone in Worktown we find the barker in full bark. Listen to a character called 'Taffy':

Hello Mrs. . . . Haven't seen you for a week or two now. How's yer hubby? Well ladies, here we are, look at these lovely undies fit fer the Queen, in fact, they are better than the Queen's an only 1/6 – no dammit I'll treat you ladies, 1/3 – who wants em?

[The trajectory of children's after-school leisure is also worth noticing.] After 4:00, when the school day ends, the child's leisure begins. Of 34 children (14 girls and 20 boys), 75 per cent of the boys and 71 per cent of the girls lingered on the way home, 8 of the boys playing football in the street together. Perhaps this is because, in its 15,280 acres of houses and factories, Worktown devotes scarely 300 acres to parks and public recreation grounds. Most of these children, however, arrived home by 5:00 p.m. passing their time in playing outside or reading until tea at 6:00 after father returns from the mill: 'We played at "hide and seek" and "running after" too. We played at "house and shop" too. We also played at "kick donkey kick" (girl 12).' After tea, 35 per cent of the girls do domestic jobs compared to 28 per cent of the boys; 75 per cent of the girls are indoors at home in the evening playing games, reading, or listening to the radio compared to only 34 per cent of the boys: most return to the street.

THE WEEKEND

[Key to the weekly routine of Worktowners, of course, is the shortage of leisure time and money. They inevitably focus attention on payday (Friday) and on Saturday afternoon, the beginning of the weekend, a time of rest as

Table 1 Rest and class

Time	Working class		Middle class	Unemployed
	Male	Female		
Going to bed	11:50	11:10	11:18	12:37
Rising	7:08	6:45	7:50	—
Hours in bed	7 hrs., 18 min.	7 hrs., 35 min.	8 hrs., 35 min.	—

much as pleasure. Observers found that working-class couples appear to get insufficient sleep.] The sleeping habits of 200 persons gave the averages shown in Table 1. Research undertaken at Colgate University (USA) suggests that persons of 20 require 8.25 hours per day of sleep. Apparently in Worktown sleep starvation may be almost as serious in affecting the health and nerves of working-class people as malnutrition is already known to be.

[But money also is a problem.] A sampling of 569 houses on weekday evenings found 73 per cent of families at home. How much people go out entirely depends on the amount of money left from Friday. On Wednesday night the 304 pubs are empty, but on Saturday night they are crowded with the 20,000 pub regulars. Dance halls, billiard halls, chip shops, clubs, the central streets, the cinemas, these and all the other institutions of Worktown's leisure come to life on Friday and die away to quietness on Monday. [Life revolves around the weekend. Here is a 'typical weekend' of the relatively well-off mill family.]

On arriving home at midday on Saturday, the spinner or overlooker swallows a hasty meal and dashes off to 'the match'. On leaving Burnden Park [about 4:30], he makes a wild dash for the Sports edition of the *Evening News*. Arriving home, he finds a well-cooked and ample meal awaiting him, and the whole family can eat in comfort together, although as the hands of the clock move towards six the younger members silently slip out, and make their way to the cinema or dance hall. After tea, the weary father of the family removes his shoes and sits by the fireside listening to his three-valve set, while mother busies herself with the washing in the scullery. The elders also may take the opportunity of going down to the cinema in the centre of the town (unless the husband succeeds in giving his spouse the slip and dodging off to the 'Spinners' Arms'). But, by ten o'clock, parents are usually by the fireside once more and anxiously wait for the return of the lads and lasses of the family.

Sunday morning is the time of rest, and the family, unless devout Roman Catholics, arise late. But, by two o'clock, mother has succeeded in producing her *chef d'oeuvre*, the best meal of the week. By three, the children have been washed and properly dressed in their best clothes; they walk in the streets or public parks. By five o'clock, every one is back again for high tea, and, as the clock hands move near the hour of six, the church bells begin to peal out merrily. There is a scramble for the family Prayer Book, and with a little effort, they are in church in time to take their seats. After eight o'clock, the family return home, and for the only time in the week, the sacred front parlour is allowed to be used. This is the time when friends and relatives drop in for a chat, though the younger members of the family usually succeed in making their escape into the streets (cinemas and places of amusement are always closed on the Sabbath day).

[But this is an idealised picture, focusing on the male. Here is a report concerning the Saturday afternoon of young female millworkers:]

On Saturdays they go home to a good hot dinner, and many seemed to spend the afternoon preparing themselves and their clothes for the evening and for Sunday. Two of 17 and 20 years went every week to a shop in Davenport Street at 2:30 for a Marcell Wave. . . . I never heard any mention of football. Saturday evening was generally spent with young men, either at the cinema or dancing.

[An observer listened in on a group of young women planning a party for Sunday:]

They were planning what games to play. One was Postman's knock; another was film stars. All the girls go out, and the men each choose a film star, such as Robert Taylor, Clark Gable, etc. A girl then comes in, and if she says one of the film stars there represented, she goes and sits with him. When each film star has a girl, the lights are turned off!

[But most of these young women rest on Sundays:]

Many lie late abed in the morning. The majority of those asked didn't go regularly to Church. Many took walks in the afternoon, either to Horwick, or in the park, or round Dean Clough. On Sunday evening they walked along Bradshawgate.

[Another centre of weekend leisure, at least in summer, is Barrow Bridge on the edge of town.] For a two-penny tram-ride to the terminus, you can be in fields. But observers found less than 1 per cent of Worktown uses this extensive countryside. Instead, on weekends, several thousands may often be found in the narrow lane to Barrow Bridge, on the half-acre muddy boating lake, at the edge of the paddling-pool which is generally out of use, at the archery range, the tea-house, and the slot machines of the peep show variety. Barrow Bridge is no longer the 'pleasant country lane' that excited Disraeli. The principal pleasure up there now is seeing other people, looking at their clothes, if you are young, looking at their bodies, and perhaps

31

picking them up. You can have a pleasant afternoon at Barrow Bridge without spending any money.

In winter there is nowhere to go. The Worktowner forgets the countryside and the moors, then barren and bleak. Then for your stroll, you walk the traditional 'monkey-walk' on the pavement of one of the main streets, endless smoke and cobble without greenness. In winter especially, the cinema, the penny, and the pint are the things thought of.

Weekend features of child life are visiting relatives, taking special care of babies, cinema going, and country walks. A group of thirty-seven schoolgirls from a working-class school were asked to rank the games they most liked at weekends [in April] – see Table 2.

Table 2 Children's games at Worktown

Game	No. of points
Rounders	45
Hop flag (hopscotch played on pavement)	40
Kick-out ball (variation of hide-and-seek)	13
Hide-and-seek	12
Tracking	12
Cricket	12
London Bridge is falling down	10

Analysis of Sunday activities of thirty-four children showed several special characteristics of that day: 63 per cent of the boys and 29 per cent of the girls go to afternoon Sunday School (parental sex climax) and 13 per cent of each sex go to the park. Longer holidays, if they are spent at home, mean principally an extension of all these activities, more visits to the parks, the playing fields, and the cinema, more excursions into the surrounding countryside. The popular games, and nearly all the popular child activities, are not only communal but conditioned by an exact social rhythm and cycle of the year.

[While these leisure patterns may be traditional, the relatively new housing estates presented new opportunities and limitations on these routines. One observer found that 'going out' in the evenings was less frequent among men but more common among women on the estates than in town. The 'deadly monotony of this estate' was one man's explanation. Women's gossiping at a neighbour's garden gate is also common, sometimes] 'till the stars come out and Henry Hall's band is ready to close down. The redeeming feature of this incessant chattering is the fact that it is the only social intercourse existent for woman on this estate – there is absolutely no other.' [The void created by an absence of a cinema, pub, or many shops was only recently filled by Mothers' meetings on Wednesday afternoons at the Methodist Mission.]

[As far as the estate husband is concerned, he has abandoned the traditional 'boozing partner' who formerly had lived nearby. The absence of pubs and cinemas on the relatively isolated housing estates severely limited this traditional conviviality.] 'His jaunts [to town] are restricted to weekends or even more infrequent intervals.' [Among the explanations:] 'new incentives to stay home by having gardens . . . and prudence dictated by a sneaking regard for the "authorities" who appear to act in a mysterious way as "distant guardians" of the behaviour of their tenants'.

[Still weekend leisure time allows a unique form of social leisure on the buses returning from town:]

The conductor knows a number of his passengers almost as personal friends, and most journeys to or from town are enlivened by the wisecracks bandied between him and his fares. This spirit of good humour . . . is particularly marked on the late Sunday night buses, when hilarity and noise reach their peak. Several of the passengers of these late buses have provided themselves with 'liveness' for the morrow, in the shape of pint bottles of beer or stout which advertise themselves by a passenger's difficulty in passing down the gangway owing to numerous mysterious bulges in the pockets of the men. Sheer drunkenness is rare. The impression created by these late buses, brilliantly lit, noisily happy as to contents . . . is a peculiar one. The bus appears to be the connecting link between two worlds as typified by the town and the estate, and is the scene of more exchanged intimacies than any other place. In this respect, it partially takes the place of the absent pub. . . . It is as if the sociability of the estate is hurled into the town at weekends, to drift back into the estates, bus load by bus load, to take up its routine until the following weekend, when the process is repeated.

INDUSTRIAL SPRING

[Despite the central role of the weekend in the cycle of life, the traditional seasons have not disappeared entirely from the consciousness of the Worktowner. Consider the role of spring.]

Modern Worktown is a place where the seasons matter comparatively little. At work there is no difference. The mills dominate landscape, life, and atmosphere. Soot settles evenly over the town. And within each mill there is created an atmosphere of tropical heat and humidity. All the year through, 65,000 Worktowners spend their days in these new tropics, and in winter, when moor-encircled Worktown is bitter cold, they go there each day before the sun, if any, comes up, and come home each day after the sun has gone down. The windows of the workrooms are frosted or otherwise made opaque, lest stray sunbeams strike the whirling white cotton threads.

[At play, too, the seasons and nature mean little.] Worktowners find everyday outlets within the town not in nature but in its football stadium, cinemas, and 304 pubs. Casual visitors find the town lovely, smoke hazing its angle in the gentle basin of encircling moors. But even in summer people scarely use the moors, something that is inexplicable to Southerners. Only on Sundays, however, is there the opportunity for adult workers to get out of the sprawling town during daylight, and then the trams do not run until the afternoon. No wonder that you forget the country around. And visitors also know nothing of the great lawsuit against the men who determined to establish a right of way across the moor, but were vindictively fought through all the courts, with financially disastrous results. Today, the memory of that case is still strong, and the Worktowner walking in the moors worries whether he is trespassing. Off the few paths, the moors are closely protected for the autumn festival of grouse shooting.

But while the seasons have in fact ceased to have recognised significance, they still determine whole fields of Worktown behaviour. This is based on a pre-industrial rythmn, now often illogical and uneconomic. The whole year is hinged on seasonal rites whose direct functions (whether propitiation, religious belief, or harvest allocation) have long since been forgotten by the masses. Instead they are devoted to the buying of clothes, booze-ups, marriage and morality, sport, special foods, and hope.

[Let's consider the festival of spring.] From age 14, the mill is the life available for most Worktowners. But at age 12 few realise it. Fewer than 1 per cent think they will go through the mill. Living near to the ground, finding beetles in crevices, having long holidays and time to roam, children can see the seasons differently. Thus a typical elementary school of thirty-six 12 year olds wrote, unassisted, poems about spring. They contain only two references to the mill-town environment and otherwise show a complete interest in nature:

> In spring the people get their hamps
> And go to sunny meadows
> And have their tea upon the grass
> Then play and roll about. (boy)

Nature and the countryside dominate the picture of spring; nature is associated with freedom and happiness in the minds of the children. But as a school subject, nature is unpopular. The wish to escape to nature is born spontaneously in the mind of the child and is still experienced when the child becomes an adult (cf. the adult's 'holiday dreams').

[But when does spring start in Worktown and does it have any connection to nature?] Said a millworking girl: 'when the trees are in bud'. But Worktown institutions show their first spring response on 5 January, when shops have all taken down Christmas signs and several already have SPRING SALES and SPRING BARGAINS. On 16 March the local paper, which reaches 96 per cent of Worktown homes, has a large SPRING ADVERTISING SUPPLEMENT. That gives the signal. The next day two dressmakers have huge vases of artificial myth-flowers in the window, and the word 'spring' gets particular application: SPRING SUITINGS, SILKS FOR SPRING, and so on.

But the key to the spring festival is Easter and the six weeks of Lent which lead up to it, even though religion and its linkage to the seasons have declined. Lent actually kicks off with two boys and two girls swinging down Settle Street early on the morning of 1 March, singing at a high screech:

> Pancake Tuesday is a very happy day.
> If you don't give us a holiday we'll aw run away
> Eating tawfy, cracking nuts,
> Stuffing pancakes deawn awr guts.

All Worktown kids know this, sing it, only on this day – the only survival of the old custom of door-to-door singing for gifts. Sales of eggs go up, but shopkeepers complain that nowadays people buy pancake powder which is cheaper. If it snows on Shrove Tuesday, custom decrees that you must mix the snow with the batter; if you can get the pancake to rise, that's very lucky. Two-thirds of the families have pancakes, predominantly those with children in the home. As a typical pair of parents put it: 'We wouldn't miss our pancake for anything. We think it's a great treat, just to watch the daughter enjoy them. Well, we can't say why we fancy them, but we suppose it's because of the old custom.'

But of belief, all that survives in Worktown is that it is unlucky not to eat pancakes on Shrove Tuesday, and (decreasingly) that you must eat one pancake before the next one is finished and turned. Strong still is the custom of leaving the Christmas holly and mistletoe up until Shrove Tuesday, and then burning them, though in most homes the resultant fire is no longer used for cooking the pancakes – owing to gas. But the next day is the big day for ashes. Ash Wednesday marks the replacement of feasting by fasting.

Though today in Worktown only one in twelve of the population goes to church, its influence seeps into every part of life. Religion determines the shape of the week as it does the year. Religion stops the trams running on Sunday mornings. And nine out of ten give up something for Lent (though rarely do they abandon dancing; even one Catholic church obtained a special dispensation from the Bishop to run dances to pay off debts during Lent).

On the evening of Shrove Tuesday, the last night for general free leisure and pleasure, one observer found seats sold out at the cinemas. The tramways manager noticed that on the following Wednesday there had been a big drop in fares. 'The public were simply not coming into Worktown.' There are distinct changes in the economy and these far exceed the small number of Catholics who have definite Lent orders. Butchers find a drop in sales of pork and sausages while fish and chip shops boom. Thus thousands of people for forty days commemorate an incident about which they know very little indeed.

[The spring festival ends with May Day rituals by children.] The children in back streets and main streets walk amongst often overflowing ashcans and privies, boys dressed as girls, girls with old sacks or discarded curtains as trains collecting pennies. And they sing,

> Dancing round the maypole
> Merrily we go
> Tripping, tripping, lightly,
> Dancing to and fro.
> All the Happy Pastures
> Round the village green
> Sparkling in the sunshine
> Hurrah for the Queen!
> Hurrah for the Queen!

And inevitably they chorus around the Queen with her curtain trails:

> She is the Queen of the May-ay-ay, the May-ay-ay,
> In the Month of May.
> The flowers, the flowers grow everywhere, everywhere,
> The flowers they grow everywhere
> In the beautiful month of May.

This final festival of spring reveals its deep industrial irony. And thence we step into the summer, with the soot falling from the long-boned factory fingers, churning out calico from a climate that knows nothing of seasons. To the children, May flowers are everywhere. But the Anglican St Augustus Church has a notice in its porch: 'Urgent. We have no money for flowers this week.'

[A world of seasonlessness still finds its seasons, but without the freshness of hand-picked flowers. The spring festival, so meaningful to agrarian people and to believers, has been reduced to a childlike longing for the spontaneity of nature but celebrated in rituals imposed on children which few understand. In fact, the year's cycle is truly organised around the summer pilgrimage to the seaside rather than around the flowers in the church. One proof is in the cycle of saving and spending. Money orders time in the way that the weather and religion once did.]

[TIME AND MONEY]

The enormous majority of Worktowners live literally from week to week. Thursday, the day before the wages come home, is based on credit. You go out to the shop and get what you need on the 'Kathleen Mavoreen'. Another system is the twenty members/twenty week club. A secretary collects, say,

1/-per week from members for twenty weeks, and lots are drawn to decide the order in which members should spend the weekly total in the shop. It is the members rather than the shopkeeper who give credit, although the shopkeeper pays expenses. In contrast, Blackpool allows no credit. [This helps explain the Worktowner's obsession with holiday saving.]

77 per cent of the Worktown sample save specifically for their holidays.[1] Those born elsewhere feel differently: 'We have never been away together for a holiday. We come from further north and there is no holiday like in Lancashire.'

This impulse to save has its origins in the Friendly Societies in the nineteenth century. These institutions created not only a 'respectable' section of the upper working class, but preserved traditional leisure values – the idea of club saving combined with communal spending on banners, initiation ceremonies, and liquor. The pageantry and conviviality remain, but now Blackpool provides the colour, the contrast, for which the year's abstinence is preparing.

Holidays are only possible if you save the whole year because the Worktown mills still do not provide holidays with pay. [But Worktowners need more than their normal weekly income:] '[I] save for holidays, so that one may spend freely without feeling that you cannot really afford it' (clerk, 47). Spending freely during the holiday makes these Worktowners feel that they are somebody:

> During holiday time, I and my sister use scented soap and never look first at a menu to find what a thing costs but just order it, because once in a year we want to smell and to behave like ladies.
>
> (weaver, 45)

To get this feeling without having a bad conscience, savings are kept completely separate from the rest of the budget. It is the function of numerous holiday clubs in Worktown to make a certain amount of money disappear and reappear in the week before the holidays.

Most churches have holiday savings clubs. In the largest church, the central Methodist Mission Hall, a holiday savings club is run by the women, paying from 6d. to 3/-. Many of the women put in without their husbands knowing, to have something for the week after the holidays when there is no wage coming in. The women evidently try to save more than is always possible. [Note the differences in Table 3 between the women's holiday club and the other savings clubs for men and boys:] Church folk tend to save more and are a minority at one-seventh of the population. The Methodists average around £8 per family for holidays savings.

The Worktown Savings Bank promotes numerous saving organisations, paying out about £100,000 in the fortnight before the holiday. In one of these, a group of coal yard workers saved an average of £3/12 (high in comparison to the wages of most cotton workers).

37

Table 3 Methodist savings clubs, April 1938

	Members	Aver. payment	No. of weeks missed		
			One	Two	Three or more
Women's	132	3/7	9	11	53
Men's	61	2/10	21	7	24
Boys'	40	1/10	4	1	18

[Poorer Worktowners tend to use more traditional savings schemes.] 'Diddlum-em' Clubs are generally run by individuals in works or pubs. You may enter at a halfpenny subscription for the first week, each week you give a halfpenny more than the week before, for twenty-four weeks, until you reach a shilling, then you go down a halfpenny each week for another twenty-four. This starts the week after the holidays, missing Christmas and Easter. When people draw out their savings the week before the holidays, they are amazed at the amount. Corner grocers also allow poorer customers to add sixpence or more on to their bills from April towards groceries for the holiday week. Finally, the 'Club Cheque', issued by United Provident Society and others, is a common way of buying holiday clothing. For an initial payment of 1/-, you can get a pound's worth of clothing from almost any shop in Worktown. Then you pay back one-twentieth a week. These cheques are now accepted by hairdressers and even by one enterprising charabanc proprietor. While 'most people are ashamed to be seen using them', these cheques are a special holiday currency for the less well off.

The Worktown holiday is a communal affair just as the savings efforts often are. In the last week in June, all mills and factories are closed and a mass migration follows. A large proportion of it goes to Blackpool, where Worktowners recognise in pubs and on promenades the faces that they have been seeing during the working year. So what they have saved together in the savings clubs, they now spend together on the simple pleasures of the holiday week. [If the weekend nourishes the worker for the week ahead, the holiday dream sustains life throughout the year and the pilgrimage to the seaside gives time its shape.]

NOTES

1 Interviews of 76 men and 124 women (by June 1939) found that 87 per cent of Worktowners claimed that they save:

	Cotton worker		Other worker		Clerical Employee		All others		Total	
	No.	%	No.	%	No.	%	No.	%	No.	%
Saves	50	67	32	73	32	80	21	62	135	71
Saves when possible	14	19	10	21	5	13	4	12	33	17
Does not save	11	14	3	6	3	7	10	9	27	13

The millworker saves less. This is probably because he is paid less. [Even more to the point is the relationship between the size of families, savings, and the declining ability to take holidays.] We undertook a personal canvas of 124 working-class homes concentrating on the poorish parts of the town:

Family size (no. studied)	Average savings	% entire family taking holidays
One (6)	41/1	100
Two (35)	99/-	91
Three (29)	91/-	72
Four (27)	105/-	48
Five (12)	118/-	25
Six to ten (15)	27/3	23

3

THE HOLIDAY DREAM

As inevitable as Sunday in the cycle of the week and death in the cycle of life is the June holiday. The holiday week is the axis dividing six months of work from six months of work. It is an extension, but with wider liberties, of Sunday. After fifty-one weeks in the mills, forges, pits, trams or the largest tannery in the country, you need 'a change' and you must have it. Work is compulsorily stopped; the town almost literally closes down for one week from the last Saturday in June.

Many in Worktown (though not nearly as many as go to Blackpool) still attend the 140 churches, because, as one worker says, 'it helps me through the rest of the week'. The holiday has a similar long-term function; it gives something to *look forward* to. In a town which offers few prospects of a better life for the individual, and where looking forward to a good afterlife has nearly disappeared, the idea of the future is largely confined to looking ahead to the possibility of a win in the football pools and the certainty of a week's leisure. These are the only two releases from the routine of life. Of course, the anticipation of death is still important, involving an average expenditure of 1/-a week in Worktown. Death is never fun for the chap saving up. But the holidays often are not much fun either, particularly if you have a family. The majority of workers get less than two pounds a week, have families, and do not at present get paid during the week's stoppage, though many have prospects of payment next year [1939]. The result is therefore not just a holiday.[1] A Worktowner writes:

> As a busy housewife, the change is best tonic. Quietness and rest from duty. To see the joyous faces of kids and knowing the happy days are giving health and relaxation to parents is enough. After a week from home, always glad to get back home. Still home to me, thankful to get back and begin saving again.

In this chapter we are concerned with just this sort of subjective data that is often mistakenly called unscientific. It illuminates the darkest territory of all social science – what people think. These subjective statements are very seldom accurate reflections of what people do actually think, but rather of

40

what they think they should think. Moreover we are mainly concerned with the working-class majority. Quite different is the salaried worker who is not employed in artificial and tropical environments; he generally has a car (3,998 private cars in Worktown in 1937) with which he can get out into the country; he seldom goes to Blackpool for holidays; and his holiday income is guaranteed.

'HOW I WOULD LIKE TO SPEND MY HOLIDAYS'

Our main source of data was from 220 letters prompted by a competition organised through the local press on 'How I would like to spend my holidays'.[2] What gives general significance to these personal statements is the recurrent idea and often the literally repeated phrase. Thus, when 102 letters raise the point of the week after the holidays and its lack of money, for many the holiday prospect is more a nightmare than a happy dream. Married man:

> I would like to sit in my garden and know that all was well and have no thought of frightening bills and demands such as have mounted up during my week's leisure at the beginning of July. . . . It isn't much I want, is it? – no! But it is more than I, as a workingman, can demand.
>
> My employers may give it to me if they wish, but, unfortunately, they are not compelled to do so. As it is, my holidays are horror days. (He actually stayed home during the holidays.)

[Others rise above these anxieties (or bury them) in an anticipation of dream magic which nevertheless is tinged with realism.] Married man:

> My mere five days rest from toil would be spent in some quiet sun-drenched hamlet far away on the Cornish Riviera (I even dream of Italian Riviera) away from crowds, dreamily wandering, admiring the majestic splendor of the surroundings . . . but alas back to reality. All this may possibly happen if I was one of the fortunate people having 'Holidays with Pay'. All I anticipate is somewhere on the Lancashire coast. (He went to Blackpool; £2/10 per head.)

Single man:

> I want to go to Oxford for my holidays. The city is steeped in history and has many excellent examples of different types of architecture. I should spend my time viewing the colleges or boating on the beautiful River Cherwell. . . . However this holiday is a dream.

And:

> Being the mother of three small boys whom I had to bring up single-handed through economic circumstances, I am just feeling the strain of 'Baby-fingers pulling at her Heartstrings'. Also the purse-strings, so if

41

some kind fairy just wafted me a five pound note [the contest prize], I would like to leave the kiddies with a kind friend and fly away with my husband to spend a long weekend at Buxton.

These holiday visions cannot fail to have an effect on people's thoughts during those fifty-one work weeks. Both nightmare and dream magic are linked closely to money or the lack of it. Worktown workers erect in their minds a lovely holiday, which is seldom practical, but from which it is possible to derive the same sort of satisfaction as from the crooner's song or the fairytale.

AWAY FROM THE OLD ENVIRONMENT

For many the holiday dream means a release from routine, a radical change from accustomed space, time, and activity. This turn from the normal is mentioned by fifty-five correspondents but is implicit in many others also. They are roughly classified in Table 4. Housewives particularly want to get away from the routine work of the home:

I am hoping to go to the North of Blackpool all being well. Just to leave the washing of dishes and clothes and baking and all the little jobs that make each day full. Just to be able to sit and knit or read, and watch my kiddies play in the sands and gaze right out to where the sea and sky seem to meet each other will make my holiday just O.K. (family of four went to Blackpool).

Millworkers most often mention the nervous strain of their time-bound work, like this card-room girl:

I want to forget the clock, the newspapers, the public – and I cannot even tell you how I want to spend my holiday, because that would be planning and all my working is done according to plan. Just this. The movements of a flow of the river almost explains how I feel about a holiday.

Table 4 Things to be avoided

	MM	SM	MW	SW	Total
Work and working environment	5	9	19	4	37
Town environment	6	5	5	2	18
Dirt/unhealthiness	4	2	2	2	10
People and crowds	5	4	1	—	10
Time/routine	—	3	3	—	6
Home environment	4	—	2	—	6
Total	24	23	32	8	87

MM = Married men; SM = Single men; MW = Married Women; SW = Single Women

Or listen to a single male worker:

> I want to start off on my tandem with my girlfriend to Wales. I want to
> camp every night in a lovely open space. We shall visit a different place
> every day and then at dusk start to find a suitable place for our night's
> rest. . . . I'm sure it will be swell to lie awake and see the moon, peering
> in through the canvas, to hear the moo of the cow and baa of nearby
> lambs, and think how different the buzz of the great engine which I see
> and hear every day.

On the whole, however, the number mentioning any specific desire to be
away from their working conditions is not as considerable as had been
expected. The feeling is less the negative getting-away and more the positive
place, the idea to-be-got-to.

So what do Worktowners say they want on holiday? The topics
specifically raised in the letters are tabulated in order of frequency in Table 5.

Table 5 Holiday themes discussed

	MM	SM	MW	SW	Total
Specified holiday pastimes	54	40	35	42	171
Rest and relaxation	29	26	43	26	124
Health	21	22	26	18	87
Gaiety, romance	22	14	27	12	75
Total change from Worktown	12	15	20	8	55
Nature main theme	10	18	4	10	52
Food and drinks	20	10	9	7	46
Novelty	7	12	12	5	36
Companionship	9	10	3	9	31

Among the specific pastimes, only a few essays mentioned intellectual
occupations. The people who want to read or listen are outnumbered by six
to one by those who seek physical activities (Table 6).

Interestingly, organised or competitive games are unpopular, although in
Worktown they dominate all forms of outdoor exercise. The middle-class
games of golf and tennis, requiring special apparatus and clothing, are
naturally rare in a working-class sample; but cricket, a popular working-
class game in Worktown, gets only one mention as a holiday wish. People
want a change. The interest of single women in sports is striking. The true
outdoor girl is a product of the post-war years. She shows almost a propri-
etary interest in dancing, bathing, and sailing. She ranks equally with the
married men in the matter of walking. Only she mentions playing games on
the sands.

Rearranging these data by type of activity, we find (in Table 7) that three-
quarters of the activities mentioned involved going into or on to the sea or to

Table 6 Holiday wishes

Intellectual activities	MM	SM	MW	SW	Total
Reading books	4	1	4	3	12
Reading newspapers	4	1	—	—	5
Listening to music	1	—	1	4	6
Conversation	2	—	—	—	2
Total	11	2	5	7	25
Physical occupations	*MM*	*SM*	*MW*	*SW*	*Total*
Sailing	4	5	4	10	23
Walking	8	2	3	9	22
Bathing	3	2	—	11	16
Chara drives	2	2	6	5	15
Fishing	5	4	3	1	13
Swimming	5	4	3	—	12
Country rambling	1	5	4	—	10
Dancing	1	2	—	6	9
Hill climbing	3	4	—	1	8
Cruises	—	—	2	2	4
Specific games	2	3	—	—	5
Cycling	—	3	—	—	3
Games on sand	—	—	—	2	2
Exercises	1	1	—	—	2
Putting	—	—	—	1	1
Total	35	37	25	49	146

Table 7 Holidays activities desired

	MM	SM	MW	SW	Total
	%	%	%	%	%
Sea	46	42	48	50	48
Countryside exercise	17	37	40	14	24.5
Resort exercise	35	15	12	22	21
Organised games	0	0	0	2	0.5
Indoor games	3	6	0	12	6
Total no.	35	37	25	49	46

the countryside away from big resorts. All groups give the sea first place. We shall presently see the difference between this wish and the reality. Still this emphasis on the not-so-vigorous activities of the sea is linked to the often stated need for rest and quiet.

This desire is well put by one who tells us what he thinks a restful holiday should be like:

As a manual worker, I would like to spend my holidays in a restful manner. . . . I would like to rise about 7:00 a.m., have a walk, then breakfast. Afterwards an easy stroll on the prom or into the country. After dinner, take a book and read it on the sands or in some shady country lane. After tea a visit to an entertainment, preferably outdoors and to bed about 11:00 p.m. This with slight variations should give rest and help me to regain wasted energy.

Yet again it is the married women who mainly think of rest: 35 per cent of the things they mention involve relaxation; a similar percentage distinctly express the wish to get away from the Worktown environment and daily routine:

I would like to spend my holidays in the country far from the bustle, traffic, grim and daily toil, no eight o'clock, just a few days in the sunshine, meals prepared for me, got out bed [sic] when I wanted, rise when I wanted. . . . That's what I would call a real holiday.

THE STILL ATMOSPHERE OF THE ENGLISH COUNTRYSIDE

Despite the dominant interest in the seaside, 24 per cent of our correspondents wish to get away to the country. Two letters best show this countryside theme.

I would like nothing better than a week in the Welsh mountains, not the seaside with its boisterous crowds, fun fairs, and noisy hawkers. I hear enough noise at work. I can imagine the spot I would choose, a farmstead in a deep green valley, with a view of mountains on every side, and there would be lake near for boating and swimming. And oh, I would love to eat my mid-day meal off a white table cloth, preferably in the garden and I would actually have milk in my tea. It sounds silly but if you could see me having my mid-day meal in the mill, you'd realise. Sat on the floor. Tea with no milk, in a thick pint pot, there would be cotton fibres settling on my food, and the mice would be peeping out of their holes waiting for the crumbs, and there would probably be a cricket chirping away too. (Married woman millworker, went to Blackpool with husband. Cost £4 for two.)

There is only one way I want to spend my holiday and that programme could only be followed in the Lake District. There are associations there for me, of youthful escapades and adventures all to be renewed. I want to climb again round hills with only the sheep and moorland birds as companions. I want to fling my tired sluggish panting body, that would be fast returning to life amid those clean fresh hills, down upon the summits and watch the clouds race across the blue sky and their

45

shadows across vallies [sic], hills and crags. . . . To see below, deep
luscious green vallies in the sweeping hills; rough moorland beneath
craggy summits; soft meadow still lower and fat round trees following
the brooks down the gentler, paler slopes to the tree skirted, deep blue
lake patched with the white of the reflected flying clouds. Or to stand
by a lonely mountain tarn, bleak and bare in the bowl of barren crags,
standing austere, black, brown and silent around. To feel again the
beat of the clean cool rain on my face up there alone, is like champagne
is said to be by those who know. (Married man. In fact during the June
holidays, he took two half-day trips to Blackpool with wife.)

[THE HOLIDAY FACT]

The letters that we have quoted paint a romantic picture. Most emphasise
greater gentleness of living during that holiday week than is in fact ever
possible at the places where at least two-thirds spend their holiday. Of the

Table 8 Holiday wishes and fulfilments

Holiday place	No. wishing	No. achieving	% wish fulfilled*
SEASIDE			
Quiet resort	24	15	63
Popular resort	45	78	173
Unspecified	38	0	0
Total	107	93	87
COUNTRY			
Lake District	6	1	17
Wales	6	4	67
Ireland	3	1	33
Scotland	3	0	0
Devon/Cornwall	3	0	0
Unspecified	24	0	0
Other districts	7	10	143
Total	52	16	30
TOWN			
London	10	1	10
Home towns	3	1	33
Sightseeing towns	3	0	0
Total	16	2	12
ABROAD			
France	5	0	0
Germany	1	0	0
Switzerland	1	0	0
Other countries	3	2	67
Total	10	2	20

* Of course, where the percentage is over 100, more went to a type of resort than actually wished to.

190 in the 220 correspondents who were followed up, 152 spent their holidays within 30 miles of Worktown, 180 within 100 miles.

Table 8 shows exactly the difference between the holiday-wish and the holiday fact: 185 people specified what sort of place they wanted to go to on their holidays in their letters; 190 of the 220 in our sample replied to the follow-up questionnaire stating where they actually spent their June holiday. The third column gives the adjusted percentage who *fulfilled* their wish.

Thus although only 24 per cent wish to go to popular seaside resorts, 69 per cent who get away actually go there. As the distance to the desired place increases, so the likelihood of getting there decreases. Still no one wishes to go anywhere which could not be visited with ten pounds or within a week. Two want to go in aeroplanes. But none wants to go to the Arctic or the South Seas. The mystical ideal of the country or healthful seaside holiday is an integral part of Worktown thought. Although most people seek quiet, few seek distant quietness. In fact, many are content to want no more than a holiday in a town of similar population density to that of Worktown. Some wish to go to the country, which would be practical and cheap, but few do so, although their June holidays would permit them. Everybody wants to go away on a holiday, but 40 per cent of adults answering these questions failed to do so in 1937.

Why Blackpool

By far the greatest number of Worktowners who go to any resort go to Blackpool. There are, however, a very large number of alternative places offered by the railway companies, charabanc firms, hotel and camp advertisers in the Worktown press. In view of the widely expressed desire to go to less crowded places, why do 69 per cent actually go there? To a great extent it is a matter of money.

By comparing the holidays of children in a middle-class school with those from a working-class school, we can see the scope of this problem (Table 9). In broad outline, the tendencies of the middle-class holiday are not very different from those of the workers, especially in the preference for the seaside. The difference is in the distance and destination: 40 per cent of our

Table 9 Percentage of school children's holidays by class

	Middle class	Working class
Stay at home	2	30
Abroad	9	1
Towns	12	3
Countryside	13	8
Seaside	62	57
Tours	2	1

Table 10 Students' resort visits by class (%)

	Middle class (280)	Working class (160)
Blackpool	16	57
Isle-of-Man	17	4
Southport	5	16
Morecambe	4	6
Fleetwood	6	5
North coast & Ireland	6	2
South coast	17	2
Other	9	8

middle-class seaside-goers make journeys involving a sea voyage or a land journey of over 200 miles; 8 per cent of the working-class group do the same (see Table 10). Said a spinner:

Blackpool is looked down on by the people who can afford to go elsewhere. It's cheaper to go to Blackpool, much cheaper. Six shillings to Blackpool; seventeen shillings at the lowest, that's steerage, to Douglas, Isle-of-Man.

A yard foreman noted:

Oh, there's a great distinction between Isle-of-Man Douglas and Blackpool. One man tried Blackpool after fourteen years at Isle-of-Man. Oh never again. It's not a holiday at Blackpool really, he said. It doesn't feel like a holiday unless you go over water, you know. That sea-voyage has a lot to do with Douglas . . . [and] not nearly so many would go to the Isle-of-Man if it wasn't so far.

The journey over the water makes a break with all the habits of the mainland, detaches one 'definitely' from the industrial scene into an old world with its castle and own system of laws. 'Go abroad in the British Isles' is the slogan of the Isle-of-Man. The most famous thing in the island is Cunningham's Young Men's Holiday Camp, whose address is 'Switzerland', Douglas. As at Squire's Gate camp near Blackpool, the bungalows are called chalets.

The difference between the island and the mainland is rather like that between the vault and the lounge in the pub. You don't naturally walk into the more expensive room, and you get a little social prestige from being in a more expensive place. There is a 'class distinction', but the people in each case are of the same origin and live in identical houses; it is an economic class that may well change from year to year with employment and wage fluctuation. All through the autumn and winter the people who've been to Douglas in the Isle-of-Man have a little more to say about it than the people who've been to Blackpool. Going across the sea by steamboat or dreamboat is the thing, even if it's only 30 miles.

The class difference is clear in the letter of a middle-class schoolboy:

> With the end of the holidays rapidly approaching for once I am not sorry because I am getting a bit bored. I usually spend more of the seven weeks away from home, but this year I had two weeks in Ilfracombe North Devon, where we had a very enjoyable time, with good weather and good company. After sleeping only one night at home, I went to the Isle-of-Man for nine days with the scouts. . . . While we were in Devon it surprised me the number of Worktown cars there were visiting it . . . we were only there for two weeks [and] saw eight.

His father is a fine-art dealer. A weaver's child could never hope for two such holidays plus the boredom. The car, of course, is basic in the middle-class holiday, and it gives the wide range of travel as compared with those tied to train fares. Thus of 4,300 vehicles coming into Blackpool at Easter Bank Holiday in 1938, only two had Worktown registration letters; they were packed charabancs.

The Blackpool habit

The holiday contrast for the worker is closely linked to the sea. Although over 50 per cent before the holidays say they want something different, less than 10 per cent in practice break away from the conventional industrial holiday which for most means Blackpool. It is the whirlpool which, if it does not draw the hearts of Worktown, draws at least their bodies and above all their money.

But there is more than its price that brings them back to Blackpool. Ironically, from the health point of view, which the holiday-maker tells us is so important, Worktown is ideal during the holiday week. It is the only time in the year that all the factory chimneys are smokeless and most of the houses too. The pure air of the moors can come down into the wide valley. In holiday week Worktown meets all the wishes of the most romantic holiday-maker. Yet Worktowners practically ignore this lovely country (there is none around Blackpool).

The Worktowner requires something more stirring. However much he thinks he wants the country, he goes to the places where the crowds are, where the rhythm is as fast and the noise almost as great as that of the mill. Blackpool is the most crowded and noisiest resort, and the railway leads straight there. Going to Blackpool for holidays is becoming as much a habit as going into a town-centre pub on Saturday night.

When asked straightforwardly which place they preferred for a holiday, without being allowed to erect any ideals, 87 working-class adult Worktowners voted as follows: 8 for the countryside and 79 for the seaside; 60 preferred Lancashire coast resorts (35 voted for Blackpool, 15 for Douglas and 12 Southport). When asked one afternoon in Blackpool why she came, a woman of 30 said, 'Well, there's everything for everybody here.'

We approached 281 working people to find out what they thought about Blackpool.[3] Their basic impressions are stated in Tables 11 and 12.

People most like Blackpool for its pleasures; children like the amusements and the sea. The sea, which seemed from earlier analysis to be essential to

Table 11 Attitudes towards Blackpool: places

| | Adults | | Children | |
	Liked	Disliked	Liked	Disliked
Sideshows	47	—	6	—
Dancing	18	—	—	—
The Tower	14	—	1	2
Shows	9	—	—	—
Pleasure	7	—	—	—
Music concerts	7	—	—	—
Release from work/worries	6	—	—	1
Winter Gardens	6	—	—	—
Variety shows	7	1	—	1
Sailing	4	—	—	—
Change	4	—	—	—
Drives	3	—	1	—
Sport	2	—	1	—
Stanley park	2	—	—	—
Tower circus	2	—	3	—
Pleasure Beach	1	1	6	—
Total	139	2	19	3

Table 12 General attitudes towards Blackpool

	Liked	Disliked
Pleasure/amusement	158	5
Health	122	5
Sea/beach	60	3
People	17	4
Economy	8	1

most Worktown holidays, now appears as somewhat less important. Perhaps it is the seaside resort, not the seaside itself, which the chaps are wanting. We shall see.

The magic carpet floats off

In Blackpool dream and reality are mixed. Perhaps this explains its success.

50

With the understanding of poets and psychologists, the Blackpool Corporation weaves the magic and the dream with the fish and the chip. The Pixies in Fairyland mine coal. As a single man wrote:

How I want to spend my holidays and how I shall spend my holidays, are two different things. I should like to be carried away by some magic carpet to a secluded spot, where work and crowds are things unheard of.

Impracticable in fact, within Blackpool the carpet is provided in theory; as ballet promoter Bill Holland advertised all over Lancashire with the caption

COME TO THE WINTER GARDENS
AND
SPIT ON BILL HOLLAND'S
HUNDRED GUINEA CARPET

Inside Blackpool you may visit all the countries of this world and the next, see a female Jesus, take the Ghost Train, or see the Last Supper (free).

One of the few we interviewed who did actually go to the country in Buckinghamshire, wanted 'new scenes, new places, new people, new ways, new cooking in fact anything and everything new'. The new people and the new cooking are Blackpool's main difficulties; it's a Worktown commonplace that you meet all your own friends in the holiday week, whether you want to or not. As another man wrote, 'Two weeks which are different, I want to see new places and new faces. Not for me Blackpool, generally spoken of as Worktown by the Sea.' But he has two weeks, a salaried worker.

NOTES

1 Many are not optimistic in looking ahead to holidays. In the spring of 1937, of 220 Worktown workers only 40 expressed any hope of getting holidays with pay and of these not one said that he thought holidays with pay would come within the next few years.

2 It was emphasised that prizes would be awarded for honesty and simplicity and that style and morals, for example, would be ignored. No indication was given to any of the correspondents as to what sort of points they were expected to raise. Those replying were then sent a series of questions to check their statements and as many as possible were interviewed. Seven experienced observers did this work, and all were of the opinion that those replying gave a fairly reasonable sample of Worktown's working-class mentality. 220 letters have been admitted as evidence:

Married men (MM): 57
Single men (SM): 64
Married women (MW): 63
Single women (SW): 36

3 13 had never been there; 15 would not answer; 20 loathed the whole place; of the rest, 23 were children and 210 were adults.

Part 2

4

THE HOLIDAY EXODUS[1]

FRIDAY

It's Friday, the 28th of June, 1938; in the Worktown mills, at exactly 5:30, the bell rings and the machines stop. The week is over. But this Friday, a year is over as well, for tonight the mill will shut, not to reopen for nine full days. Throughout the rest of the year, the workers end their day with the knowledge that they will not have more than two consecutive days off. Mostly they look forward to a few extra pints in the pub or Saturday at the cinema. Tonight is different for an adventure in an entirely non-mill world awaits them. For once in the whole working year, after the bell tonight, the lights, dusts, heat, and noise of the mill become escapable.

> The millworkers come out in batches. A man came up and in passing yelled, 'Ar tha going tonight?' with a nod another young man laughed. . . . Group of women passing, laughing and joking. Counted thirty-four with their hair covered with nets and waved. . . . On four occasions groups shout to other groups in front. Many of the women were carrying baskets. Observer followed two towards the station. They talked together and went into two cake-shops.

Routines are interrupted: hair already set, shopping after work instead of going straight home to cook. But these are not sudden changes; tonight's uniqueness has been 'coming', building momentum, for at least six months. As early as 2 February, one man was heard to mutter: 'The best way to spend the winter in Worktown is to think about how to spend the summer holidays.' And a coal-bagger commented, 'From the end of May onwards the chief topic of conversation is: where are you going?' Many introductions to lodgings are made in this way. Often workmates go to the same lodgings, and Worktown people as a rule like to go away with two or three together. Adverts for accommodation appeared in the *Evening News* in March, and a new timetable for special holiday trains appeared in April.

Still, even after all this planning – to the point of buying shirts and underwear in the January sales – this last week has been particularly hectic.

Mark's has been jammed with girls buying dancing frocks, and Woolworth's stocks are low since 'women, who never clean their teeth at home, take a toothbrush and paste on holiday.' Shoe shops have done great trade in children's shoes, but once again it seems that the men are waiting to get to the holiday site before purchasing their canvas shoes for the summer. The elaborate apparatus of saving is a continuous chain which links one holiday with the next, a demand on the income almost as automatic as life insurance. Elsewhere in the town, the library has announced that readers may borrow additional books for the holiday, although by Friday only twelve people have taken out the full limit. An insurance man works overtime to collect payments before the exodus. The *Evening News* prepares its last full night's edition and sets up to publish 'specials' next week which will be sent to Blackpool and Douglas for their regular readers. And the cinemas report the lowest weekly receipts of the year, as everyone has spent their free time on 'getting ready'.

The preparations have been thorough. Clothes have been washed and cleaned to the extent that police have to restrain the queues outside 'Zip' dry cleaners who are feverishly trying to cope with ten times their normal business. So many houses are empty that the police can't look after them all, and, as our coal-bagger puts it, 'It is a common thing for those going away to slip in on their less fortunate neighbour to ask him to keep an eye on the garden, etc. In return they may bring back a bar or two of rock. As the neighbour probably has never looked at the garden, this is about right!' Pets provide a principal problem, for Blackpool landladies want neither mongrels nor budgerigars. Some cannot cope with the difficulty, so that the Destitute Animals Shelter increases its daily lethal chamber average from 15 to 25 cats near the holidays. One paper boy is instructed by all but 8 of his 95 'usuals' not to deliver next week, and a list is made of addresses for postcards to 'less fortunate' stay-at-home friends and relations.

With all this behind them, the Worktowners have used the final few days to make themselves ready, beginning with a thorough cleaning. As one girl explains: 'This applies more so to anyone working in the mill as they are inclined to have blackheads on the body which require soaking in hot water.' Excepting the new housing estates, few Worktown houses have baths (7 per cent of 1,595 in the working-class East Ward). However, public facilities have been crowded all week long, and any friend who has a bathroom has been besieged. Once clean, there's just time for primping; one ladies' hairdresser has been booked since January until 2:00 a.m. every day of this week, and men have found themselves waiting as long as four hours for a haircut.

Shopping, cleaning, planning, and packing have made for a full and harried week regardless of those vows in December to have everything ready ahead of time and avoid the fuss. But after all this is finally done, there's little remaining but to wait for and think of the morning and what's to come. A cotton piecer explains:

The day before the holidays is generally spent in final preparations. We make out a list of things required for the holiday and tick off each item as it goes into the bags. We do feel a bit excited but manage somehow to keep a serious face over it.

Excitement, but also a certain strain, are at a peak by Friday. Still, fatigue isn't the most pressing discomfort, for there is the ever present awareness that next week there will be no wage packet. Most families have an income of £2 per week, with no pay for the holidays; for many, all of their savings will vanish in the next nine days. So the anticipation is not all so glorious.

What makes a holiday seem so necessary if it causes so much work and stress as well as excitement? An unemployed Worktowner, in conversation over tea, is convinced that people go on holiday

'to escape from the old dragon'. He pointed to a wall no more than a foot high in the back garden, and said that he felt that [wall] symbolised a boundary for him, a tying down; and it was only by walking into the country that he managed to get rid of that feeling, and his worry.

A holiday is possibly a different thing to all Worktowners, but to all it is worth it. Tomorrow, Saturday, is the big, long-awaited day, welcomed even by those who, like this married worker, realise:

When the holiday is finished, I generally find that I have almost spent up. But I have to try and raise the wind for the following week or at least my wife has. It generally takes a few weeks to get on a financial level. This thought often crops up during the holiday, and many an extra has been denied on account of this.

Work and sacrifice it may well mean, but the Worktowners do not readily consider giving up their holiday. On this Friday night in June probably 65 per cent of the townspeople are preparing to go away for the entire holiday and, counting day trips, perhaps 90 per cent will leave at some point in the week. Of these, three-quarters agree with the two men overheard outside a cinema: 'There's only one place isn't there? Blackpool.' 'That's it.'

Blackpool has the sea, the air, the sunshine, and the mystique of health that these Worktowners look for in their one week of another world. Blackpool is the non-mill, non-machine, non-regular experience. And, as a worker's wife comments: 'A large number of people go because it revives past memories, love affairs, etc. And by usage, it becomes a habit that they cannot rid themselves of.'

SATURDAY, A.M.

Saturday, the 29th of June, 1938. In a peculiar way, the day seems to start like any other. The family is up early; breakfast is rushed; the mother disappears to do the washing up; and the father prepares to go out. But instead of hurrying for the starting bell, the family wants to get to the station and get their tickets away from the mill. Breakfast is substantial – not to last a long morning of work, but rather to sustain a morning's travelling. Mother finishes the dishes and sees if the leftover milk will fit in the parcels already packed and father collects the baggage.

Things and actions today seem the same and yet are so different, like the town itself when today is over. By Monday, for the only time all year, the mill and home chimneys will be almost entirely smokeless. Fresh air will blow in from the moors, and the noise of lorries and clatter of clogs will seem minimal. But this difference will be felt by few, as the majority of Worktowners will be long since gone on their search for just these sorts of differences.

For them, the search, beginning with the journey there, offers another substantial dose of the total excitement of the holiday. Some choose to go by bus – in most cases the day trippers who make an occasion of it by 'bribing' the driver to stop along the way as the pubs open. On this Saturday, Ribble buses operate every half-hour (5/-return fare). By 8:30, the station – really only a long wooden platform with three converted nineteenth-century railway carriages for shelter – comes alive with activity. By 9:30, about 200 people are present, mainly pairs of women, with little luggage and fewer children. There's not much talking between fellow passengers, even though three-quarters of them are bound for the same place. Each somehow seems concerned with 'getting there' and devotes all attention and energy to it.

Impatience begins to build as the traffic increases. One traveller indignantly tells another, 'Our bus came in with the engine red hot and steaming and the driver said he could not go right out again. He was told he had to.' However, even overwork doesn't seem able to cope with the volume. By dinner time, 1,420 people have already left Worktown by bus.

And yet the crush here is minimal compared to that at the railway stations; for Worktowners on holiday prefer to travel by train – partly for the convenience of fewer (two) stops and no traffic snarls, and partly because trams and buses are part of everyday, workaday life. What everyone wants, according to the Blackpool publicity bureau (closely linked with the railroad company), is to get to fairyland as fast as possible. 'Come to Blackpool by rail' adverts advise and promise 'A journey without anxiety'.

The Worktowners respond. Lots of children and cases line the train platform; babies, handbags, toddlers, parcels – everyone is loaded down. Nobody moves much and the scene is a parade of all in 'Sunday Best' in honour of the occasion. Most of the women are wearing coats and hats, although one observer still notes traces of the mill on two young women 'with the mill fluff on their tams'. Men wear freshly pressed, often new suits. And the children as well, all carefully polished, are continually reminded to stay that way.

Milling slowly about – never far from their cases – occasionally commenting to a familiar face, or just staring outside, the Worktowners wait for their trains. After a while, some find more novel ways to pass the time until the trains – often being shunted from miles away – appear. A group begins to sing and their mood spreads infectiously across Great Moor St. Station to children and adults alike. One child, on the opposite platform, 'hearing the singing, began dancing about; one pretended to play the banjo. Men with accordion played "Horsey, Horsey". Some people sang. Accordion played "Count Thy Blessings, Name Them One by One". Everyone singing.'

The time does pass, and the trains begin to arrive to load up; even though they are technically on time, the crowd is anxious, for many came early to be sure to get a seat. With the size of the crowd grows the apprehension about this. As a postman notes: 'The silly buggers, they all crowd in front, they won't shift, they're so bloody frightened they won't get to Blackpool; like bloody sardines, and there's two coaches empty.' Yet, somehow, everyone gets on board, even though not everyone gets a seat. Inside the carriage, a man complains that there aren't enough corridor trains with WCs – it interferes with his pre-journey beer drinking. Children kneel on the seats and look out the windows, asking questions about the whitewashed trees that flash past. For the first part of the journey there is almost always restraint and silence. Girls read *Woman's Own, Passing Show*, or *Silver Star*; men smoke; and the train moves on to the stops at Chorley and Preston.

Then things begin to change. Preston is the door to the Fylde, a wide flat plain, roughly square, of pastoral land lying between the rivers Wyre and Ribble. Beyond Preston the traveller sees a meadow landscape unlike most Northern scenery, especially unlike Worktown with its straggling hills and slag. Winding along the coast of the Fylde, he reaches the world of sand-barrens, on which the star grass grows bending away from sea and wind. The train follows the line of the dunes and the Tower comes into view, dominating the flat landscape. No longer is the mill chimney the inescapable symbol; the 'other world' has been reached.

Inside the train, the mood changes; the travellers are now bound together as 'fellows' by this common rallying point. The restraint clearly visible at the outset has dropped from sight. When Preston is passed, the Tower stands as the key and the king of all the wide plain. Cotton and factory chimney are finished with. People in the carriage recognise one another:

Without thinking, observer hands a woman passenger a cigarette and passes them around. All men take one including a man who has slept up till now, and who suddenly comes to life. One of the women, competitively, hands around sweets to women only.

In the train behind:

Sound of an accordion being played is now audible. Then singing. Female voices, pleasant and tuneful. . . . Accordion struck up a hymn.

Three people singing in next carriage. Young man and two girls join in, 'Jesu is the friend of all'. Then accordion played 'Daisy, Daisy'. Everyone sang.

Blackpool is getting closer. A child looking out the window cries out: 'Look Dad it's the Tower!' Women notice and remark on the houses along the front – especially the new ones. The skyline has changed; the land has changed; the mood has changed. It's all Blackpool – all magic – now. The ordinary, the common, the usual is all far behind, left in the mill town. The differences introduced by the first appearance of the Tower are magnified around each bend of the track.

In trains coming in from the south few miss Squire's Gate Camp. Its chalets line the railway and stretch out across the sand-dunes to the tramway; they cluster around the Moorish Pavilion, on whose walls a stucco black cat looks invitingly at a horde of toms. Shortly after that, the Pleasure Beach, with its many struts gleaming white because they have been newly painted for the season, is passed on the seaward side. The peak of the big plunge of the Big Dipper, decorated by Mr Emberton with a conical top that looks like a Tartar's hat, is the focus of all eyes. The train dives between the backyards of tiny, grimy lodging houses, the cheapest in the town, and those who have been before know that Central Station is less than five minutes away.

By now, the compartments have really become alive; luggage is lifted down from the racks; coats are found; children's faces are wiped clean of the stickiness of sweets. One man turns around and asks the question on everyone's mind: 'How far are we now?' A second man answers: 'We'll be in a second.' The sights of the camp, the red-bricked pubs, the wine lodge, the trams, and the last-century cabs seem finally to have convinced everyone that they have made it. They really are HERE!

SATURDAY P.M.

The train pulls in. All rise. 'Good morning.' 'Good morning.' All smiling and affable. Suddenly, unexpectedly, there are references to foreign politics, practically never heard in Worktown.[2] One report was collected from overheard fragments of conversations from people passing out of the station:

> Just one pound six seven, you see
> There should have been more gravy on the joint
> Well, if we could afford
> The bloody porters on railways
> By God, same bloody crowd
> Bloody trains get worse all the time
> Well, t'Russian Communist Party
> You had all the money
> We couldn't save no more than

Can you manage?
Or course, there'll be a war and t' Chinese
Where's our Joe?
He ought to get six months
You'll get lost and they'll lock you up
They won't get me in Army

Concerns have changed: no more mill and home, but rather the new, the unusual, what is about to happen. Thoughts centre on the week ahead, like these words of a Worktowner with a sick wife: 'We emerged from the station, Blackpool Central to be exact, me feeling like a schoolboy again for it was as a schoolboy I had last been to the seaside and my wife's cheeks glowed with the salt air of the incoming tide [which] provided the first sense that were going to have a beneficial holiday.'

To come out of Central Station is to enter a pedestrian holiday-maker's realm; the exits empty into narrow Bank Hey Street, running parallel to the promenade behind the Tower. During fifteen hours of this day, there are seldom fewer than 4,000 people in the street, and cars can only hope to crawl in one direction.

The Tower is there and the mill is so far away. What to do first? Some, mostly the day trippers, with little to encumber them, answer the Tower's call and rush off to it immediately – to the 'mecca of our journey' in the words of one Worktowner. For the Tower goers, the time of day is irrelevant. Many come straight off the train, pay their shilling, and pass through the turnstile. This is perhaps the largest shilling's worth in England:

Emerged Central Station. Felt elation of being in Blackpool, breathed deeply and saw sea on left with sun on it, tide out. About to ask for Tower when I saw top of it poking over roofs of buildings ahead. . . . Did not look in any shops but walked straight towards the Tower.

A few want to see and feel the sea right away. Still, of twenty people followed out of the station by various observers, none went to the sea within the first hour. Many only look at the sea, being far more intrigued by the shops – such as the 'World's Greatest Woolworth's' where some people go straight off the train. It is on the opposite side of the road and new visitors spend from forty minutes to two hours there.

For most holiday-makers, however, the first thing to do is to find the place they booked weeks ago. The 'home away from home' in Blackpool is more than a shelter for a week – it is also a haven of relief from the routines and chores of the household in Worktown. So, for most of the travellers on the train, it is important to get settled early – and then be free to enjoy the first day in Blackpool with a home base to return to when everyone gets tired. On leaving the station, most walk to their lodgings, even if they have lots of

61

heavy luggage, rather than fight the crowds on the unfamiliar buses. Few take a taxi.

So they have arrived. Introductions are made, routines for the week are settled, luggage is put away, and perhaps dinner is eaten in these new and different surroundings. Very often there is even a brief glance back at that hour earlier in the day when it all began – when the journey from one world to another actually started. For a whole week now this will be the only link between the two. Already the journey has a certain amount of glamour and excitement. But that's looking backward already; there will be a long winter for doing that before plans are made for next year. Right now the holiday week lies ahead. The Worktowner plunges in.

NOTES

1 This chapter is based on a revision of 1930s material apparently written by Tom Harrisson and his assistant, Debra Noone, in 1972.
2 Arrival conversations reveal the following percentages: money – 24 per cent, directions – 20 per cent, politics and abroad – 20 per cent, anger – 10 per cent, home – 8 per cent, trains – 6 per cent, food – 4 per cent and 2 per cent each for jobs, women friends, clothes and the sea. Compare with only 1 per cent of 9,000 conversations in the streets and amusements at Blackpool which deal with politics.

5

[THE ESSENTIALS OF HOLIDAY LIFE]

[Observers took great interest in the way in which holiday-makers took care of ordinary life functions – lodging and eating – while on holiday. Implicit in these investigations was a comparison with these same experiences in Worktown and, more obviously, class differences and the limiting influence of income.]

HOME AWAY FROM HOME

The greatest thing to the Worktowner, and above all to the Worktown woman, is that during this one week she need not cook or serve or wash up. It is the chance to sleep longer and to be relieved of the strain of household duties that many Worktown women want most from their Blackpool week:

> It would be a joy going in to breakfast, washed and dressed in nice clothes, then rising from the table knowing that someone else would clear and wash up. I am tired. I just want a rest from everything one does and everything one sees for the rest of the year.

Organiser and dominant figure inside the Worktown home is the housewife. In the Blackpool boarding house, where for one week she will be free from the worries of running a household, the principal influence is again the woman's.

A study was made of 86 lodging houses, of every size and class all over Blackpool. In 3 of them the man was the ruling power; in 10 responsibility was shared. In the remaining 73 the woman dominated. The landlady is a central figure of Blackpool mythology. Blackpool is 'A Holy City, an island surrounded by a sea of landladies' (Palace Varieties). The husband of the house does odd plumbing jobs when the lavatory goes wrong, but it is the landlady who dominates for the six-month summer season. And from the point of view of the visiting Worktown holiday-maker, it is right that a landlord, a male, a master, factory boss, or foreman, should not be the one to receive them, but rather a woman, a mother to the family. It is into a matriarchal society that the Worktowners, themselves from a semi-matriarchal society, come for the 1 week in 52 in which they will sleep in a strange bed.

We found four main types of places for holiday-makers:

1 The hotel, licensed, generally charging over 15/-a day.
2 The private hotel, unlicensed, large, with a name prominently displayed, and generally costing over 10/-a day.
3 The boarding house or company house, unlicensed, a large private house, usually from the front looking normal, but having unusual depth back from the street, and thus 5 to 10 bedrooms. Charges about 7/6 a day average.
4 The family house (or Kippax), an ordinary home that takes in one or more guests by recommendation, has no visitors' book or legal status, and frequently breaks overcrowding regulations; it undercuts fixed rates with rooms at 6/- or less. Groups 3 and 4 are by far the most numerous.

30 observers stayed in every sort of lodging from the Metropole and Norbreck to the Girls' Shelter during the Worktown holiday but found no Worktowners over the 10/-a day level in Blackpool. However, in all the cheaper places, there were Worktowners. The better off Worktowner did not commonly spend his holidays in Blackpool. The private hotels, centred in the North Shore and South Shore promenade strips, are thus populated with 'middle-class' sort of people, but mainly from further away and from the big cities. We shall worry less about the fully licensed expensive places where guests take little part in the mass life and amusements of the town.

Most Worktowners stay in the Kippax and boarding houses. The smallest type of boarding house has 5 or 6 bedrooms, dates from before the war and is only one source of support to the proprietors. In one small boarding house, the husband has an insurance round; this is the permanent, small, family income. His wife's boarding house brings in the seasonal big income of 7/6 per visitor per day. At the opposite end of the scale are the private hotels, caterpillaring north and south along the promenade. Running these hotels is a full-time job for both wife and husband, although wife directs and husband serves the meals.

Because of cramped space, the family house (or Kippax), unrecognised officially, takes the fresh visitor right into the domestic circle. Our landlady uses this system. She has five children, never smokes or drinks, and takes everyone to her maternal bosom. When the neighbours protested because she charged her visitors 1/6 a meal, she told the visitors to spread the news it was 2/-, but left it unchanged. One thing she gives gratis is your horoscope from a teacup. She joined a mother in playing a trick on the mother's daughters:

They put itching powder in the girls' pajamas. They bought a little sixpenny poe. They put it in the girls' room and half-filled it with

64

Andrews Liver Salts. She locked the bathroom and said that something had gone wrong with the drains. When the girls went to their bedroom, all the others waited on the stairs to hear the results. The girls tried their pajamas on: they said, 'Oh I am itchy, I am itchy. I can't wear these pajamas.' Then they heard the mother say, 'Are you in bed Bina?' She said, 'Yes, I'm lying in bed naked.' Well, our landlady and the boys were bursting with laughter but they daren't make a sound. Then the mother who was in the secret said to one girl, 'Don't you want to go somewhere Vera? Because if you do, the lavatory's out of order. You'll have to use the thing under the bed.' Vera said she didn't want to. Then mother said to Bina 'Don't you want to go somewhere Bina?' But she said no. This was surprising because every night before Vera and Bina had come in at 12.00 holding themselves. Then suddenly their little brother who had been asleep woke up, wanted to go and jumped out of bed and used it. The liver salts frothed all over the floor. Bina said, 'Oh, I am glad we did it in that back street.'

This is the sort of fun that people get in the intimate circle of the small house. It is rarer in the bigger places, though it does happen. Here is a single girl, a typist from Edinburgh, at a South Shore private hotel:

Likes sitting on the narrow hotel stairs so as to be in the middle of all coming and going. Her friend married an Indian and she approves of this. She makes an apple-pie bed filled with Blackpool rock for the father of a family staying in the hotel.

However, this conviviality is abnormal in the Blackpool lodging house. Even in the gay near-illegal house, all is not happy. The women overwork and suffer for it. Let us look at the everyday routine of the small six-room boarding house. The front room on the ground floor, with its bay window, is the only communal one. Behind it, the proprietors and their help live and cook. Upstairs consists entirely of bedrooms, bathroom, and lavatories:

Bedrooms are eight feet by eight, the floor covered with oilcloth, ceiling with leafy wallpaper, the walls with pictures of Dolores Costello, crosses and scrolls bearing the motto 'I know that my Redeemer liveth' (although the proprietors of this house are Jewish). . . . When visitors want to go to the lavatory, they first peep out of their doors; and when they get in, women average $1\frac{1}{2}$ minutes, men 3 to 4 minutes. This visit is usually paid before breakfast. Visitors come down to have breakfast in a room whose most compelling decoration is its card of rules, ordering noiseless rising, forbidding piano playing before eight o'clock, suggesting an early exit on the day of departure and pointing out that to avoid mistakes extras must be paid for every night. Visitors are particularly desired to keep their children from using the piano or playing on the stairs or landings.

After breakfast, most people either spend a period sitting on the seat in the garden or go straight out.

None of five Worktowners observed in this boarding house was heard to swear. There were piano and radio, but the piano was not heard played that week, and the radio was out of date, low powered: 'On Sunday morning, man tries to get Radio Luxembourg, can get only the National Sunday service, so switches off.' The only music is the crying of the one baby guest and the 8:15 gong that calls to breakfast.

Another sort of lodging is the private hotel. Where the small boarding house is plain, single-fronted, and pre-war, the private hotel has gone up in the last ten years; it has three or four floors, rustic brick, terracotta facing. In comparison with the boarding house's tiny garden, only big enough to sit in and look at passers, these private hotels have gardens ten yards square with a grass lawn, a flower bed, and chunks of white rock, strongly suggesting waves. Within one, the furniture is dark oak, the tables small gate-legged Jacobean; there are tall cut-glass vases of gladioli, salmon-pink. Above, the oak matchboard panelling of the lounge and dining room is plaster, with semi-lunar squirls.

Still in this hotel of thirty rooms, where the guest pays 12/6 a day, there is only one bathroom. Two observers in the house for a week did not see it used. The hot water was never hot. Next door to the bathroom are two small lavatories, one gents, one ladies, the only ones in the house; but there is a jerry in every room. Pictures on the walls of this house are gilt-framed water-colours and calendars with pictures of 'The Age of Innocence'.

Although they say they want to get away from their home town, holiday-makers frequently make a point of coming to a place where they will find home town affinities, either because their pals are going there or because the management came from their home town. Landladies advertise the town of their origin.

A study by two observers in a private hotel brought up the following topics as unfailing sources of conversation: prices of tours, slimming, and getting brown. Guests here are:

1 Mrs Woodrow, a bored widow and 'life of the party'.
2 Harriet, a typist. Her mother kept a shrewd eye on her; she wanted to go to Ostend for her holiday, but Blackpool was the only place she was allowed to go to. An unwanted friend of Mama's 'looked in' to see how she was getting on.
3 An organist's wife, 60 years old who lives in Surbiton. Her husband is going blind and drinks much beer. Grown-up son tries to reform him. Spends her time crocheting a curious hat.
4 Widow Toynbee was shocked when asked, 'Do you live alone?'
5 Man, wife, and daughter of 20. Father has an ulcerated stomach. He pulls all the bedclothes off his daughter's bed in the morning.

6 A man with a wig, 60, his wife, and three other women from London.
7 A silent, engaged couple.

Groups 1, 2, 3 and 4, had formed a 'Fold' into which they drew the 2 observers on their arrival and from which 5 and 6 were excluded. 7 would have liked to have joined in, but never managed to penetrate. Exciting topic of conversation in the 'Fold' was last night's dreams:

> Widow Toynbee's dreams: 'I sometimes dream I have nothing on, or only a vest, and I walk about, and no-one thinks it at all strange. I have a nightmare sometimes of a room with water flowing all through it. . . . another nightmare is when no-one will believe what you say.'
>
> Harriet's dream: 'A black cat tries to climb up a net skirt which I wear over my ordinary skirt. I hate it. But my Grandmother likes the cat and is pleased when I am annoyed.'

After these dreams of widows and virgins, it is not surprising that 'there was much grief at our departure from the hotel. Harriet clung on to (female) observer so hard that Widow Toynbee said, "I wonder what it would be like to have a woman fall in love with you." ' But at a North Shore private hotel, another subject is reappearing:

> Old woman: 'Breaks me eart. We have both ad very good health. E says, Mind them steps and e's two years younger than me. 88, this month.' She tells history of family. Brothers and sisters died at 72, 74, 75. One was rheumatic for 32 years, bedridden for 3. Had to feed her. No tea. Milk and water. Piles. Couldn't sit on them. 'Did everything for her.' Daughter died recently of a stroke. Boy's mother tells of hunchback heiress who married Wesleyan minister, separated, and died a year ago at Blackpool of a stroke. 'Eh, it's a bad business,' says old woman.

At this private hotel, we see signs of a Blackpool health neurosis, though the sick people in this middle-class group are not thin or bronchial like many of the cotton operatives, but fat and rheumatic.

SERVICE OR FREEDOM

There are two sorts of terms you can get at a Blackpool hotel, either full board (half of which include supper) or bed and breakfast. But if you are a bed and breakfast lodger (rates from 4/6 a day), you bring your own food in to be cooked. It is hard to persuade your landlady to do this in a busy period. Moreover, bed and breakfasting entails shopping, one of the things the Worktown wife wants to avoid for a week; so families that can afford full board take it. If a prosperous year has made full board possible for the first time, they go away thinking, boarded in, the first time I have done so, but not the last I hope. I have done nothing but laze on the sands or go on the sea and go home ready for my meals, and better still ready for bed at 10:30 to sleep.

[And time is key to it all.] Said one correspondent: 'I should like my breakfast at nine o'clock, not the usual porridge, bacon, eggs, etc. Something light but nourishing.' A child in a boarding house screamed: 'I want my porridge an' I want my bread, I want it an' I want it an' I want it.'

The ordinary Worktowner need not worry. He will get his meals punctually. But the more you pay, the larger the range of time within which you may eat it. For example, the big (licensed) hotels are the only ones that offer breakfast before 8:00 and the only ones that provide breakfast after 10:00. In private hotels, the margin of an hour allowed for meals is common; in hotels, always at least one hour. The boarding house allows the least time for meals: 84 per cent have meals restricted to an exact time or within half an hour. The richer people have their two main meals with about eleven hours between them. The poor, eight hours between. Whereas at all the other lodgings dinner is the midday meal, at hotels it is from 6:30 p.m. to 8:30 p.m. The evening meal for boarders is at most biscuits, fish, or egg; they have no full meal after 5:00 p.m. (and then never more than cold meat and salad). Boarders must wait till 8:00 the next morning or fifteen hours, whereas the well-offs go an average twelve hours without food. This is an important 'class distinction'.

At home the Worktown worker eats his main meals almost always at about 12:30 p.m. and after 5:30 p.m. The tendency to a later midday meal and earlier tea in boarding houses and family houses is not to the boarders' advantage, but suits the landlady when she does not have to provides a late supper (in 40 per cent of the boarding houses.)

This enforced change of habit promotes holiday indigestion, encourages spending money on foods outside, and is one of the factors causing the near obsession with the time of day. These times, arbitrarily fixed and generally enforced by the landladies, control all the movements of people on the sands and promenade as effectively and more exactly than the tide or weather. They focus the attention of people on a punctuality from which many are seeking release.

Finally let us see people actually eating. Meal in a boarding house:

The people at observer's table are very reserved. The two couples (the table holds five) won't even talk to each other. If it should be necessary to do this, they speak in whispers, so that the people on the other side of the table, eighteen inches away, cannot hear a word. They take very small mouthfuls, so that observer has finished his food in half the time they take to do so. It is not done to unfold one's serviettes till food has been placed in front of one.

The man and wife at the table have an additional taboo in that neither starts to eat alone: they must begin simultaneously. At breakfast this morning the woman wanted to eat her porridge which was getting cold, but the man wanted to read through his *Daily Mirror* first. She had to wait till he was ready to start.

Now a private hotel (i.e. for better-off people):

The maids, assisted by Miss H., serve lunch. Mint sauce with mutton, horseradish with beef are there at beginning of meal. Most of talk confined to own table, but nods and greetings in going to and from places.

Everybody eats all they get, large quantities. Three course lunch, which about half finish with cheese and biscuits, rest stop after pudding; large quantities of badly cooked unwholesome food are served, which according to the Worktown middle class here represented, is considered very good. Coloured junket powders, cheap jelly cream packets, tinned cream, tinned fruit, etc. Potatoes always mashed or boiled, no greens, carrots once. . . . Fat and rheumatic people predominate at this hotel. They talk much of cancer and rheumatism.

Boarding houses, private hotels, and family houses have now been studied. On the basis of the eighty-six houses visited, there is an extreme difference between the service and comfort of each. Whereas private hotels provide chamber pots, shoes cleaned, baths, stationery, newspapers, telephone, morning tea, serviettes, and a list of local shows, the Kippax houses seldom or never do so. And between these is the boarding house. But in regard to liberty and individual freedom, to get up and go to bed any time, all, except the Kippax, were negative: whereas the boarding house is more restricted, the private hotel is rather freer.

In sum, we may put it roughly that the less you pay, the fewer the comforts; but the lower the price, the greater the liberty. Boarding houses and Kippax houses are equally ill-equipped with comforts compared with the private hotels. It is in regard to liberty that Kippax houses have their appeal. Family houses give keys most readily, allow their visitors in latest, and insist least on rising at the fixed time. So that what money buys at the more expensive private hotel is service, not freedom. Freedom is dependent on other than monetary factors – numbers, for one thing. The guests at the private hotel (30) are too numerous for informality; at the Kippax house (2) they are small enough for real personal contact. But the boarding house landlady, with her 10 to 20 guests, feels the responsibility of controlling them with her hanging placards of regulations.

One proof that the greater liberty attracts visitors to the family house or Kippax is revealed by the number of motorists that come to them compared to the boarding houses. When a car (a middle-class badge) comes to a

Kippax, its owners want a sense of intimacy of the family circle, of a life less bounded by regulations. Regulations in the boarding house do something to kill the idea of holiday.

Music hall comedians credit boarding houses and hotels with all sorts of liberties that aren't there. But in fact landladies frown on the first hint of the 'unrespectable'. Three girls of 16 tell an observer:

> They had always gone to the same lodging house, off Central Drive on Belmont Road; but they will not go there again. They don't like it – the landlady is too strict. She has been 'taking it out of them' for talking out of their bedroom window to boys in the house opposite.

When the good-looking blonde observer tried to get digs alone on a Sunday afternoon, she was refused three times because they 'don't take single women'. Here again, the unofficial house allows the greater freedom. One landlady recounted with some tenderness how she had slept an unmarried couple on her sofabed for a week.

Still 25 per cent of the landladies questioned acknowledged that drink was to be had, although none of them was licensed. Occasionally there is police action and proprietors find themselves in court. Keeping a stock in hand is the dangerous thing, and thirteen of the landladies make the proviso that it must be ordered in advance. One Blackpool postcard shows the outside of a house marked APARTMENTS. A blue-uniformed, red-nosed boy is arriving with a box of a dozen beers at a half-open green door. At one window is the landlady with distressed expression; at the other, with beaming faces, three round-eyed, check-suited men. The caption is 'WE'RE O.K. NOW! THE FIRST OF THE LUGGAGE JUST ARRIVING AT BLACKPOOL.'

[If this image of freedom is illusory, another longing is also seldom realised.] An overheard conversation: 'It's just like being at home.' But does it feel like being at home in a boarding house, where everything is so different from the Worktown home? It is larger; it is all in use. In Worktown, of two ground-floor rooms, the front one is only used on Sunday. In the back one, the meals are prepared, eaten, and cleared away. The backyard is the used section of outdoor living. The front of the house leads directly on to the street. If there is a patch of garden, it is not used for sitting in. Blackpool provides new scenes internal and external, a new routine of walking, eating, reading, going to bed. How Worktowners adjust themselves to a new rhythm, after fifty-one weeks conditioning in the mill rhythm, how they have their fortune told and Fun House laughter, we shall soon see for ourselves.

[STALLS AND ROCK]

Everywhere in Blackpool the holiday-maker is offered opportunities to eat. Even on the sands, as the tide goes out, on come the ice-cream stalls, sweet stalls, and oyster carts. On the Pleasure Beach, barkers shout hot dogs, waffles, and rock. All down the streets expert salesmen press rock on the passer-by. Fish and chip shops are more numerous in Blackpool than any other town of the same size. More than half the shops in Blackpool are food shops, and in our own survey of the town centre, 41 of 103 stalls were found to be primarily food dealers.

Of the various possibilities, the one of most interest at most times of the day is that which is transitional between food and drink – ice. On the beach and in the streets are the ice-cream carts. Hourly turnover of one cart on an August Bank holiday was £2/1/6. Like so many things in Blackpool, the ice-cream cart has a special architecture, with features reminiscent of the East more than the West. The carts have been likened by observers to 'little temples' or 'a large scale Punch and Judy box'. Not till the fifteenth century did Marco Polo bring Europe a recipe from Japan. Nowadays the Mediterranean associations are carefully preserved.

Off the beach, in a backstreet midway in the cheap lodging house area, is the shop of the big ice-cream specialist, Pablo. Ten years ago, Pablo made and sold ice-cream on the bottom floor of a converted stables in this same backstreet. His place became noted among Blackpool visitors for the amounts of ice-cream that they could get for a penny and two-pence. Five years ago, Pablo was drawing such profits from it that he was able to demolish his stable and build a concrete ice-cream palace, with ice-cream bars on the ground and first floors as well as in a sungarden on the roof. He told us that they often have as many as 10,000 customers a day. Pablo does no advertising. His one poster is on the wall at the head of the backstreet which leads down to his own backstreet; it simply says 'THIS IS THE WAY TO PABLO'S ICES':

> He said that a lot of new ice-cream sellers had come to Blackpool, but that the demand grew with the supply. Formerly ice-cream had been made and sold by lickspittle dirty Italians who had come to England and America to better themselves. And naturally no one had liked to buy it, but now it was sterilised and safe and doctors with any grey matter said it was good for one. . . . [H]is family were Worktown people, but his grandfather had been the son of a Spaniard and South American chief's daughter. This ancestor had a circus – Pablo's Mammoth Circus – which had been all the rage in the eighteen-hundreds.

Pablo is undoubtedly one of Blackpool's popular heroes. Our landlady constantly spoke of him as the best employer in the town. We found that his girls get tolerable hours and pay and, at the close of the season, a collective holiday in France or Holland. Every day of the season he sits impassively, with drooping mustachio, sombrero, and a grey worsted suit, at the wheel of

71

his big Chrysler parked in the backstreet, and watches the thick crowds of holiday-makers queue up at his ice-cream bars.

Side by side with the ice-cream carts are the thirteen oyster stalls. This is the one food the holiday-makers eat extensively in Blackpool and nowhere else. As with most Blackpool food there is a shout and a patter: 'Beautiful quality today, all the cream of the sea. From our own beds. Come and look at the quality.' 'Our own beds' are mostly American. An oyster stall on Central beach on the Bank Holiday sold in an hour about £4 worth. Most people use vinegar and their fingers.

'Oysters', said one vendor, 'are very good for courting couples.' Our landlady further explained that they were very 'strengthening . . . good for nursing mothers'. The more 'unnecessary' the food, the more obvious the special language, special shape, or special thought. While fruit stalls are fairly common and 129 places specialise in it, fruit was the least popular food on the stalls.

Very different are the Blackpool rock sellers, the noisiest and most eloquent of all the food groups. Observers got the impression that they had all been to one rock-selling college. A stick of rock is a cylinder of red, yellow, or green minty confectionery, a quarter of an inch to 2 inches in diameter, 3 to 12 inches long. They are rolled in paper with a view of Black-pool Tower. A stall by Central Station sells a ton of rock a week.

The rock market suffers from intense competition and undercutting. This has also stimulated rapid innovation even over a period between June and September 1937 as rock is adapted to many different shapes:

> Features not observed [in June]: Pink horseshoes of rock. . . . Green, pink, and amber round transparent lollipops on sticks. Knickers, which had only been observed as rarities, are much commoner. Mae's Vest is a nova [an impression of Mae West's upper torso]. . . . Me and My Pal is new, while the plain babies [sic] bottle seems to be going out. Most noticeable is the decline of the Old School Tie, which was far more in evidence previously.

The 'Old School Tie' is a sugar creation with realistic stripes. 'Me and My Pal', alternatively called 'The Good Companion', is a pair of sugar models flattened together on a card, twinlike, one a pink baby and the other a white baby's bottle of equal size. While 'Sally's What-Not' is a 6d. pink sugar pair of knickers with the shape of the appropriate and well-developed portion of the female body inside them; over the sub-navel area is a golden paper circle inscribed, SEAL OF QUALITY.

The holiday-maker's essential food needs do not altogether escape atten-tion in Blackpool. There is little use of foreign words on the menus of the food places of ordinary workpeople in Blackpool, nor do these people often eat chickens. At the [middle-class] Tower Restaurant 30 per cent of the items on the menu have foreign names, but this was true of only 2 per cent in

Morris's Central Pier. In the essentials, the romantic element is reduced to a minimum even in Blackpool. About money and clothes and food the Worktowner has few possible 'illusions'.

At all Prom and 'popular' places, 'Fish and Chips' is on the menu at 6d. to 10d. Out of 194 meals observed and reported from restaurants all over the town, from Woolworth's Snack Bar to the Baronial Hall:

> 33 per cent contained chipped potatoes.
> 27 per cent contained fish
> 16 per cent contained tea
> 14 per cent contained peas
> 9 per cent contained bread and butter
> 6 per cent contained sausages
> 4 per cent contained meat pies
> 3 per cent contained meat (other than pies)

Chips and fish thus easily lead the holiday-maker's eating, especially for those 30 per cent who take all their meals out. Visitors to Blackpool mostly believe that, because Blackpool is near the sea, the fish is fresh. In this belief they even buy it to take back with them to Worktown. But the fish is not caught in Blackpool, and though Fleetwood is only a few miles away, Blackpool fishmongers trade with Hull, Bristol, and Grimsby. There are 149 chip shops in Blackpool along with 106 trip shops, and 201 'popular' cafes catering to the hungry visitor.

The pie stalls are frequent links in the chains of slot machines, fortune telling booths, monstrosities, autophotos, and Walkie-snaps: 'Generally the pies are on an inclined board, and a typical stall has ninety-eight arranged in nineteen rows.' The pie-man is above all interested in the day visitor for his stalls are on the main routes to and from rail stations and are open at all hours.

Food sellers of all sorts compete vigorously by the help of barkers and enormous and elaborately worded placards, but seldom with severe price-cutting. They affect the general tempo and landscape second only to that of the amusements and slot-machines. [Food is a linkage between the essentials of lodging and the dream world of Pleasure Beach.] Perhaps this can be clarified if we digress for a moment from sociology into a poem by a sixth-form boy at the Blackpool Grammar School, entitled 'Promenade Concert':

> It is the same, the insistent voice the summons
> From the lone wheatfields factory-sown,
> That calls them
> Into an erewhon of flying boats
> To the soft-falling music of the piers.
> Gone are, forgotten, months of
> Walking desolation,

Nursing machines through months of vomiting;
Remains only the ecstasy,
The gradual dusk, soothing,
The sweat of the work of pleasure,
And the words said,
And the words sung,
And the works forgotten blend
And bloom and glow on the
Sweet wind that gently kisses the
Pie-shop windows with greased, hungering lips,
Like the cigarettes that
Flower along the lanes of occupied seats.
As the lips stay on
And the scene changes
From side-show to coffee-stall
From fairground to factory.

6

WITCH DOCTOR

[Closely related to the essentials of lodgings and food, the adjustments they require, and the mystique they create is the holiday obsession with health. Observers saw this theme expressed in many, often archaic forms and with much ambiguity. We begin with two images of Blackpool health.]

> The Duke (of Kent) took a long look at the sands southwards and northwards, and then turning to Alderman Tatham said, 'I have never seen sands looking so well. I suppose at times you will get 30,000 or more people here in a day?'   'We get 150,000' replied Ald. Tatham.
> 'Do you really?' said the Duke. 'Why, that is marvelous.' (*Blackpool Gazette*, 20 October 1937)

Or a beach patrol said:

> Yes, there's quite a lot of people ask me what it is. Some tell me outright that it's shit. . . . I had a chap at Worktown holiday week . . . and he showed me one. 'Oh' says I, 'it must come from over there' (pointing southwest). 'What are those?' says he. Well, I was forced to tell him. 'They're sewer pipes', says I. 'Oh, that should never come here, it should go the other way.' I explained to him that it was a wet day and they'd been pumping. It turned out he was a doctor.

Blackpool's sanitary inspectors periodically parade the sands looking for what they call 'floaters'. 60 per cent of the total acreage of the Borough's sewage is discharged into the sea through two 36-inch pipes between Central and South piers. This saves a great deal of money, and raises only one problem – the need for care in ensuring that the excrement is properly 'screened', i.e. broken up and desiccated so that it is unrecognisable.

The screening stations and storage tanks are certainly unrecognisable. The ventilating shafts at the Gynn are topped by elaborate stone pillars of urns and the main Central Beach outlet is the famous Blackpool windmill. One of the special Blackpool souvenir cards shows windmill, sailing ship, Dutch boy and girl in costume embracing. The windmill itself is white-walled, with delicate sails, a foreground of Dutch girls and a Dutch river in a sea of tulips on a canal bank. Under the windmill are two public lavatories. It was not till observers had repeatedly noticed larger smells than these places justified that discreet enquiries revealed a series of sewage pumps as well as a complicated set of problems that make adequate 'screening' difficult.

This economical system is undoubtedly an important factor in preventing people from bathing in the sea, and the indications are that more and more people are becoming aware of it. Perhaps this will benefit the Corporation's new super indoor bath on the front, now being constructed at the cost of £256,000.

THE BREEZE OF HEALTH AND SNAKES

Ironically the sails of the windmill are symbolic both of fresh breezes and the beauties of preindustrialism. Blackpool's air is a part of its great fame. Blackpool has 1,447 annual hours of sunshine as compared with 1,007 in Worktown; average annual rainfall is 36.49 and 47.69 inches respectively. These advantages of climate were manifest in 1790, when a visitor wrote a poem (quoted by Allen Clarke, *The Story of Blackpool*, 1923):

> Of all the gay places of public resort
> At Chatham or Scarborough, at Bath or at Court,
> There's none like sweet Blackpool of which I can boast
> So charming the sands, so healthful the coast;
> Rheumatics, scarbutics, and scrofulous kind,
> Hysterics and vapours, disorders of mind,
> By drinking and bathing you're made quite anew
> As thousands have proved and know to be true.

And health has become the main theme of Blackpool's publicity. A large advert, on notice boards all over England by Easter 1938, displays a large girl in green bathing dress with the caption: 'KEEP FIT, BLACKPOOL FOR A SPRING TONIC'. People do come full of Keep-Fitness: 122 out of 365 of our correspondents mentioned that they liked Blackpool because it was healthy.

And the moment they step out of Central Station, they become aware that Blackpool assumes their inherent unhealthiness. In every amusement area there are posters, shops, and stalls, such as this one, offering as drinks

> Back and Kidney Mixture
> Aspro Mixture
> Constipation Mixture
> Tonic Pick-me-up
> Hot Peppermint for Indigestion
> Stomach and Liver Draught
> Black Draught

An observer, who worked in a chemist's shop in Blackpool, reports how on Sunday morning, the day after arriving, holiday-makers crowd in first thing, asking for Andrew's Liver Salts and night-lights; she says the excitement, the change of routine, and the different meals and mealtimes upset a great many people. Sudden death or disease are stressed on postcards too; ill-health themes in music hall jokes are the largest single category, 13 per cent of all laugh-raisers.

The holiday-maker is most interested in the score or so of medicos, especially the 'health lecturers' with sessions eight to fifteen times a day. They favour the promenade near the piers. So let's hear one, 6 p.m., 4 September 1937:

> The herbalist sits on a chair gazing at a four foot long snake which is on the floor. After about a minute . . . he brings it to the crowd of about a dozen people. A youth of about 22 touches it, then a young soldier touches it, the rest of the crowd hangs back. 'Twopence a time to touch it', the herbalist shouts, and then laughs. . . .
>
> The crowd gathers and he asks them to come inside. 'All intelligent people will do so and I don't want to talk to anybody who has no intelligence'. . . . He asks for a member of the audience to come forward. A young woman comes on to the platform and the herbalist offers to test her on the pulsometer. 'Take your gloves off, you're not Tommy Farr.' . . .
>
> [He does the same to an elderly woman]: 'I know that your trouble is going to be your nerves.'
>
> 'I am just wondering how many people in this room would be glad to know of a cure for rheumatism or nerves.' He counts 9. A long pause here and he looks nearly as if he is going to weep, and then: 'Friends, I am just a bit upset thinking about what happened in this shop on August Bank Holiday afternoon. A little chap stood in here never taking his eyes off me. He fascinated me. I said to the people, is there anyone in this shop who would like to know of a cure for rheumatism? And he shouted, 'Please sir, I would.' Everyone in the room laughed and I couldn't help smiling myself. But when I had finished my lecture, I got him on the platform and said, 'Listen sonny, if I told you of a cure for rheumatism, what would you do with it?', and he said, 'Please sir, I'd take it home and take it to my mother.' I nearly wept. He was one of the waifs and strays of Manchester and all the time he was thinking of his mother at home. So I wrote it down for him and I am going to do the same for you. If I am talking to intelligent people, you will get out your pencils and take it down. I declare on my honour before I write it down that it is the only thing in the world that will put your stomach right. It makes me feel like a young man of 26 but instead of being 26 I am considerably older than that, I am 76.' Here he starts to throw his legs

and arms about. . . . 'It is taken from the digestive organs of the filthiest animal but when it has been sent to the laboratory it comes back cleansed, Pepsin-Porci.' . . .

'It is the most expensive medicine in the world, and if you are a panel-patient you won't get it. There is no chemist in the world today who will make you more than six months' supply up for less for 12/6. I am going to give some away tonight. Did I say give away? Well, I suppose I shall have to do it, I have not said anything that I didn't mean. I will give you six months' supply, this works out at 1 1/2d. per week. I am putting these on the counter and they are 5/-. I am not going to take any less.' His name and address are on the wrapper and if [the customer] is not satisfied the thing can be returned.

About fifteen other herbalists at the same time are attracting similar crowds. The panel-system [local health service] hit herbalists for a time, which explains their hostility to doctors. It is not till he has had the people under his spell for five minutes that he comes on to the subject of health. He interests people, first, with the snake. The snake and other reptiles are common herbalist symbols.

In the Sharma Yogi Show, the white-topped impresario, Ashworth, introduces a young Indian, who brings in a cane basket with lid which he places near the man lying on the bed of nails, near a shallow tank in which there are two or three baby alligators. The Indian takes the lid off and shows two snakes. Ashworth says:

Here you see a jungle wallah. He is immune from poison. This is a black mamba, the most deadly of African snakes. He (the Indian) is covered with bites, but they have no effect on him. Now this snake has not had its fangs removed. I wouldn't go within four yards of him.

The man who can handle the snake has the secret of life by implication. In contemporary English culture there are two main classes of reference to snakes. The first is near to the surface, and mainly dependent on the Christian story brought into its quintessential English form by Milton. This is the view of the snake as the symbol of the satanic, the cunning, and deceitful, closely allied to the idea of erring Eve. It comes out in ordinary speech in phrases like 'snake in the grass'. But though popular and familiar, it does not loom large in Blackpool. Blackpool is more concerned with the second mode of reference, one deeper rooted and older yet.

Here the snake represents life and life renewed. When the snake teeth were sown at Colchis and Thebes, armed men sprang up. In Malekula, when the first girl presented the first man to her mother, she showed him an enormous snake coiled round the house. When the medico holds up his snake, he is using a similar creation myth. But more than this. In many cultures the snake which throws and renews its skin is a token of rejuvenation and a seasonal cycle which guarantees immortality. In Blackpool, we shall constantly meet this myth of rejuvenation, especially in the seasonal cycle of spring rebirth.

THE POOL-WINNING BUDDHA AND THE LAWS OF KARMA

In the narrow densely packed street behind the Tower is the booth of Professor Aubrey Winston Grey, N.I.A., E.F., who stands in a pulpit wearing mortarboard and gown. He has a wooden pointer, an altar, seven candlesticks, and his pool-winning Buddha, the size of a large spaniel, surrounded by flowers. On the altar are piles of envelopes containing horoscopes, loose money, and a piece of paper with '53/0/2' written on it. On the right hand side are more photographs and a large caption stating that 'Euclid could not, but the Professor could' forecast the winner of the St Leger.

In Oxford accent, the lecture lasts twenty-five minutes, blackboard and chalk in action. On the basis of the date of the Crimean War, which he writes up as 1857–8 (in error for 1854–6), then the Sudan War, 1880–1, and the Boer War, 1899–1902, in rapid mathematics he shows that the war of 1914 was inevitable and forecasts a war in 1937. (This was in September 1937). Discusses Good Luck which is Faith to him:

> Mentions God's Glorious Heaven, lifting his cap. Calls on God to wither left arm from finger to shoulder-blade if what he says isn't true. Writes 10/-and £30,000 on board, talking about Irish Sweepstakes. Says you can divorce your wife with £30,000. Man in dense audience: 'Not mine, I couldn't.' Prof. ignores him. Asks if anyone has ever had a cheque from Littlewood's. Four have. Shows his for £40 and explains how he won it. He will sell models of the true Buddha, 1/-, but three conditions must be observed if it is to be successful in providing Health, Happiness, and a win in the Pools: (1) always keep in left-hand pocket or purse; (2) never lend it anyone; (3) have faith. With the Buddha comes a free horoscope, containing your lucky dates and numbers. An average of twenty paid shilling at end of each half-hour.

The link between the academic, the medical, and the astrological is far from accidental. A large proportion of present-day Oxford dons insist on what one of them recently called 'a reverence for things not intellectually apprehensible'. Another of them (Gargantuan C.S. Lewis) has written, in elaborate and tedious stanzas, a poem in which a young Queen, unhappy with her doddering and hypochondriac royal husband, is pursued through the forest by the usurping dictator and rescued by the King of Faery who whisks her away to his ageless land.

The astrologer Ellis has been established in Blackpool since 1891, the year when the Corporation ejected from the sands all palmists, phrenologists, or astrologers. So Ellis took a shop on the promenade, becoming in time a town councillor. His *Book of the Ellis Family* offers 'Advice on Health', with the details filled in open spaces by the astrologer. Here is part of the reading given to an observer:

I consider your Present state of health is
  Fair
and the part of you most liable to be affected is the
  Stomach and Nerves.
For the benefit of your health I should advise you to acquire the habit of taking a glass of
  hot water
every Morning and a glass of
  hot milk
every Night, it will help to ward off illness.

After a passage on diet prescribing total abstinence from sausage, nuts, celery, cheese, we come to section 3: 'HERBAL REMEDY FOR THE DISEASE YOU ARE MOST LIABLE TO. . . . Constipation. Medicine: Procure one ounce each of any four of the following: Balmony, Bitter Root, Buckbean, Butternut Bark, Cascara Bark.' After that, there are suggestions for treatment which encourage the patient to 'breathe through the nose, to get all the fresh air you can, but avoid draughts', and to spend forty minutes over each meal. Then we come to an important page headed 'HOW, WHEN, AND WHERE TO SLEEP (According to the Law of Repose and the Law of Magnetic Polarity)' with the advice 'to obtain the greatest benefit from your night's repose you should sleep with your head towards the' (and here comes a space two and one-fifth inches long in which Ellis should fill in the direction, but has not). These diagnoses culminate in a climax on the last page entitled: 'YOUR EXPERIENCE IN PAST LIVES (According to the Laws of Karma and Reincarnation)'.

Your experience in Past Lives has resulted in you bringing into this life much (here two and one-fifth inches space) and the reason you probably do not remember the past experiences is because you have a new physical body. The merchant, in carrying forward an account to a new page, does not always give all the details of the preceding page, but the results only.

All over Blackpool astro-medicine appears. Numerous Blackpool councillors have had astrological interests, including the late Dr George Kingsbury, 'the most picturesque of those who dominated local politics and social life 40 years ago' (*Gazette*, 9 March 1938). He rose to be Mayor of Blackpool, and 'practically single-handed, he altered the course of modern medical treatment' by developing a technique of mirror and watch hypnotism. He wrote a textbook on it and, as a result, became involved in a lawsuit over the use of hypnosis in connection with a female patient and her last will and testament. He left Blackpool in a haze and set up in London. Kingsbury was a man, as the *Gazette* says, 'in advance of his time, and he suffered the handicap of all genius'. Kingsbury was also a faith-healer. 'Healing by prayer, which has been known and debated through the ages, found in him a practitioner and powerful defender, when, later in his career, he exercised his barrister's qualifications in London and pleaded in the courts.'

Another faith-healer, whose 'Great Tent' on wasteland by the South Station is generally packed, is Revivalist Father Jeffreys. He is the biggest draw of any preacher in the industrial North. Nightly in the tent he cures those sick who have faith and preaches fundamentalist doctrine. In his sweet Welsh voice he urges the sinful to repent and be saved, the sick to believe in the Lamb and be healed. Miraculous are the cures attributed to him all over Lancashire. In many towns he has set up new churches of his sect, the Bethel Evangelical. It is the fullest and most passionate church in Worktown.

THE REJUVENATOR

All of these health attractions seek to reduce the role of human intervention. And this is accentuated by the biggest health manifestation for holiday-makers, the Rejuvenator, a tableau in the autumn Illuminations. The Rejuvenator looks like a ship's turbine into which three old people enter, a man in a bathchair wheeled by another old man in a beard and a lively old woman with a smile on her face and strutting gait. Printed on the long cylindrical machine is 'BLACKPOOL FOR REJUVENATION'. Behind this is a tank on a pedestal, marked OZONE. At the other side of the machine comes a dancing stream of 9-year-old children.

The whole thing is a sort of allegory of the idealised holiday trajectory, from leaving Worktown to return. Or, put in Worktown words in this letter:

A holiday means to me one sound of happiness. We all become as little children hearing a first fairy tale that nanny told them for the first time. We go into the enchanted garden and hear how the Prince greets his Princess and how happiness brings them closer together. Time rolls on; then they get married and live happy till their holidays returns again and they feel they are getting jaded; so rest is needed; so off they go to the seaside and the change is wonderful. Sun smiles down and tans them. It gives them all the vigour, buoys their spirits up to face the winter months.

It is another way of saying the same thing when Blackpool postcards show a bearded old man winking heavily and wheeling a baby in a pram with the caption 'IT'S NEVER TOO LATE TO LEARN'.

But ill-health cards outnumber good health cards by two to one. The most vivid presentation of the theme is in a postcard entitled: 'Upon my "sole", this is the place to enjoy yourself.' The background of the picture shows sea, sands, and bathing girls. The foreground is almost entirely occupied by two large feet with the body of the man just visible and then his face with a very red but small nose sticking up midway between the battered feet. Bright Blackpool and Battered Blackpool are shown in equal proportions, but the feet burst through the frame of the picture and protrude a fifth of an inch on each side.

The blistered feet remind us of the fifteen to twenty miles a day walked barefoot by spinners and piecers up and down between the rails in the sun-proof, noise-filled, tropically humid atmosphere of the spinning-room.

With occupational cancer and lung trouble and asthma due to flying dust (not recognised for compensation), with measurable nervous strain and exhaustion, with 6,506 families overcrowded in 1935, no wonder the Worktowner welcomes what he believes are the health properties of Blackpool.

OZONE OR WHAT?

The *Blackpool Gazette* was upset (19 March 1938) when a leading London physician told the Royal Institute of Public Health that 'the idea that fresh air, as such, has any kind of miraculous effect in sustaining the health or as a recuperative factor in illness outside of movement, temperature and humidity, is a pure fallacy'. It is, however, Blackpool's air that Worktowners count as the primary health asset. The more the wind blows, the more they like it. Of some thirty people asked on the promenade what sort of weather they liked best, two-thirds said the breeze or the wind. As one man said: 'This is bracing. I can get the sun at home. This is what I like, the breeze.' But many people say that they find Blackpool air, like old beer, 'too strong' for them. It gave one woman 'headaches and made her sick'. And a local paint advertisement: 'PROOF TO WITHSTAND BLACKPOOL AIR'.

But is Blackpool healthy? Blackpool's resident health is complicated by the tendency for retired people to come there, and the extensive, even extreme, overcrowding of most houses from July to September (Table 13). Still Blackpool's high maternal mortality rate made it a special area studied by the Royal Commission on that subject. The remarkably high cancer rate

Table 13 Vital statistics in Worktown and Blackpool (per 1000)

	Worktown	Blackpool	Eng./Wales
Birth rate	12.4	10.8	14.8
Death rate	13.7	14.2	12.1
Infant mortality	58.0	63.0	59.0
Puerperal deaths	4.6	4.6	3.8
Tuberculosis deaths	0.68	0.65	0.69
Cancer deaths	1.59	2.12	1.62

becomes all the more remarkable when we noticed practically no attention paid to it in Blackpool.

Despite the dubious health conditions in Blackpool, unquestionably people go back to Worktown at the end of their week 'feeling better' than at any other time of the year. But the physical and psychological elements are so inextricably woven that neither aerial chemistry nor astrological psychology explains it. Good health and ill-health are interwoven in every aspect of Blackpool's pleasure making. This idea of health (and sickness) is the key to the tremendous success of Blackpool and to its notion of progress. When our observer's chemist shop put up a notice 'Leave your Head-ache here', the shop assistants found more people remarking on that as 'a source of great amusement' than anything else in the shop.

Part 3

7

AROUND THE TOWER AND OUT TO THE SEA

On every Blackpool photograph, you must have the Tower somewhere in the background. Approaching Blackpool, nearly everyone points it out to each other, registering the fact that they are on holiday. The Tower's foundation stone was laid in 1891 by Sir Matthew White-Ridley, who was immediately raised to the peerage. The Tower was raised to 519 feet, 9 inches, one workman falling to his death in the process. Intended to be a British Eiffel Tower, it has become the best-known symbol in Britain. From the seahorse tank in its bowels to the brilliant lights on its tip, it guarantees good fun; and from the largest room inside, one of our contemporary culture heroes, Reginald Dixon, plays his Wonder Wurlitzer organ to the four corners of the world by radio. In Worktown, every outlook is stamped with the indelible finger of a factory chimney. In Blackpool there are none, except the Tower, a chimney which will never smoke.

In the Tower there is the grotto aquarium, the vast dance hall with two systems of galleries with angels and musicians painted on the ceiling. There is a zoo, a roof garden, aviary, criminal slot-machines, palmistry, clairvoyants, bar, tea-place, restaurant, lifts, circus, children's ballet, and palm grove.

But it is the view from the Tower that attracts many. [Observers watched crowds at the top of the Tower in the afternoon.]

> The lift opens to the west, towards the sea. 40 per cent of the groups observed walked right round to the other side to look inland, the direction of home, though they didn't spend so long looking there as over the sea. The southern side gradually gained the main interest [Table 14].

A woman, looking west out over the prom and beach and the wide blue sea, observes: 'Nothing ere'. She then moves to the south side and says, 'This is the place to look from.' They are looking over the mile-long line of stalls and teeming crowds around the Headless Woman, Gypsy Lee, the Tartar-Hatted Big Dipper, and the 'Educational' Museum of Human Anatomy with its excellent replicas of the ravages of syphilis; that is the Blackpool people want

Table 14 Views from the Tower

	East	North	West	South
How many groups look in which direction first	10	9	3	3
Total number of seconds allotted to looking in direction (12 groups)	191	320	214	717

to look at. To the west, there is only the bathing-Blackpool that started it all.

From the Tower top, the visitor sees and commands all of this Blackpool, and commonly satisfies himself by spitting on it:

'Eee, they look like bloody toys.' (spits) 'Did you see t'wind cat 'old a' your gob?'
'Look at yon bloody woman dodging through to trams.'
'Eee, I'd like to see two bloody buses have a crash from here.'

Many express a wish to drop things from the top, but few have the forethought to bring them. One man dropped something that he had in a brown paper bag; it landed plunk in the middle of Bank Hey Street. Best of all, from the spectator's angle, was the man who dropped himself over the edge. That is frequently referred to on the Tower top; 'He wanted to show those below that he'd got guts', said a commissionnaire. He crashed on to the ballroom roof thronged with dancers beneath, stuck there, and did not go through (1936). The memory of this episode is a valuable Tower advertisement.

THE AEROPLANE VIEW

The one feature of the landscape which promotes interest without fail in Blackpool is the appearance of an aeroplane. Here there is something not only metaphorically but actually to look up to. In fact, the Tower, the centre of the town, is the target of joy-flights. Five shillings buy eight minutes in the air.

These joy-flights around the Tower are a Blackpool way of indicating progress. The aeroplane is a sort of superior Tower. In the last half of the nineteenth century, Blackpool set out to conquer the elements. The three piers were laid out over the water. Blackpool thrust itself out into the sea by means of these stationary boats. Originally there was no theatre, concert hall, slot-machine or shop on the North Pier. It was not built to give access to shipping. What it did was take people nearer to the sea, give them a closer connection with it, a sense of power over it, and intimacy with it. The wooden boards of the pier were strung together with an almost deliberate roughness so that the water or sand could be seen through the chinks between board and board.

If the piers went seaward, the Tower went airward. The idea was to get up into the air, above the world, to look down on it. Just as the piers were constructed to enable holiday-makers to get nearer the sea, the Tower was built to enable them to get up into the fresh air with, at the same time, an opportunity of seeing their surroundings from a new angle.

But at 500 feet the visitor to the Tower can get no higher. The passenger in the aeroplane is taken to a dizzier height, given a truer bird's-eye view. It is a part of the Blackpool insult theme that the aeroplane should circle round the Tower only 40 feet above the flagstaff, and give its passengers a chance to feel cocky, superior to the watchers on the platforms of the Tower.

If disaster overtakes the aeroplane, the insulters are insulted. There has only been one air disaster in the history of the Blackpool airport since it was founded ten years ago. That was when Sir Alan Cobham's flying circus was flying in formation over the town. One aeroplane brushed the wing of another. It broke in half over the centre of the town. Two girls came hurtling out of the sky. As the news was swiftly passed around the town, people flocked to the scenes of the disaster from every quarter. It was like a festival, almost an occasion of public rejoicing, at the fall of the insulters. Mrs Menary's account, hoarded in her vivid memory four years after the event, gives the clue to public feeling: 'We went to look at the tail-part. We were glad we didn't go to see the front-part, because the bodies were there. They shovelled them up.'

THE SEA AND THE SEASIDE

[The Tower remains the principal vista from which to view the complex panorama of Blackpool. From its top, one can see] the main roads coming in from the east, bringing 70,421 vehicles into the town for the Easter weekend, 1938, and the three railway stations now unable to cope with the influx of traffic so that 300 special trains are needed on one Bank Holiday, which have to be shunted literally miles from town until they are wanted for midnight return. One can see also the crowds that drift along the promenade so thickly that you cannot see the pavements between them, 7,000,000 a summer; the three piers sticking out their iron legs and the oriental roofs of their shelters and theatres; and the vividly coloured trams, oyster stalls, rock sellers, restaurants, that work every inch of the 6.98 miles of seafront. The Worktowners have grown tired of looking at this scene after two minutes. They want to get down and into it again. So do we, the observers. This teeming labyrinth provides our puzzle. But we, who go in for the obvious, step out of the door and look to the west, to the sea, which phrases the seaside. So first to the sea, then to the side.

> I think I might be satisfied
> To roam the charming countryside

In touch with nature and the soil
Away from all the daily toil.
But when I think of sands and sea,
Oh dear, they do be calling me.
(Mrs I. Tonge of Worktown)

At high tide, the promenade is bordered on the west by the sea, free gratis, on the east, by over 1000 amusement devices from 1*d*. to 1/-. The sea gave Blackpool its start in life, although its position is seldom acknowledged on its posters nowadays, unless by implication from the bathing belles. But what value do holiday-makers attach to the sea rather than its side?

Lounging on prom or sands, 60 holiday-makers conversed with 6 observers about the sea. 28 answers with definable attitudes were favourable to the sea, 22 hostile, 10 ambivalent or uninterested (Table 15). Parents generally say that the sea is the place for the children. Still Worktown elementary schoolchildren weren't so sure. While 97 per cent had seen the sea, and 89 per cent had bathed in it, and 40 per cent expressed themselves as in favour of it, 60 per cent were against or ambivalent towards it. The opposition was mostly thus: 'It is very hard to swim in. When the waves come and you get a mouthful of salt water which is not very nice.' The main preference for the sea is when it is dynamic, but four people actually said that they thought the high tides and waves splashing on the promenade were 'silly'. Attitudes to the sea vary with season, light, and tide. The flat sea and the foamy sea are two different phenomena. We shall shortly play admist the foam, first enter the flat.

Table 15 Attitudes towards the sea

Attitude or issue	Like	Dislike
	%	%
General feeling	22	8
Waves and roughness	20	8
Beauty and colour	6	2
Swimming medium	2	12
Health and mental effects	2	8
Spectacle	2	2
Things in sea	0	6

[BEACH AND TIDE]

A van man, from one of the 100 or so bathing vans on the beach, complained: 'The Blackpool beach is a nudist colony. Here's chaps standing in their shirts.' In recognition of this popular trend, in 1932 beach morals at Blackpool were nominally decontrolled. So that the *Gazette* was able recently (17 June 1939) to write: 'Blackpool is probably as free from irksome restrictions as any place in the British Isles.' Far otherwise at Clevelys, for example, where a male observer was reprimanded for slightly exposing his navel.

Blackpool postcards define roughly the modern boundaries of bathing behaviour. One shows an owl-faced young man in over-sized glasses, asked by red-nosed, scarlet, bathing-dressed male, 'Why won't they let you on the beach?' His reply: 'I'm so short-sighted I have to feel my way about.' Another shows a man and woman necking on the sands in backless costumes, girl asking: 'Who said you could do all this to me?' Boy's reply: 'All the boys down here.'

Still younger observers were disappointed by the reality, and saw little of erotic interest:

Eight women disrobing amongst crowd. Bathing costumes underskirts. One takes hers off, but others shy. Proceed to lift each other's skirts off, while other resists, run away screaming. Young man takes photo. Eventually all run towards the water, dancing on the way.

But many wear costumes without going into the water. If during June the cold water kept most from bathing, during the September holidays there was no relative increase in sea-users. Any photograph of the beach front shows an overwhelming number of people along a narrow strip underneath the promenade and a mere sprinkling in the water, although more on the water's edge. Some simple counts will suffice (Table 16). A comparable survey of the beach strips in the hot June of 1939 gave identical results.

Table 16 Beach census (1937)

Date and time	Weather	Place	No. in water	No. on beach
21/8, 11 a.m.	warm/bright	440 yd beach	63	8,000
2/9, 4 p.m.	sunny/windy	300 yd beach	2	6,200
4/9, afternoon	warm	beach	113	8,000
15/9, 3 p.m.	sunny/cool	900 yd beach	8	8,000

A leading local swimmer told us that there has been a recent 'decrease in interest in swimming'. This was confirmed in 1937 when an attempt was made to bring to Blackpool a well-known Danish swimmer; a corporation official told the *Evening Gazette* (19 August 1937): 'It is probable that the offer will lie on the table. Interest, too, is declining in long-distance swimming, and an all-night swim at the baths would not be patronised.' Asked on August Bank Holiday, 'How's trade?', a proprietor of bathing vans on the best site replied: 'There used to be three sessions bathing, before

breakfast, after breakfast and afternoon, but now there's only the afternoon.' An open-air bath built at the North Shore was never used as such; it
was more profitable to lease it to amusement proprietors. The general indications, then, are of a conspicuously slight sea interest, and a scarcely greater
interest in the town's three public baths.

[If it is not swimming that brings them to the sea, perhaps there are other
attractions.] In the Royal Arms in Worktown on December 15, an old couple
expressed a Worktown sentiment:

> You've got to keep on, haven't you? It's no good trying to get away
> from it. You must go with the stream, you know. You can't kick
> against it. If you do you only get thorns and cuts, don't you? The only
> thing is to go with the tide.

[But on holiday people don't follow this advice.] It is favourite game of
holiday-makers to stay as long as they possibly can on their spot of sand
before the tide compels them to leave. Crowds gather at flights of steps and
other suitable places to watch the tide as it comes creeping in, gradually
isolating sandpits and covering them up. The scarlet-uniformed Beach Patrol
even supervise an evacuation. But not if the high tide is at night:

> Looking over the edge of the pier, the observer saw a couple kissing
> right on the edge of the water's edge. Tide is coming in, and while they
> are in a clinch, they get splashed by the water. They look at it for a few
> moments and then run back a few yards, and stay staring at it. The
> man looks up and shouts something that sounds like 'Bugger off',
> waving his right arm. His left arm is around the girl. He then resumed
> kissing.

Hundreds of people, attracted by the spectacle and the explosive claps of
the breaking waves, play at venturing as far out on the sand's water line as
possible, calculating the next wave, fleeing back from a spot which a
moment later is deluged. Thousands line up and watch the players. Laughter
and foam are the prevailing sounds. A woman correctly observed that 'they
go there in their best clothes and roar with laughter when they get them
drenched'. Of the players, about 90 per cent are under 30, of the watchers, 65
per cent are over 30.

Under such dynamic conditions, the sea evokes its maximum interest and
produces an appreciable amount of comment: 'Yes, it was a grand tide this
afternoon, did you see it?' and 'It wouldn't be so bad if this wind would drop,
it's a cold wind; yet it's better than rain. I dare say it does you as good as
sunshine.' Certainly with high seas the positive interest in the seas goes up.

The sea interest is assumed or even compelled by the Corporation. It has
placed long wooden seats, which can be used free of charge, at frequent intervals all along the promenade, arranging them so that about five seats face the
sea to every two that face inland. A study of people using these seats sheds

interesting light on the phenomenon of sea interest. The number of people looking seaward is higher, and the number per seat lower, than those facing inland.

People stay on the seats an average of about twenty minutes, as compared with three minutes leaning on the rails, and two hours in deckchairs. The people who rest on the rails for the most part gaze down on the sands and the people on them. Those who sit on the seats have more positive occupations, which differ, of course, according to the time of day and light (Table 17). On no other occasion does the Worktowner read his or her newspaper each day with such intricate thoroughness.

Table 17 Sitting activities on the beach

Activity	Soft seat afternoon	Hard seat afternoon	Hard seat evening
Sitting looking about	—	50	41
Talking	33	22	21
Smoking	—	11	—
Reading	47	6	0
Writing	0	5	0
Knitting	0	3	0
Nursing baby	—	1	0
Dosing	20	1	0
Eating	0	1	2
Necking	0	0	34

Seven miles of golden sand is the proud claim of Blackpool's publicity department. The sand is important to many who never enter the sea. Children take it home to Worktown in paper bags. Two discussed it: 'Of course if there were no sea there would be no sand.' And 'I only play about in the sand, and build sand forts. It's alright in them boats, though.' Sand-patterns for children were overwhelmingly castles or plain cones. Sand-drawing is usually done by trailing a stick or bamboo pole in an unorganised way.

The critics of Blackpool tend to exaggerate beach congestion. A women from Bredbury wrote to us as the result of a broadcast:

[Blackpool] might be a thrill for people 'up from t'country' but to townsfolk it can be reminiscent of Manchester on a Saturday. Manchester hasn't got the sea: no, perhaps not, and according to my ideas neither has Blackpool, for all one can see of it for people, both in it and beside it.

But on a fine day in September, a careful count done by observers (one with a Cambridge First in mathematics!) showed 10,000 people on the sand along this frontage. Maximum estimates for Bank Holidays by observation were 40,000, a liberal figure. But the Corporation claims 400,000 were in Blackpool then. Most sand-goers stay on the sand at least one hour, often three at a stretch. [So apparently relatively few visitors take advantage of these golden sands.]

A full day's observation of a strip of beach between the first and second flights of steps north of Manchester Square shows there was greater density of people in a small section of sand within the first channel; this runs about 25 yards off and parallel with the promenade. However, the much larger sand strip, expanding with low tide up to 500 yards beyond the first channel, is sparsely populated. At no time during the day are there 50 people in the large section, while there are constantly over 100 in the smaller. The similar tendency to accumulate along the land-line is apparent in connection with the land projections into the sea, i.e. the piers. The density on each side of the pier reaches a maximum from 10 to 20 paces on each side of the pier.

Just before tea on a typical afternoon within the first channel, 50 per cent were sleeping or snoozing, 25 per cent were looking, 10 per cent playing, 10 per cent supervising children, and 5 per cent talking. Here women predominate over men and children together, though the female dominance disappears as we get near the sea, where children form up to a third of the whole population (Table 18).

Table 18 Beach census

	Men	Women	Children	% Women
Inside the channel	144	241	79	52
Outside the channel	114	109	110	32

On the land-side strip are crowded the deckchairs; on the outer edge of this strip are lined the oyster and ice-cream stalls, the Giant Tea-Pot, ventriloquist, and Punch and Judy. The beach is the territory in Blackpool of the person who comes to rest his or her body and has only a few square yards to do it in. Not all interest in the sea has to do with the sands and water. Focal interests are the Punch and Judy and the donkeys on this narrow strip of beach.

PUNCH AND ARSE

A box, 8 feet square, wide enough to house a man, covered with cloth striped brilliant red and gold. On one side an opening, 2 feet square, with a wooden stage at the base. Written above is 'Prof. Green, No. 1 Brown St Established 1881'. The start of the show is announced by beating a drum. A crowd gathers quickly, mainly children. Each show is allowed 30 square yards of sand, for which the proprietor pays the Corporation. As one said, 'We have to follow the tides, they are our masters here.' Show lasted average of 20 minutes or less:

> Enter Punch, with his stick. . . . Punch slaps his own bottom (applause) and sings. Enters house while Judy looks through window. Judy in frilled cap and dress of the Victorian period. Punch: 'Oh, what a little beauty.' They kiss . . . and dance. Judy becomes coy. Punch slaps her. Judy descends and comes up again with a baby. Punch delighted. They play at tossing the baby from one to the other. Judy leaves Punch to mind the baby. Baby cries. Punch beats [the baby, shouting], 'Stop it, stop it, stop it,' and then throws it out of the theatre. Enter Judy, and goes for Punch, slaps him, bites him, gets his stick and belabours him soundly. He kills her. 'That's the way to do it.' Enter policeman, almost modern dress, navy blue, not the 'Beadle' of some sets. 'Ere, I say what's all the noise about, I'm here. You've killed yer wife Judy.' 'What's that to do with you?' Kills the policeman. 'That's the way to settle im.' Sings 'We all go the same way home.'
>
> [After several other violent encounters] . . . Crocodile sings below, enters, frightens Punch, bites his nose, gets him by the banana, swallows Punch's stick, proceeds to drag him down, growling. Children growl. This is the only time that the children have joined in, although they have laughed at all the good points, especially when Punch was hit, or anyone fought.

The show concludes with Punch being dragged off, hitting his own bottom to the laughter of the children. At the end the children vanish as quickly as they appeared.

Prof. Green has a nose slightly curved – not unlike the traditional Punch. 'I am the oldest entertainer on the Blackpool sands', he says. His father was a gymnast, the first in the country to introduce lady acrobats. He is trained as a somersault thrower; he picked up Punch and Judy by himself and has been coming to Blackpool for fifty-four years. 'You can have all your pictures, but there's nothing that the kids like better than Punch and Judy. They all laugh and enjoy as they have ever since I can remember . . . ; the grown-ups laugh as much as they used to.' The Professor has twelve children: 'They were all brought up on Punch and Judy, they've not done so bad out of it; one of them is an engineer, another a chemist; there is only one of them who is doing the Punch and Judy; he is down south.' Two were killed in the war. 'I go to Church sometimes, I know what's what. . . . You know the entertainers' life, they look at it like this, a short life and a merry one, they are not like the ordinary folks.' He gets bronchitis badly in winter.

Punch has not changed very much since he appeared in England at Bartholomew Fair in 1703. But whereas then he apparently fought on behalf of all the oppressed peoples of the world, now he is more a symbol of personal anarchy and wish, overthrowing constabular and marital order, mixing up reptile and herbalism, in a way that symbolises well enough much of what happens on land in Blackpool.

'Give it a kick on its arse,' says a little girl on a donkey. And 'it's lost its feathers,' as she pulls its tail. The donkeys take little notice. There are about 200 in Blackpool. They have green and red woollen bobs suspended from straps passing round their heads; coloured leather straps go around the bodies. A strip of sand the whole length of the beach is kept as a donkey-run and deckchairs may not pass on it. A boy runs behind to wallop the beast. Each donkey knows when to turn on this strip at a point about 200 yards from its standing place.

'All children', said a donkey woman, 'look forward to a ride on Blackpool sands.' But 36 per cent of the riders observed were adults. Adult riders come in groups. It is traditionally childish to donkey-ride, and thus adults need the sanction of numbers. Generally small boys come alone or with other small boys; girls come with parents. Children take it more seriously:

> Four adults and two small boys (age 5 and 6) sitting on beach. Boys were digging, asked several times for ride. Mother says: 'Oh, let them go. They've mithered all week to go on.' [Father to the other boy:] 'You go on the small donkey and I'll go on this,' pointing to brown one. . . . Auntie of the group decided to go, too. She took off her coat and amidst much shouting got on the donkey. The father led off the boys. The mother left in group bawled to the donkey-man: 'Give her (auntie's) donkey a real good crack.'

One of these donkeys wears a medal, 'Presented by the Royal Society for the Prevention of Cruelty to Animals. Award of Merit, 1912'. The RSPCA got headlines in April 1938 through the Donkey's Charter of Dr L. C. Floyd-McKeon, Ph.D., urging: no donkey-riders over eight stone, no whips or sticks to be used, eight p.m. curfew, and one hour's rest, unsaddled, at midday. The Worktown RSPCA inspector was emphatic that a 'donkey should only work eight hours a day', but thought they could carry eleven stone for that time. Though 'like a human being, it should have a day of rest', donkeys work all Sunday.

The donkey owners speak with great affection of their animals. They cost from £3 to £14 each. Observations showed an average taking of 1/3 per donkey per hour at ordinary busy times. Mornings were the most profitable times, said a donkey woman. To augment income, her son is a bricksetter's labourer during the winter. The chap on the next set of donkeys is a labourer; this business didn't keep him entirely, 'but I feel like this: I'm my own boss.'

There is a widely held Worktown idea about donkeys that they never perish. Jesus rode on one into Jerusalem. A donkey woman, having made friends with an observer, took her up to a grey donkey, lifted the saddle, and said, pointing, 'There you see the cross of Our Lord Jesus on its back.' On its ear she pointed to another black mark and said, 'that was the mark of his thumb, where he held on to the ass'. 'You see,' she said, 'Our Lord rode on one – therefore you must never ill-treat a donkey.' The wallop, however, she thought, was essential. She said, 'people say you never see a donkey die – well, they do'. She lost one or two every year.

You can ride on many different things that will shake you up and excite you in Blackpool, but of these only the donkey is alive. Immortal ass, arse, or Bottom, is loved now by children, giving to adults the giggle of youth. The kindly Ph.D. has not yet timetabled the Christ-marked ass, whose clock is the tide, and the winter, to which he alone gives way. And when the tide goes out, the donkeys are the first back on the sand, standing in steady clusters, before the food stalls or the Punch and Judy come down.

Inward (within the wide sheet of asphalt which belongs to the tramlines) is the main promenade motor road, bordered on the inland side by a dense labyrinth of stalls, side shows, slot-machines, cafes, and palmists' dens. Probably at any one moment there are as many people on this front as on the sand, and all evening and at high tide a great many more.

The promenade was first financed about 1828 by a special levy among landowners in the neighbourhood. In 1899, Parliament sanctioned a 60-foot widening. The extension of the promenade and its powerful buttressing against the sea required a huge-scale accretion of sand, largely carried in suspension from dredging operations in the Mersey and Ribble estuaries. Thus Blackpool has changed the face of nature as well as of nature lovers.

Such conquests are part of progress. Blackpool's coat of arms has as its main central theme eight waves, and a seagull flying across them, over the motto 'Progress'. This is a recognition of the town's first dependence on the sea, its early advertisements as a bathing resort. It was only when the visitor had come to Blackpool for the sea and the air that other diversions were developed like [Punch and the donkeys].

There is, as we shall presently see, an intensification of development and interest on land and inland; this takes largely the shape of things to come and is often made of concrete. There are only a handful of pigeons on the first of the three piers. These piers were the first definite achievement of Blackpool in imposing its larger wishes on nature by the technique of science with the language of superstition. There are no trees anywhere along the promenade to complicate the new million pound development scheme. [And thus the seaside prevails over the sea. And so now we will turn from the west to the inland view and see what the promenade has to offer.]

8

[THE PEOPLE'S PLAYGROUND]

The origin of the amusement park is in the village fair. There used to be no transport to take the villagers away to amusements, so the amusements came to them. So the village fair was mobile, and therefore simple in structure. But with the arrival of transport the inlander began to visit resorts, and it was now possible to introduce something more advanced in structure. The fair, a relic of the Middle Ages, was noisy and filthy. Our problem is that of clearing-up, of putting order into chaos.

(Interview with Joseph Emberton, architect at Blackpool)

FUNERAL OF WORK

The holiday, a brief release from the routine of the year's life, implies that standard routine is arduous and inadequate to human needs. This is especially true of the class whose toil is imposed by necessity; for these people, the brief regular holiday is vital. In the Latin Saturnalia, the slaves were thus released for an outburst of temporary freedom, in which they reversed the roles of the year and played the part of masters. We have already seen that this is precisely what some Worktowners (especially housewives) expect from a holiday: 'Instead of preparing meals for my family, it would be a real holiday for me to be waited on. I would love to stay at a hotel and have *everything* done for me.' But fifty-one weeks of work set up a rhythm which is psychologically impossible to dismiss in the short space of a week, however much another rhythm may attract. In Blackpool, as in so many other places and times, an intoxicating medium is sought to create the release.

But what distinguishes the industrial holiday from its forerunners is the mass trek to a chosen place. The trek itself dates from the practice of the religious pilgrimage, in which the devotions at the holy tomb gradually ceased to be more than the nominal goal; the journey, with its jovial companionships and fresh sights, became the important thing. Rapid transport arrived to diminish the time of journeys, and consequently gave back to the town at the end of the journey its old supremacy as a holiday goal; expanding transport also facilitated the movement of masses. The wealthy masters of the eighteenth century had gone to the spas and the seaside; a growing concern for the less trammelled aspects of nature placed the emphasis away from spa on to sea; therefore when the working people won the means, they followed to the seaside. Doing so, they partly achieved the reversal of role essential to saturnalia.

About the same time, the fair also had a revival. Lewis Mumford sees that rebirth in the growth of the London pleasure gardens, Ranelagh and Vauxhall, and in the great trade exhibitions of nineteenth-century Europe. In the boosting of trade amid the surroundings of the fair, a nostalgia for the Middle Ages, exploited in the contemporary pre-Raphaelite art, was fused with the politics and economics of a technological age. Blackpool was to become a combination of the seaside and the fair. In the beginning there were scarcely glimmerings of it. Towards the end of the eighteenth century, the growing interest in the seaside brought the Fylde coast to notice. And when a little trickle of life started towards it, the fair, travelling from town to town in Lancashire, came to Blackpool and from then on made fortnightly visits. In 1810 the gypsies came and pitched their tents on the cliffs in the north, drawing incomes from palm reading until a rival amusement centre began to grow up at the southern end of the town. Here a London company had built a switchback on the edge of the sand-dunes. The tide of money turned that way, and the gypsies followed, establishing their new camp near the Star Inn.

On the sand-dune frontier of Blackpool, Pleasure Beach grew. With its total area of thirty-three acres, its wide avenues separating the blocks of sixteen major mechanical amusements, especially 'Ghost Train,' 'Big Dipper,' 'Reel,' 'Whip,' and 'Noah's Ark', it was the first of the contemporary amusements to be planted. The other places in the centre of the town arrived later, but more quickly they were given their distinctive shapes. Central Beach, a quarter of a mile strip of promenade, begins with the arcade called Toyland and strikes south along a line of stalls, amusement arcades, and 'food brothels'. Its landmarks include Luna Park, a brown stucco Moorish palace dominated by a green half-dome with a crescent moon. At the southern end is Coney Island, where choirboys gaze (free) at the waxwork tableau of the Last Supper. This is the part of the Blackpool amusement scene that visitors meet first when they come out of Central Station. 300 yards back from the promenade and directly inland from the Tower is a more recently promoted area – Olympia, with its lighthouse and searchlight, the only amusement area of the three to be covered. Housed under its one roof are the Motor Dodgem, Over-the-Top swings, Speed Thrill, and Speed-Boats in a grotto supported on rocky granite pillars and where a notice guarantees that the dark waters are pure.

A WAR BETWEEN JAPAN AND HERE

A microcosm of the pre-1938 Blackpool amusement world was Luna Park. In it, Abyssinians breathed gas, danced on broken beer bottles, and kept green lizards. At its doors, an Indian yogi man talked to the crowds and a snake-charmer soothed his pets. Promoter of this enterprise, as of the Honeymoon Express at Brighton and Ghost Trains all over the country, was the Japanese, Kamiya. He told us:

> The sillier the thing, the more it gets the people, something like a golliwog, for instance. If the thing is educational, they're not interested. They want the *curious* and the sensational. . . .
> Half of the people who come here don't go on the sands at all. More people pass in front of those windows than in any other part of the world. Some people just go round paying for shows and the others follow them. When I used to attend stalls, I used to be able to judge people's wants better than they could themselves. In the mornings, they would be eager for me to open, they would knock down the shutter of the stall, and . . . there'd be no time to arrange anything. So we'd close down for half an hour and there'd be a bigger rush than ever afterwards. I would shame the cheeky ones by giving them prizes. They'd say, 'What do I do with this?' I'd say, 'Would you like one of these?' always a good fellow; in arguments there were always some on my side – 'Oh, he's a good fair chap.' My instinct for psychology, it just comes in this business.
> Our business is like backing horses. Once it's opened and the first day over, I can always tell if it will succeed. Sometimes I wish I had just a stall again.

As Kamiya knew by experience, the vicissitudes of the amusement trade are manifold. Blackpool Orient had to suffer. In mid-season, 26 August 1937, Luna Park was destroyed by fire, the third in a short period:

> Observer saw no cases of panic or running at this time. The crowd, arriving from the north (where a late dance at the Palace had just broken up), did not hasten; but all waited. . . . By 2:30, the glow had gone out of the fire. . . . Observer went to hot-dog stall which was doing big business. Owners had been woken up and came out to open stalls. By 2:50 there were only eighty people watching and leaving quickly; mostly with smiles and laughter.

In fact, no one in Blackpool was depressed by the gutting of Luna Park. Said a housewife, 'You don't know what they might be doing it for. They might be trying to cause a war between Japan and here.' The *Evening Gazette* announced that Luna Park was the property of the Tower Company. Kamiya was nominal owner and their manager. It printed a facsimile of an anonymous threatening letter, received by Mr Kamiya shortly before the fire, with implications of arson and a mysterious oriental hand. The Kamiya brothers were anxious, they said, to rebuild at once and reopen that season. But with the Central Beach Clearance Scheme, the central amusement district will shortly disappear to make way for sunken gardens and squares. We have to regret that Luke Gannon, Blackpool's individualist thinker and lover of the bizarre, has evacuated in favour of Clevelys.

SIXTH FLOOR, REGENT STREET

Left supreme will be the Pleasure Beach, the new Blackpool. Listen again to Joseph Emberton, architect, of 136 Regent Street, who came from the 'oil and warehouses' of Newcastle-under-Lyme to build publicity architecture at Wembley, Blackpool, and the Paris Exhibition:

> The promenade is the worst thing in Blackpool. Of course, it's the lodging houses that spoil it, but besides that, it's uninteresting. They should have sunken gardens with fountains playing. They will tell you that fountains would splash the people when it was windy, but put them in glass. We have unbreakable glass now, you know. And the swimming bath. They've plastered it with terracotta so that you can't see a thing. You ought to be able to see in from the promenade, that would give it life. . . . If we clean up the Pleasure Beach, we may get the inlander to clean up his backyard.
>
> The better class does not think of visiting an amusement park, unless for a binge. There is too much noise and filth and touting. This I want to remedy. A switchback appeals to all classes with its sensation of speed. In replanning the Pleasure Beach, we have tried to intersperse the big attractions with the small stalls, such as darts, where they can win prizes.
>
> . . . . [On new buildings] we have tried to remove the pretence at pagodas and Indian temples, which have nothing to do with the amusements, have they?

Or have they? Emberton himself, who has taken away the obvious crescent moons, green minarets, and palm-tree motifs, has brought in a new symbolism for old ideas. Into the religious festival scene, the merchant came knowing that, among the dense crowds, custom was waiting. But the church kept a grip on the holiday. The sideshows at the fairs did not digress from the religious story. One of the *Jovial Poems* (1632) gives this catalogue of the attractions at Bartholomew Fair:

> Here's the women of Babylon, the Devil and the Pope,
> And here's the little girl just going on the Rope.
> Here's Dives and Lazarus and the World's Creation,
> Here's the Tall Dutch Woman, the like's not in the nation.

We have already seen the tall Dutch windmill and the Stratosphere Girl going on the rope off Central Pier. Later we shall see a rector roasting in hell, prodded by the devil. In periodic outbursts, the church endeavoured to restrict the fair entirely to scenes like these, by expelling the hawkers and vendors who persistently returned to mingle with the religious fantasies and worship of the miraculous. Explorers, bringing back prodigies from Asia, the New World, and Africa, made it easy to procure exhibits to tempt the curious. The objects of curiosity in holiday week, the summer week of Sundays, are basically the same, although they wear the clothes of different periods and tastes. We shall see how when we dip into the dark passages of Noah's Ark and the Ghost Train.

UNDERWORLDS AND OVERWORLDS

The promoters of amusements have taken the best sites along the central portion of the ribbon of promenade, on that interesting borderline where town merges into sand-dunes. Adding year by year machines of greater ingenuity, better and better adapted to toss, turn, shock, and shake, they have elevated, decorated, and vocalised them so that as you pass, from two to four of your senses are assaulted. [And so we enter this realm of underworlds and overworlds.]

The children are taught in Blackpool elementary schools that in the beginning came Dr Cocker, the father of Blackpool borough. He was its first businessman and its first mayor, functions often united in municipal politics. In 1874, Dr Cocker converted Sir Reginald Heywood's mansion on the seafront into an 'Aquarium, Aviary and Menagerie'. In 1891, with great profit, he passed it over to the Standard Debenture Company of London who were looking for a site for an English Eiffel Tower. If that was the age of stark criss cross girdered engineering triumphs like the Eiffel and Blackpool Towers, it was also the age of Darwin, and therefore when the Tower was reared above it, the aquarium was still kept open to the public. The entrance to the Tower on the inland side leads straight into it.

The aquarium is an oblong about 40 yards by 20. From floor to ceiling, occupying most of the central space, is a square rock with the glass faces of tanks on all four sides. They seem to be filled with yellow-green light, coming through the still water in which the fish swim or hover motionless. The effect on a Worktowner was well expressed by a young man who rushed straight into it from the station. For him, it was 'a kind of underworld or undersea with artificial stalactites with faint red or yellow lighting'. No one speaks in loud tones in this dim room where a shout would reverberate, but there is a feeling of suppressed excitement which perhaps comes out in these almost whispered comments picked up by observers:

Little boy: 'Is them sharks in here?'

Woman: 'I don't know. That's cod. How do y'like being in here?'
Man (to boy of 6): 'It's just a case of flapping their wings.'

No one is indifferent to these fish which can be watched living private lives under public gaze. People pressed up against the tanks often do their best to make the fish aware of and responsive to their presence by tapping on the glass, talking to them, and even (apparently) making little offerings: 'An empty packet of Nuttal's Minties is put in front of the eel on the ledge outside, showing the Keep-Fit series side.'

The fish in this aquarium, the first chronologically of Blackpool's amusements, derive their interest from the fact that they can be seen living and moving with none of the consciousness of the actor. But the major tendency is the replacement of the living actor by others mechanically propelled.

DISNEY IN BLACKPOOL

Fairyland is a grotto on the central promenade some 400 yards south of the Tower. Out of its tunnel on the right comes a car, its head shaped like a rearing sea-serpent, coloured seaweed green. The ten seats of the car form the body of the serpent. The dragon turns down a dark passage revealing various lighted scenes. Here are some examples:

Scene 1 A fairy on a swing, with leaves and coloured lights on the ropes. It is suspended from the bough of a tree, and in the background is a painting of a castle on the Rhine. There are two gnomes, one on each side of the swing.

Scene 2 A cottage raised on bricks, at the side of which is a waterwheel; the stream turns the waterwheel . . . and is crossed by a wooden bridge. Dwarfs are at the windows of the house, at the door, crossing the bridge, and chopping wood in the foreground. There is a large white terrier further still in the foreground.

Scene 7 A coal mine. On the left of scene is a pit shaft with two cages in it. . . . Dwarfs are pushing trucks filled with coal. . . .

Scene 11 A camping scene. Seven dwarfs are grouped round a cooking-pot suspended over a fire. Two are at a table with cups in their hands, raising them and putting them down again. . . . In the foreground is a card bearing the words 'Good Health and Cheer'.

The manager shed limelight on the ordinary process by which scenes such as these are selected when he told our observer that the Rhineland Castle and Fairy on the Swing were copied from a postcard. By casual routes, then, the parts of the dream are formulated and put together; and, pointedly, they are brought into conjunction with scenes that have a homing ring to the Worktowner, scenes taken from the bottom of a coalpit. It will be noticed that in this grotto we live rather in the past in a saga-land, among dwarfs and castles; yet the scenes of today of the scout's campfire colour dream with more than a mist of reality.

The grotto pattern keeps recurring throughout Blackpool amusements. Among the many at the Pleasure Beach is the Grotto, designed particularly for children. Whatever Boards of Censors may pronounce, English practice rarely keeps the child from scenes in which thrills of horror are shot through the fanciful woof. Whether in a Disney fantasia or in a children's grotto, there is the excitement of animated deformity; the suffering trees in one scene have a long tradition reaching through Disney's Snow-White to Spenser, Dante, and Virgil.

Much more prominent than this at the northern entrance of Pleasure Beach is Noah's Ark. The exterior has considerable variety and interest both human and animal, modern and biblical. Here is an observer's view of it:

> A model of the Ark, rocking on a rugged granite rock. The deck of the ark and the clefts of the rock are thronged with animals and other figures. . . .
>
> Policeman in front of steps up, against a Belisha beacon, has long beard, hand up to stop (or bless), and at regular intervals knees bend as in gym. A rhino is chained to a robed, bearded male, Noah (?). Procession of animals is: elephant with rabbit on back; stork and chick; frog and anteater; polar bear and foxhound; kangaroo and lamb; swan; cat and pelican; cow and wasp; emu and koala; camel and hare; top-hatted ostrich; white puffin and snake. Looking from windows: Mrs Noah with rolling pin and giraffe.

Around the base of the Ark, a light-blue billowy line of sea is drawn. Swimming in it are fanged flying-fish, sharp-nosed goggle-eyed seahorses, and the Loch Ness monster rearing a goggle-eyed head, its open mouth and rows of teeth like a horse's. The figure in the attic has changed twice since it was recorded as king and queen in June 1937. By August 1937 it was a clock. By Easter, 1938, it was a yellow-jerseyed mulatto.

From a different observer comes the following account of what happens:

> When, having paid your sixpence at the generally crowded pay-box, you pass directly into the Ark and cross a sort of gangplank of round wooden stepping stones. These tip up as you tread on them and you slip into about six inches of water. More dark passages – steps that bump up and down. A gangplank that bumps you to and fro like the cakewalk. On to upper deck where there is a donkey in a stall whose tail shoots at you as you step on floor by stall. A rocking pig with the caption: 'Thus it is written in Noah's log, Oft the crew were on the hog.'
> . . . Passages [go] down into bowels of ship – sharp slopes and sudden corners, all pitch dark, more bumpy stairs, etc. Finally, as you step on a board, a whistling draught blows in your right ear. As you step

quickly on to the next bit of floor, it gives way with a loud clank. The whole ship pitches constantly in a very realistic way. During forty-five minutes, never more than two parties were inside at the same time. Of the parties followed inside during the same period only one separated inside. All the others clung together screaming in the dark.

On the whole, observers agreed that Noah's Ark was the most terrifying mental experience on the Pleasure Beach.

But people seem also to get up a comparable heat of excitement about the Ghost Train. At night it is internally illuminated with a dusky blue light apparently shot with smoke and flame. A skeleton stands upright in it, legs apart, right arm bent downwards, left raised like a policeman's signalling traffic. Visible from many corners of the pleasure city, the skeleton by day, the flame effect by night, helps to draw possible customers towards trolleys that take couples through winding corridors revealing, for example, a red-eyed dragon, a coffin, lovers on a bench, and a gallows scene.

CLOWN AND SAUSAGES

Those who are tired of short exciting trips down dark passages may enjoy the Fun House where duration of stay is not limited to a few minutes. This white concrete palace provides you with six preliminary ordeals, which you can only enjoy once on your way in. But, once inside, there are eight games which you can play as long as you like and as many times as you like. From the pay-box you go down a narrow passage which leads between iron tube-railings and one cannot avoid the coming ordeals. On the stage there is an attendant, dressed and made up as a clown, who points the way to be followed, and occasionally slaps girls' arses as they pass with a flexible rubber truncheon (the conventional clown's string of sausages?). Then, one by one, come the ordeals. For example: three rows of disks in the floor, revolving in opposite directions. When you cross you have to execute a kind of Charleston-step dance. Or: the cakewalk. Two planks moving parallel to each other, and always in opposite directions.

After this, you step down into the main hall. There you see 96 seats (6 rows of 16). From these seats people watch and are entertained by the antics of those suffering the ordeals. At the end of each stage of the ordeals are little holes in the floor through which a terrific current of air blows up at the people stepping over them. As the females pass over, this provides the spectacle.

The reactions of females seen at 9 p.m., 3 September [1937?], are catalogued here:

1 A blonde about 18. Used the puffs for exhibitionist purposes with some sense of stage effect, facing her audience and adopting a slinky step, posing, smiling coyly. 2 An effective puff raised tremendous

cheers in the case of one girl, but there was even more cheering, and this time clapping, for two fat old women ('Mother') – here it was notably the kids who were screaming with delight. 3 One plain girl, housemaid type, became completely hysterical with giggles at puffs, leaning on to railings, head falling forward with inward palpitations. 4 Little boy, 10 or 11. Goes through ordeals alone, is not holding handrails, very skilful. Some applause from other boys. 5 Three girls and two boys. Boys push each other, one boy carries his girl over the wind-puffs. 6 Two glum-looking girls in identical paper hats go slowly and sulkily. 7 Girls' knickers show when skirts blow up. Yells of applause. Boy says, 'That was a good one.' 8 Elderly woman cheats by climbing through railings at back; cries of 'Go back'. She laughs but goes on. 9 Large party all cling together.

Among the games on in the main hall are a giant slide, an inclined wooden revolving table, and the 'Social Mixer'. This last is a large bowl entered via a gangway.

The people sit in a circle with their feet towards the hub, and the bowl is rotated at increasing speed. Everyone is churned up. Fifty lads and girls are in it. It gathers speed. Boys . . . crawl around centre and are rolled towards the other groups. Girls sit round the side, with knees drawn up, holding skirts down. Speed becomes dizzy. Minor orgies develop between males but in vicinity of females. As it stops, one can see that several people are feeling ill, and three are violently sick before leaving the Mixer. Another woman staggers towards gangway, skids in the vomit, is nearly sick herself.

Next door to the Mixer there are chairs, full of boys and girls in pairs. These chairs are fastened to a baseboard, which is operated by a man who stands rather like a workman operating a crane in a raised controltower. When set going, the baseboard slides to and fro with an emetic motion, only less pronounced than that of the Mixer. No one is sick after.

A general impression recorded by many observers is that the effect given by metal cylinders, metal basins, wooden chutes, and platforms resembles nothing so much as a mill. Their remark does not differ widely from Wordsworth's when he saw Bartholomew Fair, once England's premier holiday centre as Blackpool claims to be now:

> All moveables of wonder from all parts,
> Are here, Albinos, painted Indians, Dwarfs,
> The Horse of Knowledge, and the learned Pig,
> The Stone-eater, the Man that swallows fire,
> Giants, Ventriloquists, the Invisible Girl,
> The Bust that speaks, and moves its goggling eyes,
> The Wax-work, Clock-work, all the marvelous craft

106

Of modern Merlins, wild Beasts, Puppet-shows,
All out-o'-the way, far-fetch'd, perverted things,
All freaks of Nature, all Promethean thoughts
Of Man; his dulness, madness, and their feats,
All jumbled up together to make up
This Parliament of Monsters. Tents and Booths
Meanwhile, as if the whole were one vast Mill,
Are vomiting, receiving, on all sides,
Men, Women, three-years' Children, Babes in arms.

(*The Prelude*, A-text, VII 679-94)

Work structures and pleasure structures have become more complex since Wordsworth wrote, but the relationship between them has altered more slowly, if at all.

Outside the Fun House there is a small glass case. It contains: a large clown, holding on his right side, on his knee, a smaller specimen in nautical rig; both with faces powdered, large mouths that laugh in bursts of mechanical hysteria. . . . One elderly woman with two others became infected with the laughter and began to imitate the figure. Another woman told her not to laugh.

Long periods of observation on people's reactions to the laughing clown established two facts: that large numbers of people stop to stare at the laughter and that practically none of them imitate it. In a 45 minute observation, 2 people were seen to laugh. Photographs of different groups watching the clown show 2 of them laughing. The rest have expressions tense, concentrated, curious.

RECURRING

In the mass of Blackpool amusement events, there is no easy way to compare one element with other. Account has to be made for the confusing factor of differing dates. Still, it is possible to disentangle the strands of time and see how some symbols of holiday fun have consistently endured through 100 years of Blackpool and how some have altered or given way before the advance of technology, speed, international crisis, and quicker communication with the far away. Table 19 does it best.

As far as possible the five amusement areas are arranged in roughly chronological order from left to right, based on the year in which each was either built (if unaltered since) or altered to its present shape. What is striking is the declining curve of interest in the rural scene or the water scene. To be sure, in 1938, in the booth once owned by Gannon (on the promenade facing the well-watered sea), a diver was on exhibition in a tank which was advertised in bold letters to contain 'Real Water'. But the show did not survive into a second season.

107

Table 19 Amusement park themes

Symbol	Place and form in which it appears				
	Fairyland	Grotto	Noah's Ark	Ghost Train	Fun House
Fish, water, ship	Pond, stream,	Sea, Mermaid	Waves, sea-horses, Loch Ness monster	—	Gangway, ship's rail
Reptile & batrachian	Toad, salamander	Crocodile	Snake, frog, brontosaurs	Dragon	—
Cave	Tunnels, mines	Tunnels	Tunnels	Tunnels, cylinder	Tunnels, barrels
Fairies	Fairy, gnome, dwarfs	Witch	Loch Ness	Dragon, Mephistopheles	—
Wind	Watermill	Windmill, draught	Whistling	Hooters	Wind lifting frocks
Nature	Lilies, rose, rustic pub	Trees, village	Chickens	—	Barrels, sacks
Industrial	Coalmine, blacksmith	—	Radio, Belisha beacon	Railway signals	Crane
Distortion	Dwarfs	Distorted trees, roasting missionary	Room of mirrors	Mirrors, turning cylinder	Mirror, 'cakewalk'

Replicas or suggestions of the industrial scene from which the Work-towners have just come have intensified; the cave motif has continued strong; distortion, principally by the aid of mirrors, has become increasingly popular. For example, one meets the distorting mirror in the Hall of Magic of Tussaud's Waxworks. Wind, which was previously linked to the rural scene to do useful jobs like turning windmill sails, is now more fierce and frisky. Stars, important to the astrologers elsewhere in Blackpool, are found once in these amusements, but the herbalist reptiles are frequent.

One aspect of feeling for the rural persists – for the animal. Even so, the animals are alive in one building only. At the entrance to the Tower there is a notice in large caps:

> MONARCHS OF THE JUNGLE
> BIRDS FROM THE TROPICS
> WONDERS OF THE DEEP

But there are very few birds from the tropics in the Tower, and, strictly speaking, no wonders of the deep. Nevertheless there is a Zoo, with lions, tigers, bears, puma, leopard, and monkeys. All the animals are carnivorous or manlike. Monkeys, of which there are most, are the biggest draw. Two women were followed:

> They only glance at the majority of the animals, but stay and stare if there is a crowd. They watch the monkeys particularly, pointing at them and laughing at their strange antics. . . . But . . . many people walk through without stopping at any exhibit.

With the newer mechanical animals, the species can be varied very widely, and brontosaurs, rhinoceros, pelican, emu, and koala, difficult to obtain for the Tower Zoo, are easily brought on to the scene. Where they lose is in the amount of things they can do. No exciting tricks to entertain the watcher; the regular performance of the same tinned tune and the regular march round the Ark find their limit.

The general scope of the development within the amusements can perhaps be summarised very briefly. In Fairyland, the journey was made in a dragon from which you passively saw the tableaux. So too in the Grotto, but the range of distortion in the things seen increased. In the labyrinth of Noah's Ark you felt things as well as saw; you could not avoid feeling them. Same in the Ghost Train. The Fun House differed from all these because you could select, go where you please, avoid what you please (except the labyrinth by which you first enter).

A holiday-maker who was imaginative might equate these joys and perils with experience of the unknown and wonderful. We are now going on to look at a class of amusement in which the barker insists on reminding them, explicitly, that they are being brought into contact with the mystery of things.

9

FOURTH DIMENSION

Shops around the Tower and stalls on the piers specialise in the whole bag of tricks. No. 228 of a Blackpool catalogue of jokes is captioned the 'Mystery of the Fourth Dimension'. No. 193 of the same series is headed 'Cards De-Materialised by Thought'. 'Parsons are particularly keen on them,' one male salesman told us. On any dry afternoon an expert on Central Pier is demonstrating them to a crowd of onlookers. But pocket mysteries like these are more individual and more expensive (range 6*d*. to 2/6) than the public mysteries which are loudly boosted in Olympia, Luna Park, Central Beach, and the Pleasure Beach. Here there are mysteries concentrated into the persons and behaviours of human beings – fakirs, ecstatics, and holy men.

In the minds of English people, the mysterious and superlunary is often closely associated with the oriental; the fortune of being born in an exotic climate is tacitly assumed to have permitted easier access to the spiritual centre of things – an assumption not peculiar to the uninformed, but evident in Cambridge mystics and the eagerness with which T. E. Lawrence donned a burnous or Trebitch Lincoln, the Buddhist habit. So that the faith of audiences in Blackpool may not be clouded, the yellow-skinned fakirs never speak. They have their spokesmen, very often playing the part of sahib to his native, in topee, ducks, and a semi-consular accent. Over the porch which leads to the place where Sharma reclines on a bed of nails are capital letters with a question mark superimposed, 'WHY DO THEY DO IT'. The barkers are pictured with some of their actors – Tajan with muscular arms and lidded basket of snakes and Rama with turban, glasses, and double chain of beads. Tajan stands with his back to the notice: 'See how the holy Men of India pay penance. Their faith defies all pain.' In a neighbouring booth we see the words, 'Baffling SCIENTISTS & DOCTORS the HEADLESS GIRL.' The booth next to this has a poster which shows the head of a cow bursting through a sheet of paper. The words ALIVE are printed vertically on each side of it. Above and below: 'THE COW WITH 5 LEGS – THE SIGHT OF A LIFETIME.'

Simple but effective artifice gathers the crowds for the Blackpool shows as we saw when the herbalist played with his dormant snake. This is how an Arcade African chief brings people inside to his show:

an . . . African lays a small totem on the pavement, covers it with a cloth, kneels down and bows his head to the floor in front of it. He rapidly picks up the cloth, recovers the totem, and goes back inside with it.

At the expense of little energy and time he draws the curious back with him. Even when the more energetic work of the spieler is the principal means of attracting folks' attention, a parallel simple parade of esoteric costume or esoteric behaviour is considered vital. Thus the Ashanti War-chief stalking in front of the dais where his spieler (introduced as Explorer Evans) talks:

His black face is painted in white blue lines. His head-dress, roe-deer antler in leopard skin. . . . Round his throat, Tahiti beads. . . . Coloured bead necklace across his chest. Cheetah fur at front. Skull hangs from his waist. In his left hand, is a yellow-faced human head. In his right hand, a big sword, blue-edged. . . .

Often a gillie-gillie man in native costume sits silently beside the sahib, fixing his eyes on the audience; sometimes he handles a snake, or gently beats a tom-tom. Though equally simple, the sahib's narration to the people who pause from promenade or Olympic wanderings to listen to him is carefully contrived to exploit certain potent words which the times favour. Here is a sample of how key words are placed attractively:

Outside the Indian Temple, Pleasure Beach. The sahib is a fat, well-preserved man over 50, wears blue suit, bow tie, spats; has a very pukka sahib voice. He struts about while he talks. 'This beautiful girl (girl stands up) is going to dance the famous Ceylon Temple dance. This dance was banned until a few years ago. People thought there was evil where none was intended. But if you are interested in an artist performing with that rare and wonderful grace of the East, you will appreciate her performance. Out here she is going to show you how snakes are tamed in India. . . . We have surprised everybody, even ourselves, by the audiences we have drawn. If you go inside you will find Gogia Pasha himself with all his performers. All are artists, all are performers. There are none that just squat on the floor. Two Congolese brothers will juggle and do such acrobats as you have never seen. There is the bicycle wonder-man of India. None can beat his tricks on a bicycle. Royalty has seen and wondered. Step inside. The show lasts half an hour, but in that half-hour are packed such a wealth of beauty, mystery, and wonder that it will seem like an hour and a half.'

The appeal is to the spiritual, yet the spielers also draw on the citizen's respect and appetite for education. [Let's now look a little closer at the shows themselves.]

INDIAN THEATRE

Until 1938 a grey square castle stood at the south end of the Pleasure Beach, scanty of exterior decoration except for battlements and an anchor device on the front wall. Shortly after the War, this building housed a spectacle called 'The Battle of Jutland'. The Battle soon went off in favour of an Indian troupe, who called the place the Indian Theatre and played in it for many years without altering its architecture.

Inside are steeply rising tiers of seats. No orchestra, but a piano played all the time. A six-foot high model of an elephant stands in front of the backset, where a rather Mediterranean bay and blue sea sweep round with palms and minarets. The star men in the performance are the fakir and conjuror Gogia Pasha. Here is the fakir:

> Dressed in slight loin cloth. Very old. Laughs all the time. Prays. In contorted postures, e.g. legs behind head, hand on privates. Has book (Koran?) in hand. Reads it resting on upturned sole of one foot. (Woman in audience: 'Oh, I'm not looking.') Then Gogia Pasha himself appears: comes on in flowing robes. 'Messieurs and mesdames. Now ladies and gentlemen, I shall show you Mr Cupid and his bow and arrow.' He shoots at a string of flags of different colours. 'Red indicates danger, that's Russia. White indicates peace, honesty, the League of Nations. . . . Now don't be frightened, ladies. I shant shoot your hearts with my darts.' Then he goes among the audience producing pennies from pockets and heads of members of it. 'Now ladies and gentlemen, I will show you truly how I do it. . . . I say Ba ba ba bun bun, bun bun bun bun bun bun.' Gogia finally feels in boy's waistcoat pocket, takes out pair of pink panties. Loud laughter.

A good deal of everyday acrobatics and tap-dancing are mixed with oriental tricks on this stage. If applause is the index, there is little audience discrimination between the two types of entertainment.

WITH MORE POINT

But the adulteration of oriental ecstasy with bits of variety stage does not often occur in Blackpool. A serious tone is preferred. It is analogous to that prevailing in the herbalist's meeting, where the vital topics of health and disease, youth and age, the past and the future, make the facetious a breach of manners. So also with Sharma:

The spectators looked down from a platform which surrounded a pit about four to five feet deep. In the middle was Sharma lying on his bed of nails. At his feet was a radiator. At his head two rags were rolled to form a cushion. The bed is announced as consisting of 4,000 six-inch nails.

Sharma's booth at Olympia utilises a popular Blackpool set. The pit is associated with suffering, whether in the form of glass to be danced on, fire to be burned in, fasting and self-control to be studied, or Sharma's bed of nails.

Sharma had a very brown skin, black hair going grey, and a greyish moustache. Round his neck were two links of brown beads, very much like a rosary. . . . He continually passed the beads through his fingers, and muttered in a low voice. At intervals he startled everybody by shouting 'Allah'. Inside the pit was another native, Tajan, an elderly man, grey moustache, horn-rimmed glasses, red turban, and red calico bound round him and reaching to his knees. . . . He addresses the crowd as follows (his voice very low, his English peculiar): 'Ladies and gentlemen, in India are many holy men; some do penance; some bury themselves up to the neck in sand; others sleep on broken glass; or walk over hot ashes. They are never harmed; they are Yogis. Why do they do this? They are holy men who believe that to achieve great life in the next world they must do penance in this. Their souls will pass into a higher animal according to their deeds in this life. They have FAITH. This is essential, you all know this. Your doctor is no good unless you have faith in him. . . . In England there are towns where the water or the wood had special powers – e.g. Holywell and Holyrood. Now ladies and gentlemen, look at the bed of nails. Sharma does fifteen hours a day on it.' . . .

Then Tajan shook a drum. The noise brought in Mr Ashworth, who now conducted the performance. He introduced a young Indian who brought in a cane basket with lid, which he placed near bed of nails. In one corner of the pit was a sort of shallow tank, containing water, in which were two or three baby alligators. . . .

Mr Ashworth said: 'You know that India has a famous river called the Ganges, regarded as holy. People wash themselves in it. When people die their relatives cremate them and try to scatter their ashes on the banks of the Ganges. On the banks grows a plant which has red seeds. Now Rama will bring them round in a tin, and I want you all to take one. If you like, you can drop a coin in, but don't let that stop you from taking one.' About two people didn't drop coins in. Then Mr Ashworth said, 'These seeds are lucky. And there is an old Indian saying, if you are feeling truthful your prayer will come true. . . .'

When we entered there were thirty-six people present. . . . There was scarcely any conversation, as people had to listen very carefully to hear what was being said. It was not long before two people made a move to go out, and they were followed by several others immediately, so that only twenty-five were left. After this, the interest of the people began to flag.

Holy men cannot keep the Sabbath in Blackpool, where the working week is seven days. The middle of the night and early in the morning are the times Sharma comes off the bed. On a Sunday morning, an observer saw the ecstatic staring into a boot-shop window. He can't have used much shoe-leather in his job.

HEADLESS AND OTHER DIFFICULTIES

These entertainers have no hesitation in making a mystic marriage of the languages of science and religion. For most people there is, in fact, no hiatus between the miraculous and the scientific; electricity and television are their miracles. But the predominant theme of human suffering has its origins in a pretechnological age. In many periods, a mystic might furnish himself with a bed of nails or a woman have her head removed. [And this interest survives into the modern world.]

The oligarchically minded pioneer student of crowds, [Gustav] Le Bon, remarked: 'The notion of impossibility disappears for the individual in a crowd' [*The Crowd* (1896), p. 20]. In our Blackpool experience, however, the individual even in a crowd displays a proper scepticism. Thus in Olympia at the Headless Woman booth where a Chinese girl is 'guillotined':

When the headless girl was revealed, one man said, 'I bet she would show it, if you offered her a drink.' The women giggled. There was silence for several minutes, while a 'professor' showed us how the girl was fed, how she breathed, etc. One woman went up to shake her by the hand. We came out; the men were obviously sceptical, and one of the women said, 'I don't think it's right to show such things.' Her husband said, 'Oh, she's a contortionist.'

Among local youth this act raises perhaps more controversy as to 'How It Is Done' than any other single trick in the gamut of amusements. Not the least singular explanation heard is that when the girl comes for the decapitation, she is in fact a mummy which is regulated by electricity or radio.

But another venture of Le Bon's is perhaps relevant: 'Crowds will hear no more of the words divinity and religion, in whose name they were so long enslaved; but they have never possessed so many fetishes as in the last hundred years, and the old divinities have never had so many statues and altars raised in their honour' [*The Crowd*, p. 66]. The old divinity in this case is Isis who, because she loosened the fetters laid upon the defeated Set, incurred the vengeance of Horus: 'He became like a raging panther of the south with fury, and she fled before him'; he pursued her and smote off her head. Later, Thoth, the divine intelligence, gave her a cow's head in place of her own. The cow, which is for this reason the animal sacred to Isis, stands in a neighbouring booth, with five legs.

In many of the performances, human beings are viewed in circumstances which should cause great suffering yet apparently occasion none. In Tussaud's waxworks things are different but only because the people on view are now not flesh-and-blood but shiny waxen. The inner chamber of Tussaud's Central Beach waxworks is the Chamber of Horrors. A catalogue offers educational instruction: the rack 'is mentioned by Demosthenes (330 BC), and was used on the Continent throughout the Middle Ages, and by the Spanish Inquisition, its object being to extort confessions'.

Tussaud's also adds a political lesson in very exact terms. The catalogue thus describes this contemporary object lesson:

> SPANISH REVOLUTION SCENE, showing the Church of the Monastery of La Rabida (Huelva), where Christopher Columbus prepared for his expedition. This world-famous monastery was gutted by the Communists without regard for its Art Treasures and Historical Associations. The Priests were shot in cold blood, their heads cut off, and were specially arranged in rows, and erected on spikes, etc. The Management, at very great cost, and much forethought, are endeavouring to place before our every year patrons some idea of the present every day atrocities, which are now taking place in Spain.

Congratulating the Management on their forethought, we may simply note that in no other Blackpool amusement has implication given place as yet to unequivocal statement.

Other tableaux include a Chinese execution, the Turkish Gin-Pole, the Torture of the Hooks at Algiers, and Dr Buck Ruxton and his library. Blackpool and Tussaud's pulled off a scoop when they secured the Ruxton furniture. The catalogue goes into the history of the haul:

> Dr Buck Ruxton, aged 35 years, a Parsi and a true type of the Orient, was born in Bombay, and came of a well-known Hakim family, in 1925 married a girl of his own faith and class, but in 1938 went through a form of marriage with Isabella Kerr, the woman who was to become Mrs Ruxton, and whom he afterwards murdered. He was executed at Strangeways Prison, Manchester, on Tuesday, May 12th, 1936. Fragments of two human beings were the only clues upon which the authorities could work, and it was the laboratory which solved what became known as the Moffat Ravin murder riddle. Dr Ruxton, himself a qualified surgeon as well as physician, so dismembered the bodies of his victims that at first even their sex could not be determined.

The exhibit stands as No. 29 in Hall No. 3, the Chamber of Horrors. People passing are divided in opinion:

> Two women come up. First woman: 'Eh, it is a library, isn't it.' She reads out the card. 'He doesn't look much of a black, does he?' Second woman: 'No.'
>
> Two women: 'E was an Indian. What can you expect?'

With what joy must the editor of the catalogue have handled his copy when he spotted the great fact that Ruxton was both oriental and medico. As we have seen, these themes together attract the crowd as no other.

THE ABSENT JOKE

Leaving out of account the effigies of Tussaud's, the dramatis personae of Blackpool shows are dancers (some dancing for happiness, some for devils), tightrope men, a blindfold archer, a conjuror, holy men, a snake-charmer, a doctor, a king in his own country, and a headless woman. Though the Indian Theatre hasn't an idol, its model elephant stands at the back of the stage; and, though nobody there eats fire, Gogia Pasha belches up quite a lot of things, including the Red Flag, balls, and coins. Bell, drum, and Koran are indispensable, together with the sharp ascetic points of knives or nails. These props on the side of the stage, and faith on the side of the audience, mean money to many.

And some, like Albert Ellis, become local figures and believe what they preach. The high seriousness that attends on these performances is, in fact, one of their distinguishing features. Both from patter and action the conspicuous absentee is humour. Leaders of the higher criticism, accustomed to teach that tragedy requires a tincture of comedy, may frown at this Blackpool popular art. [But then the Gogia Pasha offers more than entertainment. This is also true of the Blackpool fortune-teller.]

10

PENNIES FROM HEAVEN AND FROM EARTH

[The Mass-Observers took a special interest in the plethora of fortune-telling services, both gypsy and mechanical, as well as the 'skilled' amusements of the slot-machines, all of which claimed the pennies of Worktowners.]

On the cover of the *Book of Ellis*, given to every client of this renowned seer, is this scene: at the top is a streamer emblazoned with THE ELLIS FAMILY, above which are the words, TRUTH, WISDOM. From the streamer, a globe is suspended in a cloudy sky. Below it on the right is a desert scene, with the Sphinx, the pyramids in the distance, and palm trees. On the left is an Ionian pillar, around which winds a serpent, whose coils bear the letters, 'KNOWLEDGE IS POWER' and 'FOREWARNED FOREARMED'. At the base of the pillar are the following words, 'PHYSIOGNOMY, PATHOGNOMY, GRAPHOLOGY, ASTROLOGY, NUMEROLOGY, and OCCULT SCIENCE'. At the foot of the picture are two ancient tomes. The first is entitled 'PHRENOLOGY' and shows a man's head in profile, with the crown of the head divided into sectors labelled, 'Moral, Aspiring, Domestic, Selfish, Refining, Reflective, and Receptive'. The second tome is called 'PALMISTRY' and shows a hand with the lines well marked.

Page two lists 504 human characteristics. Ellis underlines in pencil those he considers relevant to his client. 41 numbers were marked for the attractive blonde observer who went to him first on a series of visits to the Blackpool palmists and occultists (October 1937). She found Ellis on the promenade where he first took a shop when the Corporation expelled occultists and herbalists from the sands in 1891. Here is part of her report:

> There are three shelves in the shop window with seven phrenological heads. On the indoor shelves, too, there is one large green glass ball, a marble egg, three round crystals and one oblong one, some crystal rods, and small glass balls. A pencilled notice says, 'Members of the Royal Family have not thought it beneath their dignity to consult the Ellis family.' There is a photograph of Mr Ellis telling fortunes forty-five years ago.

Inside the shop is an office desk, with a lot of papers on it and piles of the *Book of Ellis*. . . . Also, a lot of . . . dusty medical and psychology books and a three foot plaster cast of a man showing muscle system.

Ellis's age was about 75. Very clean fresh face, round. . . . Clean collar and blue shirt, spotted bow tie, black suit. He was wrapped all round in a warm rug. His hands were very clean and well looked-after. He looked . . . mostly at [my] left [hand], and sometimes took up a magnifying glass to look through. He first asked for 2/6, then he took one of the booklets and started ticking off numbers and paragraphs and occasionally writing in it, looking at my palms between each tick. I said to him, 'You do a good deal more for your money than those ladies who glance at my hand and say, my lucky day is Thursday, my colour blue.' He chuckled and said, 'Yes, I do; but it would take me a good ten minutes of hard work and concentration for me to tell you what your colour is. Of course, I could tell you anything just to satisfy you and pretend I know. But that isn't my way at all. This is my fifty-first year at Blackpool and my forty-seventh on this very spot and I know my powers and use them properly.' 'You must have seen a lot of change in that time.' 'Yes, I have', he said, 'and not all for the better. Nowadays we have to cater for the masses instead of the classes.'

I asked him if he thought people were becoming more or less interested in phrenology and palmistry. He said, 'Oh, certainly more so. A few years ago there wasn't much interest, but nowadays people are becoming more and more aware of the psychic forces around them.'

These are the words of Ellis which he wrote in pencil in the *Book of Ellis*:

You have quite a good change in the near future, when your money lines are better. You have signs for voyages and you will probably go abroad and do well there. . . . You have good abilities for mental and educational work and fancy and artistic business. . . . Advise piano or voice, but it should be thoroughly understood that although you have the necessary capacity for music, I do not expect you to be a musician without training. Persons likely to prove enemies: stout short fair women, small sunken eyes. Persons likely to prove friends: plump rather dark women.

THE TWO GYPSY SMITHS

There are two Gypsy Smiths in Blackpool, and both claim to be 'The Real Gypsy Smith' and both read palms. Here is the first, age about 55, untidy short brown curly hair and wearing a bright orange knitted jumper with an enormous blue enamel silver brooch. She has her booth behind a shopwindow:

Hanging on each side of window are four sets of impressions of palms, white on black [under which were named]: William Whiteley, Sir Rodgers Bulwer, Dame Melba, Austen Chamberlain (a prominent member of the House of Commons). . . .

When there was a session on, the curtains were completely drawn. . . . On white wall opposite the window were two paper Union Jacks pinned on wall with shining gold edges. Over blue curtain at the entrance was a large coloured framed picture of Queen Elizabeth. Small table in corner with green cloth, silver stand for crystal, vase of four artificial flowers. Saucer full of rubbish, pencil ends, buttons. Blue knitting on table. She invited me in and I gave her a shilling which she put in her pocket. She asked to look at both my hands. . . .

'You've had some terrible things to contend with in your life. No one but yourself knows what you've been through. You're a great one for worry. You meet trouble half-way, you understand. Things get on your mind and keep you awake at night. You've got near relations that say things to your back that they don't dare say to your face – you understand. You're very outspoken and you've said what you think to them. But it's done you no good, dearie. They've done you a lot of harm. But it's over now. There's sunshine ahead of you; there's prosperity ahead of you; there's security ahead of you. I can see you've been married before. Have you been married twice?' Me: 'No.' She: 'Well, I can see two marriages in your hand and you're going to be married again before Xmas. There's great happiness ahead of you. For 2/6, I'll tell you the name of the man.' Me: 'No, I think a shilling is enough for now.' She: 'For ten shillings I'll look in the crystal and tell you some planets.' Me: 'No thanks. I'll probably come back later.' She: 'Well, dearie, you've had an awful lot to contend with, with your last husband – something awful – you understand. No one but yourself knows what you've been through. . . . I'll tell you a lot more of your future and what trouble to avoid for eighteen pence.' Me: 'No, thank you. I can't possibly spend more than a shilling today.' She: 'You came here not minding where you went, didn't you, dearie? You just wanted to get away, you understand. Well, you'll soon have some good friends. You'll be alright in the future, you understand!' She let go of my hands. I asked her, 'Why do you have Union Jacks?' She look absolutely at a loss. . . . She said, 'Oh, they stand for truth – the Union Jack always means truth. I put them up at the Coronation.'

Gypsy Smith No. 1 was right about the marriages. This is what Gypsy Smith No. 2 did for her money. Her booth is on Central Beach behind a mass of stalls, hidden away:

A dirty blue striped beach tent. Outside, a notice saying: 'Step inside and consult the Real Gypsy Smith, Romany Palmist.' Inside, two

119

chairs and an orange box. This Gypsy Smith is a tall dark woman, 50, very black eyes. Brown dress and black coat, shabby; red silk handkerchief round neck. A gold necklace, very thick gold wedding ring.

She said after I had given her a shilling: 'Cross your hand that way to take away bad luck. Cross your hand this way to bring good luck. Now you didn't wish for anyone else's riches, did you, love? Well, what you wished for will come true and sooner than you expected. You make up your mind very quickly and act accordingly. Well, next time you have to make up your mind it will be a very important decision. Do just what your heart tells you. That will be the right thing and don't let nobody interfere. There's a man a shade darker than you, and you've had a lot of difficulties to contend with to bring you to him. But you'll be together sooner than you expect. There's a small amount of money coming to you. You'll have to sign papers for it. You're never going to want and you're going to live till a good old age.'

Of course the occultist atmosphere affects the resident as it does the visitor. Take our landlady, for example. She often read observers' teacups, including, one Sunday evening when she and her family came back from Mass. An observer turns his teacup on to his saucer, and passes it to the landlady when the tea has drained off. She says, 'Has one of your friends got an aeroplane? A tall, very tall man?' 'That's Lord Trevelyan.' She says, 'Yes, well, he's coming, and you're going for a flight in it. I see your life is a clean book. There'll be no sin in your life.' (Six-foot-two surrealist Julian Trevelyan has no aeroplane, but he does have 'aeroplanic' views.)

ROBOTS

[Like everything else, the occultist is being replaced by the machine.] This would be the civilised development from the gypsy and pyramid to technology and Unilever. One step from the gypsy giving your lucky number and health forecast is 'Telepathic Robot, the Scientific Miracle'. According to its spieler on Pleasure Beach, it is a

miracle of modern mechanism with a mysterious radio-brain that will describe all manner of your possessions and answer any question that you put to it. It is baffling, bewildering, and uncanny, and it is the topic of argument wherever it goes. How can it know so much about you? By what means can it so actively and quickly tell you the answer to your most perplexing problems? You will find yourself coming back time after time to stand and watch and wonder how it is done, and just when you think you have discovered the secret, it will say something that explodes your theory.

It is built like an enormous weighing machine in Martian-human form. Where the dial of the weighing machine would be, there is a glass front revealing electrical coils and other gadgets inside, and in particular two electric bulbs glowing green with an effect of monster's eyes. A spieler gathers a crowd around the machine:

'Let me introduce you to the most wonderful piece of mechanism the world has ever known. I expect many of you will remember that I personally had the honour to introduce it at the Exhibition at Wembley, at the World Fair in Chicago, and at the International Exposition in Paris, and in many other places. Now I am not going to bore you with a technical description of how this truly amazing machine works, but will content myself with showing you a few of the things that it can do. But first let me convince you that I am not, as is often suggested, a ventriloquist. You know that it is not possible to say two things at once – not even your mother-in-law could do that. I am going to ask the Robot to talk, and then talk myself.' . . . [After this] he goes around the audience, about sixty in number, and asks them to show him small articles, and these the Robot describes. . . . 'Let's see if we can get something tricky – anything you like from a battleship to a brassiere, the Robot will describe it'. . . . [The Robot] describes someone wiping his nose, a paper with music on it and the composer's name, Schubert. . . . He now says, 'Well, ladies and gentlemen, you must admit this machine is very wonderful. But what you have just seen it perform is nothing. Today this machine is progressing many stages further. It will actually describe you. In the form of a horoscope it will give character delineation. It will describe you better than your own mother could hope to describe you. Nothing private will be disclosed. It prints your character by electricity. But my time is short. The Robot gets overheated very quickly. So please have your money ready.'

First a woman, 55, gave him sixpence, and he asks the Robot to describe the coin. Then he makes the Robot name the woman's lucky number as he goes to the machine and draws out a paper which he folds and hands to her. . . . Then he goes back to the Robot and repeats his speech from 'a correct horoscope and true delineation of your character. All your love affairs, all your business affairs. . . .'

Throughout 1937 and 1938 observers heard this speech continually, and it never altered. The character charts dispensed are constructed in the same way as the booklets at the Ellis booth. Eighty-six possible characteristics are typed and crosses are put in against certain of them. A four-line analysis of character appears at the top of the page under which appears, 'For Amusement Only':

You were born under a lucky star and should make the best of every opportunity that presents itself. Life holds good things in store for you, but do not abuse the gifts that are offered you. Keep bright and cheerful and optimistic.

Most of characteristics marked are complimentary but there are also 'self-opinionated', 'fond of criticising', and 'have your share of troubles'. In four tries, all mark 'You are very good company'. On its average prediction for age, payers would live to over 72; none below 70. An hour's observation showed Robot's turnover at £3/10.

How its answers are engineered is a thing we failed to find out after a season's attempts. A familiar method where answers are involved is the use of a code, although we have not yet traced one here. One of our observers asked the Robot, 'What am I?' Reply: 'A Mass-Observer'.

THE MASTER MIND

Near to the Telepathic Robot is a whole range of prediction machines which occur all over Blackpool, along the piers, in the Tower, Olympia, Winter Gardens, Pleasure Beach, and all along the promenade. They require no human intervention, charge a penny, and have names such as the 'Green-Ray Television Wonder'. Television has fitted excellently into progressive ideas of spirit and magic, and two observers who have televised find it gives them almost superhuman status among many Northern folk. Other efforts: 'The Robot King', 'The Radio Analyst', 'Electrical Crystal Gazer', 'Vocal Radialist', and 'Professor Renerb's Master Mind'.

Take the Professor. One of his many and slightly variable machines is in Olympia. Next to it is the stall selling Violet Ray Ozoner, which ensures relief for 'Catarrh and Asthma as recommended by Sir R. Paget and Prof. Kowarschick'. The Professor's mechanism is housed in a 6 feet by 3-feet by 2-feet box, with a large 'Silver Crystal' – i.e. silver-painted globe or 'witch ball' – and below two glass globes set side by side, representing the Professor's eyes. 'Look into my eyes,' says one notice. More fully another claims:

> Professor Renerb's Master Mind Can Read You Like An Open Book. My delicate mechanism responds to every thought. And my tape machine types what I observe about you. For your benefit inventive brains are built into this machine with deep knowledge accumulated by years of study. Insert penny. Hold the divining rod and look into my eyes. My tape machine will type what the mechanical master mind thinks about you.

When the penny is inserted a yellowish orb rotates, flickering inside each eye. Between the eyes there is a window into the machine, revealing a sort of circular metal toasting grid, with a link of thin chain lying on it (the brain?).

Observer was unscientifically laughing at this performance, when he received a long strip of thin paper with typewritten words on, starting with an admonition from the eyes, 'Don't look so serious.' But another strip from 'The Robot King' gave a professional hint: 'Muster your powers of observa-

tion especially between Thursdays and Sundays.' Renerb is always excep-
tionally progressive, and his latest development in 1938 was in the form of a
NERVOGRAPH, on a telegram slip: 'NEXT TIME START IMMEDIATELY
BETWEEN THE LINES – PLEASING TEMPERAMENT – JOLLY GOOD
SORT – USUALLY GO STRAIGHT FOR WHAT YOU WANT – WAVE
OR ZIG-ZAG ALL SAME TO YOU – KEEP THAT HAPPY
FEELING – OTHERS ENJOY COMPANY – ESPECIALLY ONE – NINE
TIMES OUT OF TEN RIGHT – SEE AGAIN SOON – CHEERIO – PROF.
RENERB.'

The 'crystal' to take the gaze is the central and most conspicuous part of
these machines. Telepathy, robot man, and television's curved 'viewing-
screen' are mechanisms for bringing the remote, the invisible, and almost
incredible right into our Worktown lives. When you are invited not only to
look into the crystal but to put your hands on it, you are playing the seer a bit
yourself. One of the newest and commonest machines is 'Scientific
Automatic Palmistry'. For a printed reading, you place your hand on a small
square plate covered with little metal studs. On insertion of coin these
tremble up and down in erotic ways, tickling and stimulating your palm.
Then out comes a yellow card with a design of a palm on it, and your character. The oldest ideas of prediction have persisted in these modern
developments.

One observer collected forty-three different machines' character or palm
readings on the same day. He was thus able to score his lucky day on every
day of the week and every date of the month. In the representation of his
character, he found little with which he could disagree. Every phrase can
refer equally to people of any age and either sex. The machine readings are
vaguer and less elaborate than those given personally. But in terms of
quantity, you get about six times better value for a penny inserted into a
machine as per penny of your half-crown for the medium.

None of these machines ever tells you anything about your future, except
in the vaguest terms or as regards length of life. In fact, the penny card is no
more than a statement of your character. It tells you what you are like and
gives encouraging advice, sometimes tempered with a little sternness such as:
'To see things entirely different from the rest of humanity leads to misunder-
standings, and you should try to be more generous and less impatient in
dealing with others.' But the card immediately grows more kindly and
encouraging: 'Success may be attained by you through some active business
enterprises or management. Do not expect to pass through life without a
mixture of good and evil.'

Both the machines and occultists offer only personal advice. There is no
social aspect of prediction. And the advice is directed towards making the
individual feel good or better about things as they are; any change must
come from within oneself, and that is already predetermined and
predictable. There are certain modifications possible through the exercise of

free will, but in general the date on which you are born and the position of the planets and stars at that time are the crucial factors. This is the essential and fundamental assumption of all such astrology and prediction. These cards, like psychoanalysis, to which, in a mass-produced way, they approximate, assume that the only changes needed are those within the individual.

From these machines the Worktowners read about their personalities, clearly themselves because they put the penny in the machine and made it work. Those things which are true about them, and which they admit to themselves as true, will not be news to them. Those things which are, in their opinion, untrue cannot be easily ignored and may well bring from the back of their minds some new, if small, self-understanding.

In one sense, the Worktowners, who have none of these machines in their own town, are paying to get the machine's opinion of themselves. In this one week, during which they are free from work, they are out of their familiar environment; they are not associating with all the people they would ordinarily meet each day at work, in the tram, in the backstreet and the corner-pub. In their social contacts they are thus bound to behave 'abnormally', and in such circumstances the opinion of others grows especially important.

In another sense, during this week the normal trajectory of working life is suspended: there is no payday and no washing day. This accentuates the moment and the future, which for this week is not turning on the endless chain of industry. For unemployed Worktowners and those who feel that their jobs are insecure (the latter appear to be continually increasing), the future offers little sign of improvement; thus, it is easy to grasp at any straw or star.

Clearly people do not regard these machines simply as a joke. Mediums and clairvoyants charge half-a-crown. Even at a penny with the machines, there isn't much of a joke about it. There is no field for skill, competition, seeing something, laughter, or prize winning. It is the experience of observers that the great majority of people who patronise the occult believe in it. Often they profess scepticism or mild disbelief, but the words that they have heard or read about themselves nevertheless have their effect. Hundreds of observations on people using the 'Hand-Impressionist' showed everyone placing his hand correctly on the studs. Observers from the South tended rather self-consciously to fool about with these; sometimes one would get several readings from the same instrument, sitting on the studs with his behind. But for the Worktowner the machine still did its work, reading the Mount of Jupiter, Line of Love, and Line of Life.

SLOT

An unusually candid comment from the only one of 220 letters in the 'Holiday Dream' survey [who mentioned enjoying the slot-machines]: 'A

Table 20 Slot-machines

Types of game	Prize	Pier and Pleasure Beach (sample of 96)	Central Beach (sample of 74)
		%	%
Sport	1*d*. or 0	27	27
Ball games	Gifts, 1*d*	24	34
Info. about self	Words	19	15
Grabs and swag	Gifts	12	10
Shooting and throwing	Gifts or 0	10	4
Peep	0	6	8
Babies and moneys	1*d*. back	1	2

day amongst the hundreds of automatic machines, watching the faces of those who swell the machines with pennies. It is an education in itself.' We made a detailed census of slot-machines along the promenade and other amusement centres. Our analysis is in Table 20. In this wealth of slottery, people can play games more simple and immediate and even more profitable than those available for the rest of the year in Worktown. And they do play.

Commonest of all slot machines is the 'Football Game'; the highest concentration of these is on the piers, and most of the football machines are visibly aged. Less common are 'Hockey', 'Polo', and 'Golf'. In all these games, either two players compete or (rarely) the player matches his own skill against a standard set by the machine. He cannot win more than he puts in.

But when you start playing with human effigies, always male, juvenile or simian, you may hope for some more material profit. In 'Play the Red' you flick a ball by a lever identical to that in the football game into 1 of 7 cups. If you get 5 reds, you get your penny back and another free turn; in some cases, it is possible to win more money than you put in. This is the only machine of its sort in Blackpool, and on the Pleasure Beach there is an arcade largely filled with them. Similar in conception is the 'Prize Wheel' and the 'Spiral Machines' in which you whisk around 5 balls for a penny, aiming for numbered holes, 0, 20, 30, 50, to win 5 cigarettes for over a hundred points, 10 cigarettes for over 130.

The spiral idea is developed in 'Skee Ball', where long low machines slope upwards away from the player, with concentric rings of 50, 100, 150 at the end. On the Pleasure Beach, a long arcade is filled with ranks of Skee Ball tracks, 3*d*. to play; an illuminated indicator shows your score, which must be at least 260 for a woman to win, more for a man.

The active socialisation of these and all ball games is attained in 'To-Win', where a long row of players sits each side of a system of pigeon holes laid flat; from a dais, a man directs the play through a microphone, telling everyone

125

when to throw their next ball. All throw each ball simultaneously, and the first who gets a row of pigeon holes filled with balls in a straight line is announced a winner. Two turns cost threepence, and the first prize is generally a box of chocolates. 'To-Win' is generally working at full blast all evening, with people waiting to take the places of those who have finished; some play for an hour at a time. The microphone patter runs on:

Come and try your hand at a real sporting game. . . . It's not a race. You all have a chance to win. You're not competing against each other. You're competing against luck, and luck's on your side. Come on. Come on. Show your girls what you can do.

This patter contains all the elements fundamental to these slot-machines and ballgames. Although, in fact, you are competing against one another in 'To-Win', in feeling, you are competing against luck. But you must show your success, if any, to some other human being.

Probably all these amusements originated from bagatelle (or billiards), which is now scarce in Blackpool, but appears as a slot-machine under the names of 'Kings', 'Roly-Poly', 'Sure-Shot', and the 'Big Game-Hunter'. The slot-machine tendency is continually to elaborate and to introduce fortuitous factors. But invariably the higher the number, the better the score.

The idea of aiming at the highest number or centre in a circular pattern is equally basic in another important group of amusements and slot-machines, the shooting and shying type. In 'Pussy' you aim with a fixed pistol at five white grinning cats with red tongues hanging out on a painted brick wall, with a backcloth of houses and chimney stacks. Five lead bullets for one penny and no prizes.

Crowds gather around the games where you throw a ball at a target. There are no coconut shies in Blackpool and no skittles; the objectives are more closely associated to the release of holidays. Thus at 'Crazy Kitchen' you throw to smash crockery; with 'Belisha Beacons' you throw at the middle of traffic signs. Or you kick a football at the glass windows of a house; or you shoot with rifles at beer bottles suspended on strings, against a background of luxuriant palms and South Sea islands. At the Belisha Beacons, the barkers cry:

Come on, come on. Any prize you like. All for threepence. Have a whack at one. You must have wanted to do it. Here's your chance. Have a bang at the ruddy things.

Observers continually noticed the epidemics of interest and disinterest in these shies; sometimes they made control experiments. For perhaps an hour no one would play. Then one man would start, and in a few moments a section of the constantly flowing tide of people would gather, congest the passageway, and within a minute there would be a dense crowd. Others would start playing, and the place would become a temporary centre of activity.

In the slot-machines the figures to be struck are males; but in the prizes, which are nearly always given by men to women, the dolls are female, and the animals are domestic or petsy. The dolls are dressed as Miss Muffet, Dutch Girl, Beach Girl, and Columbine. Everyone wears trousers, and indeed the animal prizes, too, are equally unsexable. In 1939, with the Pandas at the Zoo getting newspaper headlines and photographs, at Blackpool large stuffed Pandas appeared as top prizes.

[Into these slots, holiday-makers pour millions of pennies.] One manager told us his machines cost £200; in three years it would be worth £30. 'But it's popular, and I can afford to spend 40 per cent of the takings on swag.' 'Swag' includes scent bottles, small tape measures, powder puffs, packets of cigarettes, large black cats (these are often the most difficult things to win and much the most played for), packets of sweets, packets of five cigarettes, ashtrays, penknives and shellac cigarette cases. [Apparently Worktowners believe that they get their money's worth.]

11

THEATRES AND CINEMA

[The attractions of Blackpool are not merely the modernised extensions of the traditional seaside pilgrimage and the fair, but the Victorian entertainment of the music hall and the more recent cinema. These pleasures reflect both the trend away from the sea and towards the 'side' and the taste of Worktowners.]

There are 4 theatres and 5 pierrot halls; during the season, all but 1 of these is doing a musical show. These are 19 cinemas, of which 15 have a seating capacity of 20,548. Adding the Circus, the Marina Ice Rink, and the Indian Theatre, we get an approximate total seating capacity, taking 2 houses an evening, of about 70,000. This enables everyone during the peak week, when 400,000 holiday-makers are claimed by official statistics, to see an evening show. In practice, the big central places are full and queuing all the time. Weather makes little difference. Neither cinema nor theatre can be harmed by the warmest outdoor weather. But in the event of rain, all the big places put out posters, 'MORNING PERFORMANCE AT 10:30'.

For George Formby's King Cheer show at the Opera House, observers generally had to pay 3/6 if they hadn't booked well in advance. A lesser star like Reg Bolton at Feldman's, 'Punch and Beauty', cost only 1/9. Here are some examples from the Feldman's show:

'The Judge's night-gown'. . . . The curtain shoots up on the court and shows the chorus girls packing the jury box. Enter Bolton as the judge. . . . One of the juvenile chorus enters, as the boy disputed in the case. . . . The women claimants appear. Bolton addresses one of them. 'Are you the mother of that—?' 'Ten years then.' 'Any evidence?' 'Only my motherhood.' 'Have you got it with you?' The house roars. . . . A lawyer with an enormous paunch rises and says, 'I rise.' Hysteria. . . . Repeats, 'I rise.' Bolton, 'Well, don't rise any more.' Hysteria. All this time Bolton keeps slapping the policeman's helmet off, creating a stream of hysterical laughter. Bolton to the lawyer, 'Sit down and get on with your knitting.' The second woman claimant says, 'See my likeness to the child.' Bolton replies, 'Oh, he may grow out of that.' A general fight ensues, particularly between the two women claimants.

Then Bolton leans over to the lawyer and hisses, 'So you won't talk, hey?' He knocks the lawyer down. Bolton, 'A child can only have one mother, though it can have four fathers.' The house shrieks. Bolton as the judge decrees that the child shall choose its own parent. It selects him. Down comes the curtain, leaving Bolton and the child on the front stage. . . . The child calls out, 'Are you Lord Nuffield?'

['My Little Buckaroo' is the title of the next item.] Little Eva and a singer are in cowboy costumes. The singer rocks little Eva on her knee, and tells her, 'Go to sleep or you'll never be a man like your daddy,' and then begins the song, 'Close your sleepy eyes, my little one'. In the foreground grow cacti by a log cabin. The prairie recedes into the distance. 'And remember Buffalo Bill was once a kid like you.' Little Eva yawns, spreads her arms in a circle, half-lights, shadows. Piano arpeggios on top octaves against a violin tune. Little Eva at last asleep reclining on the mother's shoulder. The mother spreads out the fingers of Eva's hand, and pulls it against her own cheek. Curtain.

Bolton enters as a window cleaner. The curtain goes up on an artist's studio. On an easel is a female nude, the back view. The artist's model makes her entry. 'I love you', Bolton tells her, 'with a passion that spoils my football coupons.' The artist enters, distinguished by a black velvet coat and hat. The artist's model goes behind a screen, and one by her clothes are slung over the top. A garter comes first. The artist complains that it will be half an hour before the marks of the garter wear off. Corsets follow. The artist makes the same complaint even more strongly. Bolton stands on a chair and looks over the screen and . . . says to the artist, 'Did you say that it took half an hour for the marks of the garters to come off? Then you might as well pack up for today – she's sitting on a cane-bottom chair.'

Boot boy tells how he can never remember the number of the rooms where the shoes come from in his posh hotel, so he marks initials of the people on the door in chalk. When Jimmy Maxton came, J. M., that was alright, when Neville Chamberlain came, N. C., that was O.K., too. But there was a hell of a row the next morning from Winston Churchill.

Song and romance alternate with comedy and parody of politicians, lawyers, artists, teachers, doctors, homosexuals, teetotalers, dead royalty, and dictators. The Feldman's show, like any other, has an emotional trajectory:

A. Spectacle. Atmosphere. Everyone on. Strip-tease.
B. Comedy. The background is liquor.
C. Song and dream. The background is the sea, ships, the tropics.
D. Children. Sentiment through cuteness.
E. Comedy. The background is sex.

F. Song and drama. The background is nature, putting up a vain resistance against the onslaught of commerce.

G. Comedy. The background is lavatory humour and deformity humour. The subject is the futility of politics.

H. Song and comedy. The background is the plantation, and the comedy is a defence of the plantation and class differences. The subject is regret for *le temps perdu*. Interval.

I. Song and dance. The background is Holland in tulip time. Spring and rusticity.

J. Comedy. The background is the kitchen, the subject is the levelling power of domestic pleasures.

K. Children. The same appeal as in the previous instance, but sharpened, because the cuteness involves actual mimicry.

L. Song and dream. The background is the old-world garden and the Italian scene. The subject is memory of youth, more lament for *le temps perdu*.

M. Comedy. The background is the law court, the subject the futility of legal proceedings, the instrument for debunking the court is sex (described above).

N. Song and children. The background is nature, the wilderness of the prairie that develops men. The appeal again depends on the cuteness of one child, but less uniquely.

O. Comedy. The background is sex. The subject the futility of art.

P. Spectacle. The background and the appeal alike based on patriotism.

Q. Song. The background is the Blackpool oyster. The purpose of the item is to complete the work of bringing the audience into complete liaison with the stage and its attitude.

R. Spectacle. Ties up the end with the beginning, and stresses the dreamboat element in the scene and on the programme, which concludes: 'The Punch and Beauty Company bid you Au Revoir with the wish that YOUR Dreamboat will come home.
GOD SAVE THE KING.'

In Table 21, 427 jokes that made people laugh in 8 shows are classified. One ill-health joke appeared in three shows simultaneously: 'I wish you had a hotel with 1000 rooms.' 'Why?' 'So I could come down tomorrow morning and find you dead in every one of them.' 35 scenes (13 within England) and 101 costume parts by the principal actors were described in Blackpool music hall shows (see Table 22). Although there is no industrial scenery, 22 per cent of the leads were dressed as workers; of these 5 by the hero or heroine. On the other hand, of the 11 society and high-class characters, all were the hero or heroine.

Table 21 Music hall jokes

	South Pier	North Pier	Central Pier	Palace	Leslie Henson	Feld-man	Opera House	Total
Ill-health	7	1	19	3	10	11	3	54
Royalty	6	2	15	—	5	8	—	36
Domestic affairs	3	3	6	1	3	11	5	32
Local Blackpool	5	5	10	2	1	3	3	29
Sex	16	1	5	1	—	5	—	28
Domestic objects	5	2	3	1	5	6	1	23
Art	3	1	10	—	7	1	—	22
Food	4	4	1	1	4	6	2	22
Money	4	1	8	2	1	4	2	22
Clothes	5	1	8	2	1	4	2	23
Alcohol	4	4	6	—	5	—	2	21
Religion	2	1	6	1	5	1	2	18
Sport	8	1	1	—	—	3	3	16
Law	—	—	5	—	1	7	—	13
Jobs	4	1	6	1	—	—	—	12
Lavatory humour	3	1	—	1	2	7	1	15
Abroad	—	—	5	1	4	1	—	11
English towns	3	—	3	2	—	2	—	10
Live big shots	1	—	2	—	3	2	—	8
Education	—	—	1	—	4	3	—	8
Dead or mythological	—	—	3	—	2	—	—	5
War, politics, science	—	—	1	—	4	—	—	5

Table 22 Music hall themes

Subject	Backsets	Style of costumes worn by principal actors
Industrial	0	22
Asiatic or African	6	13
Professions	2	13
Rustic	4	12
Society	2	11
Continental	9	10
American	5	7
Domestic	1	6
Religious	4	5
Marine	2	2

BIG SHOT

But the biggest heros of the working class are 'their own' Gracie Fields and
George Formby. Both constantly behave and talk working class (her word is
'lass' just as Formby's is 'daft'). Gracie was born not far from Worktown in
1898, and started her career as a cinema vocalist there in 1906; she performed
first as a single act in 1913; and in 1914, at an adjacent town, she was Princess
of Morocco in 'Dick Whittington'. As Sally Perkins in 'Mr Tower of
London', she went to the front rank in its seven years of success. Honorary
freeman of her home town, benefactor to all sorts of things, founder of an
orphanage at Peacehaven, Sussex, she is even more easily still 'an ordinary
person' than George Formby.

George is a Gracie Fields fan, constantly referring to her with admiration.
Once a stable-lad, he says in the *Empire News* (March–June, 1938):

> I don't know a note of music. Where music is concerned I am
> completely dumb. I can remember the time when I first went on a
> theatre stage and the conductor of the orchestra said to me, 'Give me
> the cue.' I looked round for a stick because I thought the chap was
> talking about billiards. Eh, I've always been that daft. . . .
>
> I have no desire to work in America. British studios are good
> enough for me. . . . I have certainly been wonderfully treated,
> having good stories for my clowning, which is the life and soul of
> every comedian.

This is the Formby of the songs, shy but sensible. And it is music especially
that brings the crowds to the Blackpool theatre. Dominant songs in 1937
were:

'A Star Fell Out of Heaven'
'When Did You Leave Heaven'
'Pennies from Heaven'
'Chapel in the Moonlight'
'Choirboy'
'When My Dreamboat Comes Home'
'I Saw a Ship a-Sailing'
'September in the Rain'

'A Star Fell Out of Heaven' contains nearly all the brand features of
popular jazz songs: 'A miracle had happened as they sometimes do. A star
fell out of heaven and turned out to be you.' And the year's second most
popular Blackpool song:

> A long time ago, a million years BC,
> The best things in life were absolutely free.
> But no one appreciated a sky that was always blue
> And no one congratulated a moon that was always new.

So it was planned that they should vanish now and then
And you must pay before you get them back again.

This interpretation of economic history has received the widest acceptance among contemporary Worktowners, and is the same as that promoted by Blackpool's astrologers, Sharma Yogis, and Noah's Ark. Time, whether as a recollection of time past or regard for time future, is the theme of these jazz hits; and in all of them there is a movement of some person or object between the earth and sea or sky.

But Formby's songs are noticeably different, containing few of these 'escapist' elements. Professedly the Lancashire man, Formby brings things right down to earth. Compare the symbols (Table 23) used in ten of his songs with those in three popular songs in Blackpool.

Table 23 Music hall songs

Symbol	Formby	Others
	%	%
Dreams and time	7	26
Beauty and religion	8	24
Domestic affairs	42	20
Love	24	17
Country and abroad	5	12
Town	4	1
Sport	5	0
Important folk	3	0
Others	2	0

Thus Formby reverses the symbolism or metaphor; he brings up home, policemen, ordinary kissing, sport, and town life. There is nothing in the jazz hits comparable to the typical Formby opening to a song, in typical simple rhythm with ukulele played by himself:

> 'In My Little Snapshot Album':
> Now I'm a young inventor, a chap with good ideas,
> I made myself a camera; it took me years and years.

> 'Noughts and Crosses':
> I could never be poetic;
> I could never write a song.
> But a simple game for two
> That I can play with you
> I'm as happy as the day is long.

> I'd rather play noughts and crosses with you
> Than take you to a French non-stop revue

133

I'm very daft at dancing, at moonlight and romancing,
I'd rather play noughts and crosses with you.

Formby has a lot to say about what you can see when underclothes slip or
aren't there. For example:

> On the swingboats when you ladies go;
> Mind the crowd below
> Take care what you show.
> Hold tight! KEEP YOUR SEATS, PLEASE!

> She pulls her hair all down behind;
> Then pulls down her never-mind,
> And after that pulls down the blind
> WHEN I'M CLEANING WINDOWS.

> I've got a picture of a Nudist Camp,
> All very jolly, tho' a trifle damp.
> There's Uncle Dick without a care –
> Discarding all his underwear.
> But his watch and chain still dangles there.

> A lovely bathroom and all brand new,
> You splash me, yes, and I'll splash you,
> We'll see quite a lot of each other, too,
> When we feather our nest!

Blackpool has no opera, though Formby occupies its Opera House. Blackpool culture means the old waltz, stars falling out of heaven and dreamboats,
and Reg Dixon's Mighty Wurlitzer organ. Even in the ballrooms there is little
enthusiasm for the hot American stuff. Formby, the big shot but nevertheless
the ordinary man, the near-Worktowner, the man who tried to climb the
Tower but was stopped by the police, synthesises the whole position even in
the title of the Lancashire Toreador, and with his 'Hindu Howdoo, Hoodoo
Youdoo Man' merges east and west in the Chinese Laundry way; and his
attitude to Americanisms he states in 'Do De O Do De O Do':

> In modern music some clever guy
> Has started a brand new craze.
> A fellow must put do-de-o-do
> Into all he sings or plays.
> Now some may think this foolish
> But I'm not one of these.
> For I attach importance to
> Those do-de-o-do-de-o-do's.
> Now you can't be rich; you're poor instead –
> Without the do-de-o-de-o-do.

CINEMA

Whereas in Worktown the star generally appears after the interval in a musical show, in Blackpool there is a first-class star who ends the show as a grand finale. [The same stress on the big shot is present in the cinema.] Cinema boss Mellow, speaking for the powerful Tower group of cinemas, remarked to an observer: 'We deal with the biggest film producers, and look for pure star-value; that's more important than story; small artists mean nothing to the Blackpool crowd.' By contrast, the manager of the small and independent 'Imperial' says, 'We do best with humourous shows than thrillers. Musicals also popular. George Formby and Gracie Fields are the two surest draws.'

The Clifton and Palladium each had their biggest successes with romantic and musical films. They showed 17 of these during the season, 8 comedies, 14 crime and political, 4 adventure, and 2 westerns. Flops were 'The General Died at Dawn' (Gary Cooper), 'Land Without Music', and 'Men are not Gods'. Manager Burgess of the Palladium said:

> The crowd you get here doesn't like anything that makes it think . . . prefers mostly blood and thunder and sophisticated comedy. Spencer Tracy and Gable get over well. The Marx Brothers fall flat; they just don't see the point. What I think is the best policy is just to get people into a seat and simply pour entertainment into them. We have 1,500 seats.

And showing his film list to us, he commented one word on all films except one – 'Pennies from Heaven' – against which he observed, 'Believe it or not, a success'. We believe it.

12

THE FRINGE OF OUR LAW

[The trend away from the natural setting of the seaside and towards the manufactured space of commercial pleasure is revealed in the observers' study of the new holiday camp and hydro, self-contained living and play places standing on the fringes of Blackpool culture.]

The Tower, incorporating behind one pay-box an aquarium, dance-hall, slot-machine, restaurant, and bird's eye view of Blackpool, was the first Blackpool within Blackpool. It only does not include lodging. To make a place for whole-time living (as well as playing) was left to promoters at the fringe of the Borough, near enough to the centre to be Blackpool but far enough away to keep an internal integrity. To the north is the Norbreck Hydro, like a vast Elstree castle, to the south the Squire's Gate Camp. The south is for those who want their holidays cheap, people like this Worktown girl:

> There is only my Father and I and we wish to spend our holidays together so I think we can't improve upon our choice of the last two years, namely a Holiday Camp. Here we can both enjoy ourselves in our own way and make friends suitable to our different ages. The tennis, swimming, putting, and dancing (all available within the camp-grounds at any well-organised camp) appeal to me while the whist drives and the motor coach drives and the general sociability appeal to father. We both like the good fellowship and the utter absence of any snobbishness we have always found in these camps, whilst the separated chalets provide the privacy and comfort without losing the freedom and open air life of ordinary camping. The food, well served and cooked whilst plain, is varied and wholesome, and the homeliness of the Dining Hall makes meals a real pleasure. This holiday is also quite reasonable (£2), well within the reach of most working-class people.

Cunningham's Camp at the Isle of Man and Butlin's at Skegness set the pace for the growth of camps all over England.

136

SQUIRE'S GATE

Very Mediterranean-looking is the Squire's Gate Camp with rows and rows of tiled chalets, centred on the largest building with a bell turret, 'The Moorish Pavilion', a cross between a Spanish hacienda and a Swiss chalet. The 1,400 chalets among the sand-dunes, the manager calls 'Californian chalets'. The alleys between the blocks of huts are named, from the manager's several years' experience in California, 'Hollywood Avenue', 'Santa Monica', and so on. The cheaper sort of chalet is like this:

Four single camp beds, blue iron legs. Room is fifteen feet by nine feet painted cream. . . . Triangular canvas roof lashed on to wooden walls. . . . Right of door is small cupboard with grey electric cooker. . . . Two folding wooden chairs. Enamelled wash-basin, ten inches in diameter. . . . Lavatory near railway line. No pictures. Straw mattress and pillow case. Holidayers mainly criticised the shilling a day in the meter for electricity. Otherwise, 'It's so free and easy. Nobody cares what you do, or whether father gets drunk.' To which father replies: 'That's all you can do when it rains. You may as well get wet inside as outside.'

Confirming its status as a compendium of all amusements, the camp issues a recurrent weekly programme, including:

1 Dancing – In the Ballroom with Jenny Millar's Senoritas' Band, twice daily.
2 Squire's Gate Follies – Three shows daily.
  Physical Training Class – All guests invited to participate. No charge.
3 Treasure Hunt – On the sports field on Monday at 10:30 a.m.
  Beauty Contest-Class I, single ladies. Class II, girls aged 3 to 6. Class III, men. No entry fee.
4 'Go as you Please' competition – Singing, crooning (with use of mike), conjuring. . . . Competitors are allowed four minutes each.

Orchestral concerts, whist, miniature golf, tennis tournaments, dancing instruction, and field sports are organised. Church services, Sunday, 9:15 a.m. and 8 p.m. For the sports, all the chairs are filled at 2d. a time: sack-race, three-legged race, wheel-barrow race, shoe-race, balloon-race, and egg-and-spoon race. Then:

A ladies' beauty competition for ladies in bathing costume got no entries. Man waives bathing-costume rule. Twenty seven ladies enter after persuasion. One white-haired old lady is first entrant and stands half a minute before anyone else comes forward. Parade round field.

137

Five entrants drop out as they go round. Judged by hand-clap. Old lady who entered first wins hands down. Receives chromium 'Ship'. Next, beauty contest for little girls, 5 to 11 year olds. Thirty enter. Little baby falls as parade goes round. Mother dashes out and carries her round. Judged by hand clapping, and baby who fell wins hands down. Other children were much nicer.

The dreamboat song all over Blackpool in 1937 was particularly appropriate to Squire's Camp, for the 1938 camp brochure claimed: 'Squire's Gate is different. It is the Beach of Dreams Come True!' But the dream has rules: a maximum of five in the chalet, only one at a time in the lavatory (washing your legs in the basin is prohibited). Still, here you have much greater freedom than that which you receive in the lodgings, and you are liberated too from traffic noise and dense crowds. Camps inside the Borough are controlled by the local authority, but Squire's Gate is actually just over the boundary of the Borough in Lytham St Annes. Thus the camp is in a strong position for doing as it will. This has been partly responsible for the fable of its immorality, a legend encouraged by the decorations round the sportfield, a wall and six arches of Moorish design, surmounted by models of tomcats, tails erect on two arches, while on the corresponding pair of arches are she-cats glancing round at the toms. The myth undoubtedly attracts young people to the camp, while it does not appear to keep others away. Witness a group of elderly women talking on the veranda of a chalet:

'This place is getting awful common. The young uns seems to think they can do owt they mind.'

'Aye they get away with owt nowadays, showing all their legs an carrying on with young fellows.'

Observer asked if they had ever seen anything wrong: 'What's that luv – you've seen nowt? Ye want to come round back of railway . . . don't go round yourself. It's not safe for young girls.'

But on no evening during the week were there more than five couples in the famous 'back of railway', often described as the scene of wild orgies. Camp management has its own vigilance corps, led by a giant ex-police officer.

People buy this self-contained holiday for cheapness and liberty only equalled by the Kippax system in Blackpool, but in addition it provides a family or groups of friends with a self-contained community of their own in the chalet. The commonest unit is the man, wife, and two children; only here is the couple without children a minority in Blackpool. Campers are typical Worktowners and the *Daily Dispatch* has the biggest circulation in the Camp.

NORBRECK HYDRO

The camp lacks the vigour and violence of the central Blackpool scene. There are no barkers or stream-lined trams or food brothels, and space does not convert people into crowds. After Pleasure Beach, it may sound a little dull. At its opposite number, the Norbreck Hydro, the rhythm is faster, with nearly 1000 people sleeping under one roof. But the idea is the same: 'A Seaside Resort in Itself'. This camp is a castle or rather two twin castles, one pre-war, the other an addition of six years ago. With castellated roof, turrets, and four flag-poles, from a distance the place looks like the set of a British film studio. The effect of antiquity is somewhat disturbed by the drainpipes exposed on the face of the wall. It is, says the coloured brochure, a 'land-ship of healthful pleasures', not a 'common inn' but a 'LUXURY LINER ON LAND minus Mal-de-Mer plus links and lawns'. The boat-like trams which run past the front door take you from the ship into Blackpool: 'There is always Blackpool, a pleasant cliff-car ride away, to fall back upon for first-class shows,' notes the brochure, 'but Norbreck is all-sufficing and self-contained.'

> For 17/6 a day inclusive, you get a room like No. 45: Sixteen feet by nine, about nine feet high. The wall-paper is mottled buff. Half the floor is bare board, unstained, the other half pink lino. . . . Central heating. Small basin in corner with hot and cold water-taps. No mirror or shelf by basin. Two chairs. . . . No pictures. Copy of house rules. Double bed. . . . No bed lamp or bedside table. . . . Under the wash-basin, a metal slop pail, light enamelled tin. One dressing-table, with looking glass [and] wardrobe.

On each floor of the new wing there were lavatories. The first thing you see on entering the hall is a fortune-telling machine. From the hall through a lounge runs 'Main Street', a long high passage with red plush benches running down a continuous chain of rooms past the Amusement Arcade culminating in the dining-hall.

Luncheon conversation. Miss Y from Newcastle, plain, 30, staying alone in the hotel:

> Observer: 'Why do you think people come to this hotel?'
> Miss Y: 'Oh, because of its notorious reputation, I think.'
> Obs: 'Looking round, I should say it's a bit exaggerated, don't you think? It seems healthy enough.'
> Miss Y: 'Oh yes, it's healthy alright.'
> Obs: 'Have you been to Blackpool yet?'
> Miss Y: 'No, not yet.'
> Obs: 'Have you been on the beach?'
> Miss Y: 'No. The sea looks so dirty. In fact, I've never been on the beach, though I've been here three times.'

No Hydroist was seen on the beach at any time. Miss Y brings up the Norbreck myth of a bell having to be rung at 8:00 in the morning so that people could get back to their own bedrooms. This false story undoubtedly attracts people there, and outsiders readily circulate or believe such stories as a satisfaction for frustrated wish and curiosity.

Norbreck, like the camp, is in one sense a hamlet with a law unto itself. The hotel has never applied for a licence, so that the police have no right of entry. All drinks are brought in from across the road. A good deal is drunk, especially in the unique Bachelors' Quarters, entered by a special stairway. Most of the drinking is done after the dancing is over in the evening. The largest party that our observer found in one bedroom was twenty-one.

Near the big dance hall is the Sun Lounge, fifty feet square. In the wall is set a tank of fish. Coloured glass depicts a balustraded court-yard on which five women are grouped in togas or bath wraps. The adjacent wall has a Mediterranean harbour scene, a lake with small islands on each of which is a small town with steeples and towers. The scenery is closely similar to the backset of theatre scenes and the 'Reel' on the Pleasure Beach.

In addition to evening dancing (on average 80 dance, 100 watch) and drinking, there are film shows – 175 attend on Monday – and entertainers such as Mr Tom Sherbourne, described on the hotel noticeboards as 'The Man with X-Ray Eyes', who offered an act of magic and mass prediction. The biggest activity anywhere in the Hydro was on the writing tables in the lounge. At no time on Tuesday morning was the observer able to get a place at one of them. People were mostly writing postcards. The *Daily Mail* heads the newspaper circulations, followed by the *Express* and *Mirror*.

Norbreck guests present several different types. George represents Norbreck's public character No. 1:

Age late 30s. Big – almost six feet tall. Fifteen stone. Healthy complexion, large hands, well kept, little thin on top, manner very hearty. George has been here about ten times and always on the same week. He is an Irishman. His first appearance was at dinner on Monday.

Attention was first caught by George's loud cry to the head waiter, 'Hello, George here.' This caused a number of remarks at observer's table: 'George is a lad.' 'George is a card.' Throughout the meal, George clapped his hands, whistled, and called out to catch attention of people whom he recognised. Nobody came over to him, but all smiled back or waved a hand.

He was next seen at lunch. George passed behind a very old lady and a middle-aged lady. . . . George . . . concentrated his attention on the old lady, who responded by laughing and talking. A little later, when ordering from the waiter, George said, 'One for me and one for my girl friend.' She liked this immensely. 'George is a one, isn't he?' said a man at observer's table.

It may be noticed that without making any enquiry our observer knew all about George. His is what the brochure calls 'the old face' the visitors like to see again.

In contrast is a second type:

Miss A was about 35, spectacles, plain, severe, touchy, dressed in tweeds or blouse and skirt, from Durham.

Arrived Monday night.

Spent Tuesday indoors.

Did not go out once.

Breakfasted at ll a.m.

Read a book.

Went to conjuror and a dance.

Bed at 12:30

Spent Wednesday morning in bed reading.

Up at 9 a.m.

Breakfasted at 9:30.

Had been introduced to seven people, knew none of their names.

George is the Hydro type in the sense that he personifies the ideal brochured, 'happy family' spirit; Miss A is another type which predominates.

CASTLE AND CAMP

In the castle, there are very few children and men predominate. Many during the holidays came from Worktown to the camp, but visitors from all over Britain and even Ireland came to the Hydro. In contrast to the camp, the castle had no fish and chips, different newpaper preferences, ten times as many tennis courts for a fifth the number of people, and no church. This reflects the economic ('class') differences between the camp and castle. In both, however, one can spend a full holiday week without ever going out of the place. Each has its own entertainments and reputation. Yet these places are Blackpool and admit the fact. Blackpool values get in whether as sea-apathy or postcard frenzy, alcohol intensity or X-Ray Eye.

In 1937 people were beginning to speak of the future covered-in Blackpool. The new million-pound improvement scheme, passed since then, will be a step in that direction, sweeping away the labyrinthine system of stalls and slot-machines along Central Beach and Bank Hey Street; and implicit in any such tendency is a movement away from nature, in the form of the sea, a most unreliable and unprofitable phenomenon.

These communities within communities suggest another form of development along the same lines, one that is in a sense against the main Blackpool trend. Here the community is able to make its own code of laws, and here your holiday home is for once your castle. The removal of the law from the outside is as important as the removal of routine from inside. Blackpool offers its holiday-makers many new liberties and sanctions in how they behave outside, as we shall soon see. But the Blackpools within Blackpool are able to furnish even more. They also provide some of the peace and quiet which so many of our holiday-makers wanted. And just because of that, the pressure on moral rights and liberties is not as strong, or as noticeable.

IN FACT, IN GENERAL

We have now described the Worktowner on holiday in Blackpool, what he does openly and what there is openly to do. We presume that those readers who have survived this far have also got a good deal of information about the covert behaviour and mentality of the Worktowner and of Blackpool in general. Our concern is with fact and with trying to present it in such a way that others may later verify it, correct it, may at all times draw their own conclusions from it. At this early stage in the sociology of our own civilisation, we are very ready to take the risk of being called mere collectors of endless facts. A leading sociologist and opponent of Mass-Observation once wrote that our facts 'simply multiply like maggots in a cheese and leave no shape behind them'. But nothing is easier than to impose a shape from a pleasant room in Exeter College. But the shape the social scientist seeks is the shape of things as they are.

So we will shift from the plane of simple economic behaviour on to that which can loosely be termed moral behaviour, involving the laws written and unwritten of this culture. This will take us dancing and bring us into fighting and maybe the gutter, to snooping on 10,000 conversations, and we can hardly avoid concern with Blackpool's employees, its cultural heroes, and the working of its business interests. But groping in the sand-dunes in search of clinical material on the couple, we hope not to lose sight of the stomach and sleep, the lodger in the lavatory, and the penny in the slot.

Ultimately in this book we are concerned with Blackpool's motto of progress and with the question – what is progress? – and thus the question – what is industrial civilisation? But for now we present this book as a casebook of ordinary life in now-a-day England.

Part 4

13

DAY ROUTINE

We have now covered the absolute needs of seaside holiday life. We have seen that the things people eat and drink and live in are different from those they get in Worktown, mainly in the direction of greater elaboration or size or time. It is outside the sands and the boarding house that we come to the territory of pleasures which are absolutely unobtainable in Worktown. These are found in Pleasure Beach, in the theatres, where real stars like Formby and Fields play, in the waxworks and great ballrooms, and in the Indian Theatre and palmist parlours. It is through these tangles of pleasure that the holiday-makers, a minority of whom play on the sands, spend most of their seven days' release.

[But, how do they spend their time and with whom?] In the pendulum of the day and week, what you do and how you do it depends largely on whom and how many you are with. It is therefore necessary to understand the units of outdoor pleasure in Blackpool:[1] 1,802 of these in Blackpool have been studied and, as a comparison, 3,261 groups in Worktown were also identified (Table 24).

In Blackpool, above all the couple predominates. Of the groups of three in Blackpool, three-quarters (183) included a child, whereas of the quartets, only a fifth (32) included any children. Of the 1,802 Blackpool groups, a total of 249 included children and of these 10 were of children unaccompanied by adults. Only 7 groups included more than 2 children. Of all people counted, only 9.5% per cent were children.

The main difference from afternoon to evening was a decrease of single women, pairs of women, and pairs of men, as compared with an increase of mixed pairs and single men. But at all times of the day, the predominating unit is the couple. For days we followed pairs about.

A DAY IN THE LIFE OF THE *DAILY EXPRESS*

At Blackpool, Worktowners step into a new rhythm of life. Hours of rising and spacing of meals are changed. More than this, the space between meals is no longer to be filled in as someone else dictates. Now the people have to

145

Table 24 Social groups

	Worktown	Blackpool
	%	%
Males only	45	21
Females only	29	29
Mixed	26	50
One person	43	27
Two people	43	48
Three people	9	14
Four people	4	9
More than four	1	2

work out their own routine. The better-offs are liable to see so much pleasure in Blackpool and take it for granted that chaps are able to have 'one round of pleasure'. In fact, the ordinary worker, if he drinks a bit, has an oyster or two, reasonably good lodgings, and his wife along, can hardly manage on less than £8. [This severely constricts his pleasure as we shall see] in the following account of the day of two married couples at Blackpool. So here are Mr and Mrs A, Mr and Mrs F, not quite 30. They are staying at a large boarding-house just beyond North Station. All four work 'in the mills'. It is 11 August 1937 (weather warm, dull). A report from an observer at their digs starts the day: 'They rise a little after eight o'clock, uncalled. . . . All four come downstairs together, 8:35, go straight into the front room. Mrs F then comes to kitchen to give landlady bacon and eggs to be cooked for breakfast. (They are not boarding).' Each time the group went out, they acted as if they had a definite purpose in mind. They took the quickest route to where they were going:

> The four people left the boarding-house at 9:48 and walked slowly up the street towards the promenade. Mr and Mrs F were about 5 feet 8 inches tall. He had a broad pleasant face with a snub nose. She had a red jovial face and dark hair. . . . Mr and Mrs A were about the same height but slimmer. He wore grey worsted flannels and a light sports jacket; she, a cream-coloured linen skirt and a pink woollen blouse. They went down a passage beside the Imperial Hydro and so out on to the promenade. Where possible the two couples walked together, each couple with arms linked. . . . Having reached the Gynn Square, they went up on the cliff walk. Mrs A put on a pair of sunglasses, although the sun was not shining very brilliantly. Mr A appeared to be imitating the movement of one looking at his wristwatch although he was not wearing one. He repeated this movement three times. When they reached the boating pool near the lift, they went without hesitation

146

down the slope to it. . . . They selected deckchairs in the front row overlooking the water. Their walk from their lodging house had taken them 29 minutes. . . .

Mr F opened a *Daily Express* across his legs and began to read. All four looked up at three yellow RAF planes as they passed over towards the North. Then they leaned forward and began to discuss them. Mrs A leaned back with her head resting against the back of the deckchairs. She had very restless feet which were always twitching and tapping. Mrs F passed the remainder of the newspaper to his wife and took out a packet of cigarettes. Slowly he selected one and lit it. This action took him about 35 seconds and observer, experimenting himself, found that it could be done in 18 seconds.

Mr A passed his part of the newspaper to his wife. Mrs A spread the newspaper on her knees and looked at the front page idly. Mr A strained his neck to look at it over her shoulder for a minute and then sat back. Mr F was now reading his part of the paper again. He finished his cigarette in about 10 minutes. The only conversation was a few remarks between Mr and Mrs F and Mrs F and Mrs A. Mr A hardly spoke at all. He picked up part of the newspaper discarded by Mrs A and was reading it again.

The sun came out more strongly and Mrs F leaned back several times resting her head on the back of her deck-chair. She never kept this position for more than a minute. For a few moments, she rested her head on the top of her hands and played with her hair. Mr A passed on the newspaper to Mrs A again. Mr and Mrs F gazed up at the Isle of Man plane which was passing over. . . . At 11:55 . . . all moved away. . . . The four straggled up the slope to the cliff walk in a ragged line about 15 feet apart. They paired off at the top and walked south. Both men lit cigarettes along the cliff walk.

They stopped near the Gynn to stare at some donkeys coming up from the sands. Later Mrs F lagged behind to watch a beach patrol calling in the bathers. The party returned by the same route that they had gone in the morning. Their wives had called in at the fish-and-chips shop to buy the food for dinner. After dinner they sit in the front room and talk for ten minutes. Then, upstairs.

At 1:30 they went to the south end:

All rush across the promenade to catch a tram-car. Mr and Mrs A get seats. Mrs F sits on Mr F's knee. Mrs A picks the skin off Mr A's nose. Conductor comes round, and Mr F says, 'Two to the beach.' Mrs A says, 'It's a thruppence each.' A long pause. Then: 'A lot of damned thieves. . . .'

All four get off tram at Victoria Pier, and all go on the pier, keeping to the right side, all four walking together, the two women kept looking in the shops. As soon as they get to the end of the pier, they all lean over the side and look at the water. Three of them sit in deckchairs and Mrs A walks to the kiosk and looks at postcards and magazines. . . . Then all . . . wait for pierrots to start. Both women go to sleep. The two men look around and watch people coming to the show. Mrs F sits up and says 'Oh I am tired', and goes to sleep again. Meanwhile both men fall asleep. Show starts and all sit up and observe. Mrs A keeps looking at Mr A and smiles at him. . . .

They leave before the pierrots have finished though near the end. Mr F seems reluctant to go, and lingers behind and looks at them. Then he runs up and catches them and all four walk off the pier. Eventually all get on a tram and sit on the top. Mr A says, 'To the Carlton.' All get up and off together. They walk in a block of four till they reach a small grocer's shop. Women enter. Mr F stops and looks at pictures with babies on them; then on to their digs.

Their afternoon has followed a similar trajectory to their morning. They have gone to one place, and come back the same way. They show no enterprise in finding a different way home. In each case, their return involves calling at a shop to bring in the food for their meals. That is a disadvantage entailing the old business of domestic worries which they have been trying to get away from. However, it's a matter of money. Our two couples have to cut down expenses at every turn.

When they come out of the house at 6:15, the first stop they make is at the booking office of a chara firm and look in passing at boards advertising trips. Then

they cross the road to the picture-house. They go straight to the box-office where Mr A takes four 1/-seats and pays for them. (The range of prices was 6d., 1/-, 1/6.) They sit in the same order as before. . . . The two women rise and go to the toffee stall at the back. . . . They return with a big bag of caramels. They take one each and hand the bag to the men. The film, 'The Isle of Fury', based on a Somerset Maugham story, begins.

In the film, there comes a fight with an octopus; Mrs F closes nearer to her husband; he passes his hand across his mouth. Mrs A sits still sucking her finger. A love-scene; Mrs F makes motions towards her husband; he scratches his ear.

After the interval, a Joe E. Brown film follows, 'A Natural Salesman'. A funny incident, the house shrieks. Mrs F first shakes a little; then remains still; then scratches her right cheek with her right hand. . . ; [then she] puts up her left hand and bites her fingers, then is still, then puts her left hand behind her neck and scratches.

The restlessness which all of the party manifested in the morning cannot be overcome easily after fifty-one weeks of automatic motion in obedience of a regimented routine.

> They stand during the 'King', walking out of the picture-house. They turn right to walk gradually towards the promenade, the two couples walking separately. . . . Mr and Mrs F look in a chemist's window with Kodak photographs. As they come on to the promenade, Mr and Mrs F meet another man and women, stop and talk to them for twelve minutes. Mr A looks impatient waiting for them. . . . Mrs A yawns. At last Mr and Mrs F come up trotting; all four move on southward down the prom. . . . Their pace slackens where the promenade becomes more crowded opposite the Central Station. They had a little conference, walk on to Manchester Square. They turn around there and walk back by the route they went to Clifford Road. As they approach the shops near their boarding-house, the two men go ahead for hot pies. They are all back at their lodgings by 10:15.

Basic in the day's routine chosen by these people is the amount of money they spent. These are the recorded items (excluding food for meals): 22*d*. cigarettes, 1*d*. newspaper, 6*d*. deckchairs, 1/-tramfares, 4*d*. ice-cream, 6*d*. on pier; 4/-cinema; 8*d*. caramels, and 2*d*. lavatory. The total sum is 11/3, the cost per head of 2/9.75. The best value for this expenditure in terms of time was the l*d*. spent on the *Daily Express* in the morning. Every one of them got something out of this in the course of 98 minutes sitting.

SEVEN HOURS, EIGHTEEN MINUTES

Of supreme importance is the problem of rest and restlessness as industry tends to be speeded up and keeping fit increasingly emphasised. 120 correspondents, in a total of 220, asserted that holidays for them were synonymous with rest.

[As we noticed in the chapter on 'Work',] based on a study by Colgate University, working-class people in Worktown get almost an hour less sleep than needed (at seven hours, eighteen minutes) while the middle class get half an hour more than needed. Most workers have risen soon after seven, and the housewife who gets up first to make the fire and breakfast has been up a quarter of an hour before. Even on Saturday nights, they only average eight hours sleep.

This is altered at Blackpool to the advantage of labouring Worktowners. Holiday-makers in all our observed places averaged nine hours sleep, and varied little from that average. Only in Blackpool can the housewife get away from the routine of rising before seven to prepare for a worker's new

149

day. The common rule in boarding houses, door locked at eleven, further encourages thorough sleep. According to the inside observer, when our two couples arrived back indoors, 'They went to bed at 10:45, half an hour earlier than the women would have done at home and an hour earlier than the men. They rose just after eight o'clock.'

But once downstairs in the morning, is the beneficial rest equally realised? The activities of the group followed show that they try to realise it, seeking nothing strenuous, making their way to deck-chair sites and pierrot-shows. But once they are seated, restlessness intervenes. They wriggle or they scratch. The look at watches they do not possess. The fact that very few do succeed in getting continuous rest suggests some internal factors. The biggest thing in the holiday week is that for one week you rest as much as you *like* but also only as much as you *can*. If you are out early, you can get a deckchair until the tide comes in, and then, perhaps with some waiting about, find a place on a bench on the promenade. But there aren't too many places for resters, for they aren't buyers of Blackpool's commodities.

Of all the groups followed in Blackpool, our two couples contrive to stay longest sitting down in one place. By contrast with their 98 minute stay in the deckchairs, the following showed a quite different rhythm of rest and move-ment: 4 other groups (3 of which were workers) were followed on a fairly windy day in early September 1937. The first group (3 men and 3 women) rested 6 minutes in an hour stroll. The second (2 men, 2 women, 2 kids) rested only 2 minutes in a 145 minute wandering around the amusement parks. The third (consisting of 2 men, 3 women, and 3 kids) rested 8 minutes in 2 hours strolling around shops and the piers. The fourth group alone was middle class, an elderly couple. They rested 33 minutes in 82 minutes in a walk along the cliffs. In a total of 407 minutes spent by these 4 groups, 43 minutes were for resting, 22 minutes in amusements, and 20 on trams. Notice the typical effect of children on group restlessness, a fact recognised by many parents who are torn between wanting to give their children a holiday and to have a holiday away from their children. Note also the predominance of time walking. The average distance walked was 2.5 miles per hour. (The As and Fs did about 9 miles of walking in their day.)

Blackpool sanctions walking and especially watching. The third group spent 47 minutes, more than a third of the time they were under observation, watching the dancing. They never participated. When people behave chiefly as spectators at amusement places like the Pleasure Beach, it can often be attributed to their want of money:

> I took the kiddies on the Pleasure Beach but I was a bit disappointed there as to have a ride it would have cost me 6*d*. and 3*d*. each; and to have had two or three rides for all of us, well it would cost me a little too much; but anyway we enjoyed ourselves all the same watching other people spending their money.

But once you are on the Central Pier it costs nothing to dance – dancing is what many people go on the Central Pier go for – so that when they watch here, it is by choice. When they watch the Stratosphere Girl for 15 minutes, they do so without spending a penny. Watching and walking are dominant Blackpool activities, occupy a big portion of everybody's day, and it is the massing of thousands all doing these same things that makes the amorphous mob.

But much of what they do is what they would do at home. Two young men followed for 85 minutes did nothing except walk and talk until they reached a motorcycle shop in Lytham Road.

> They continue looking at the same cycle five minutes. I go up and say, 'That's a fine job.' Yes, answers one. They develop a highly technical conversation on camshafts, capacities, . . . and discussing price.

They could do this just as well back in Bury. It is difficult for people to set up a new routine for themselves. The new routine they do assume is that imposed on them from an outside source, from the landlady with her times of closing the door, of morning meals, of meals during the day.

Relevant to the question of the modification of Worktown routine is that of dress (Table 25). The boot almost disappears, the clog entirely does. In Worktown the clog is still used, although the percentage of its wearers has decreased in the past few years (5 per cent in one sample of men, with black shoes and boots comprising 71 per cent and brown 24 per cent). It is used by working people during working hours. Holidays see it laid aside.

Few people take the opportunity to go barefoot or wear sandals even on the beach where samples were also taken. What does increase as expected is the number of girls who go out with bare legs (29 per cent compared to 2 per cent in Worktown in samples of 100 and 145 women). In a survey of 373 males in Blackpool, 48 per cent wore hats (46 per cent of which were caps, 45 per cent trilbies, and only 8 per cent bowlers) whereas, of 308 women counted, 77 per cent wore hats. Still men were more formal. At Blackpool a

Table 25 Footwear at Blackpool

	Black	Brown	White	Other	Sandals	Bare	Boots	Total No.
	%	%	%	%	%	%	%	
Males								
Over 35	53	27	7	—	—	—	13	15
Under 35	51	29	17	3	—	—	—	39
Females								
Over 35	28	36	36	—	—	—	—	11
Under 35	28	22	30	14	6	—	—	36
Children	21	50	21	—	—	8	—	14
Total	37	32	22	7	0.8	0.8	0.4	115

count of 100 young men on the promenade in the middle of a fine afternoon found 82 wearing collar and tie but only eighteen with open necks.

One major aspect of the day's walking is that you are bound to come across some old Worktown pals sooner or later. You do not try to avoid the old faces. You look out for them. Indeed this phenomenon of hundreds of thousands of people wandering about all day can be likened to a search for familiar patterns in this unfamiliar life of one week. In fact, extremely few people make new friends in Blackpool. In the Holiday Dream letters, the category of companionship came low. The age group that does make new contacts is the unmarried under-25 year old group. A party of girls, for example, made a pick-up with a different party of boys on five out of the seven days of the week. But apart from this, there are practically no records of people previously unknown to one another meeting and banding to form a new group in a day routine.

The competitive spirit is operating somewhere here. One correspondent gave it as his opinion that people going away are always anxious to display themselves to their less fortunate neighbours who are not. A similar sort of thing is present here. People are on the look out for one another to prove to one another that they have come too; then their neighbours cannot claim superiority.

[But holiday-makers want to do more than walk and watch.] Listen to this unmarried female from Worktown:

> I want to go to Blackpool. Many hundreds of holiday-makers flock to this popular resort but here there is always a spirit of cheerfulness and gaiety. My mornings would be spent on the pier dancing and watching seaside pierrots. In the afternoon, I would discover new places and visit old haunts such as the popular Stanley Park and the Pleasure Beach. In the evening I would stroll along the prom, and later prepare myself to go dancing in the Tower Ballroom. This is the holiday I am wanting.

The wish fulfilment though, depends on money. The less of that, the more the walking about and looking at others fulfilling your wish – and reading the *Daily Express*.

NOTES

1 The first thing we checked in Blackpool was the prevailing unit in which the crowd moved. The method used to check groups was as follows: observers working in different parts of the town, on the promenade, in the park, in front of the Tower, on the edge of the tide on Central Beach, under the pier sheltering from a fall of rain, by Madame Tussaud's, in a Community Singing Booth, on the far South Promenade in the private hotel area, recorded, at given times morning, afternoon, and night, the groups that passed them.

14

CHILDREN

By examining the Worktown child in Blackpool, perhaps we may get a clearer understanding of the holiday's meaning and some of its deeper stresses and conflicts. In Worktown the child lives largely in a free industrial culture, in many ways approximating in its interests to those of the adults during their Blackpool holiday week. And many Worktown adults explicitly wish to grow younger for their holiday week, a feeling most conspicuously symbolised in the Rejuvenator, and clearly expressed by this married workman:

> This is how I want to spend my holidays: forget all about my work and other things that I am responsible for, take my wife and child to the seaside, play with the youngster in the sand, and be a kiddie myself once again just for the holidays.

SANDS, THE MAGIC CARPET

Blackpool publicity associates the sand with children:

> Picture a golden carpet of seven miles long . . . of gleaming golden grains of clean, firm sand. Look upon it as a nursery carpet of Brobdingnagian dimensions, for here is the Paradise of Kiddies, their El Dorado of every happiness. Budding architects cheerfully construct fantastical castles and blissfully knock them down again. Childish demands are fully satisfied by thrilling donkey rides, Punch and Judy with Dog Toby, and ventriloquists bringing forth shrieks of laughter from the tiny little souls who are in their seventh heaven of delight. And who cares if their skirts or trousers are just a little splashed when they paddle; who cares what they do for they are healthy and happy? And not only do the kiddies enjoy themselves, but the grown-ups return to their second childhood and romp and play completely irresponsible of everyday worries at home.
>
> (*Blackpool Holiday Journal*, 1937)

Table 26 What they like about Blackpool

Sea and beach	27
Pleasure Beach	19
Amusements and shows	12
Piers	5
Ice-cream, rock, etc.	4
Tower	3
Toys and games	3
Punch and Judy	2
Animals and fish	2
Park	1
Baths	1
Cinema	1

[But what is the child's experience and expectations? As we saw in 'The Order of Time',] in Worktown the popular games and nearly all the popular child activities are communal; they are conditioned by an exact social rhythm and cycle of the year, set by school and bedtimes and the weekend. In Blackpool the street gang and the local convention compulsorily collapse. So how does the seaside routine compare with the holiday-at-home routine? What do the children themselves think about Blackpool? 48 kids in 4 Worktown elementary schools told us what they liked (Table 26).

The things at the top of the list are just those things which are most peculiar to the holiday environment. And the cinema, which looms very large in Worktown, practically fades out in the Blackpool scene.

[FATHERS AND MOTHERS AT BLACKPOOL]

Two adults give their holiday wish. First, a mother:

> I am hoping to go to the north of Blackpool, all being well, just to leave the washing of dishes and clothes and baking and all the little jobs that make each day full, just to be able to sit and knit or read, and watch my kiddies play in the sands and gaze right out to where the sea and sky seem to meet each other will make my holiday just O.K.

And a father:

> Being a married man with wife and family I should . . . go to some place of interest miles from our present abode, the kiddies first ride in a train, then there's the 'sands', aye, even the father can show them his knowledge of pie-making he learned in his childhood days.

At Blackpool alone is the family the child's constant social unit. An observer studied 543 groups of children on the beach for two days in

154

Table 27 Children on the beach

Size of child group	No. seen	Percentage of total
Units	407	75
Couple	108	20
Groups of three	24	4
Groups of four	4	1
Total	543	

September [1937]. 86 per cent of these were accompanied by a parent or guardian, and 57 per cent of them were 'units' separate from other children – either entirely alone or accompanied only by adults. Groups with more than two children are rare (Table 27). Observation of two Worktown parks on holiday showed that 27 per cent of play groups were of four children or over, as compared with 1 per cent in Blackpool. The average number of children in these groups was only 1.31 in Blackpool compared to 3.32 in Worktown.

The continuous parental contact on holiday, the absence of their usual companions, and the games they play are major factors in the child's Blackpool visit. They offer an escape from the routine of errands, backstreet, and Sunday School. Table 28 shows what children did while playing on the sands.

Play is not generally organised. Castles are popular, nearly always moated, conical, and often with a post or flag on the top; in over half the cases, there is a cave at one side, and this is frequently extended, the child trying to pierce right through the castle without causing the structure to collapse. The average size of the groups playing games is 1.46, and of the children building sandcastles, 45 per cent are alone, 40 per cent are in pairs, and the remaining groups consist of three children.

Table 28 Children playing on the sands

Game played	Unit M.	F.	Couple M.	F.	Mixed	Group M.	F.	Mixed	Total* Children
Sandcastles	14	13	2	4	6	—	2	1	60
Tossing balls	—	1	—	2	—	—	—	—	5
Sand drawing	5	2	—	1	—	—	—	1	13
Paddling	4	—	—	—	—	—	—	1	8
Bathing	—	—	—	1	—	—	—	1	5
Football	2	2	1	—	—	—	—	—	6
Running with windmill	—	1	—	—	—	—	—	—	1
Total	25	19	3	8	6	—	2	4	98

* Totals in this column include individuals in the group column.

155

The creative interests of the children are satisfied in sand, but often the parents intervene, especially the father:

> In all the sandcastles observed, thirteen were being built with the assistance of the father, one with the assistance of the mother. . . . There were five where the father himself was building the castle and the child or children digging aimlessly around or making 'pies' or subsidiary 'castles' of their own.

The next day, there were 41 fathers helping children build sandcastles compared to 31 who left their children alone and 6 mothers helped compared to 66 who did not.

The beach, where whole families settle for hours at a time, allows the family, as a play group, to develop in directions which are not possible in Worktown. Back home, fathers do not play with their children in the backstreet and very seldom in the park. A half-hour study of children's expressions on the beach opposite the Tower indicates the child's reaction to parental interest (Table 29):

Table 29 Children's behaviour

Child's expression	Male		Female		Total	
	Acc.	Unacc.*	Acc.	Unacc.	Acc.	Unacc.
Undefined	47	17	54	17	111	34
Laughing	3	13	1	8	4	21
Jumping and dancing	1	13	2	13	3	16
Shouting	2	7	—	7	2	14
Crying	4	1	10	2	14	3
Talking	4	4	8	—	12	4
Singing	—	4	1	2	1	6
Quarrelling	—	—	8	—	8	—
Quarrelling with parents	3	—	5	—	8	—
Smiling	3	—	2	—	5	—

* Acc. = accompanied; Unacc. = unaccompanied.

General observation confirms that high spirits, laughing, dancing, singing, and shouting are most evident in unaccompanied children, while accompanied children talk more and tend to be more quarrelsome. 71 cases of children changing their clothes are suggestive of paternal involvement:

Undressing   17 mothers undressing children.
                    10 fathers undressing children.
                    0 both fathers and mothers.
                    0 children undressing themselves.
Dressing   19 mothers dressing children.
                    22 fathers dressing children.
                    2 fathers and mothers both dressing children.
                    1 child dressing himself.

Figures were only taken where both parents were present. A snap count (5 September) of children accompanied by only one parent on the sands showed 34 with father alone and 19 with mother alone. Unquestionably, father has a special function of guide and friend to the holiday child, while mother – who has this job all the weekdays for the rest of the year – takes a comparative rest, and leaves games almost entirely to father.

[The general acceptance of this holiday code is revealed in the following report of a case when fathers neglected their temporary roles as child tenders:]

> Group of three women, four children followed from Central Pier to New Inn. Conversation centred around the lack of interest that fathers show in children; one woman points out that interest finishes when he gets out of bed. Continual calling to children to come here. Children will persist in running down to sand from prom across road near New Inn. [The mothers] stop outside and give warnings of trouble to come to children if they dare to move away whilst mothers go inside and 'find their fathers'. Fathers found in vault and [they were] told they seem to be enjoying themselves 'whilst we are lugging the kids about'. Fathers forced out of vault to a more 'respectable' room. When seated in room, Guinness and beer ordered.
> Conversation: difficult time the mothers had with kids, fathers cursed for selfish attitude, 'boozing while we are struggling'. [The women were] so worked up they drink deep and one finishes Guinness before men finish beer. . . . At different intervals, one of the fathers leave to see that the kids are alright.

THE FAMILY HOLIDAY

The child feels the changed life of the holiday week at least as much as the parent, and the amount of childish bad temper, crying, biting, and smacking is noticeably greater in Blackpool than in Worktown. A Worktowner, a father himself and a highly intelligent sometime-observer, put the position clearly:

> When I was younger, I found the holidays with the family more enjoyable. There may of course be physical reasons for this. And young children are better company than grown-up children. I have had cricket holidays, climbing holidays, and tramping holidays as well as the more conventional holidays with the family. The most disagreeable holidays, however, were undoubtedly those I spent as a child with my parents. Horrible!!! And now I am wondering if my children have suffered as I did.

157

And a mother writes about her holiday dream:

> After tea, another hour on the sands, and then, if you have a kindly
> landlady to keep an eye on the children while they are asleep, to go off
> on your own to see the shows we know so well, thanks to the wireless.

It is in no sense a reflection on Blackpool to point out that there is much bad
temper between child and parent. To the mothers especially, as we have seen
in earlier chapters, the holiday is anticipated as relief from the continuous
routine, from the rigours of domestic and family obligation, whereas to the
father it is more commonly a simpler release from industrial work. Children
add to the expense, add to the worry, are unwelcome in many boarding
houses, and are in constant danger of becoming lost.

Blackpool has one creche, on the Pleasure Beach, where children can be
temporarily left by parents. There are several boating lakes, 'Take a Trip on
the Silver Swan, Fare 3d.', but none reserved for children and only one
special kid's roundabout. The publicised Kiddies' Corner of the Tower Zoo is
a small section with no special distinctions, but an emphasis on monkeys.
From the Worktowner's point of view, the real importance of the holiday
child in Blackpool is the additional routine imposed and the additional
expense. Of 12,408 tickets sold from Worktown to Blackpool (4–7
September 1937), only 982 were for children. Yet the census returns for
Worktown in 1931 show that 23 per cent of the population are under 14 years
of age. The larger the family of working-class people, the less money it has
for holidays. And the less money there is for a holiday, the more the family
tends to go to Blackpool. Well over 50 per cent of the children do not get
away for a full holiday. Larger families who may be argued to need holidays
most are the least likely to enjoy its benefits. Because of the place of the
holiday in the mental trajectory of the year, adults may associate the large
family with a little holiday and the little family with a large holiday.

15

THE MOB

[The Mass-Observers not only focused on the isolated individual social unit and the daily routine, but recorded the more amorphous movements of the crowd and its 'release from the constraints of time'. They begin with some of the varieties of crowd behaviour.]

In an arena formed by a crowd of perhaps 2,000, we see a comic act:

Three red-coated guardsmen, one with another attached as a horse, blow squibs at a policeman in uniform. Policeman has a cannon firing squibs . . . Then appears a fusillade from the rear end of the horse. Eventually chaos. . . .

Policeman now comes among the crowd. Red rose, white feathers on hat, etc. greeted everywhere with fun and laughter.

Woman: 'Eh, you've lost yer suspender.'

Policeman, two finger gesture, and simpers: 'Yer can't do that there here.'

The policeman is the good fairy of the crowd. And everything in Blackpool is dominated by the dense crowds with the innumerable incidents which go to make up this vast pleasure as much as any sideshow or postcard. Little whirlpools appear everywhere:

Four men and three women singing, 'Underneath the Arches'. Sham fight between them, after a mock blow one leaning head on the other. All laugh, sway.

Other incidents are bad natured:

Egerton St. A front bedroom window suddenly thrown up by a man – tall, dark hair and moustache – who leaned out, waving his fists and shouting, 'I hate him, I hate them, dirty beggars what's what they are, seven thousand of them, I hate them, I hate them.' He slammed down the window, snapped the catch violently.

In this mass go the rough accordion players and gangs of lads with mouth organs. And stumping his way through the 700,000 said to be in town one

159

summer week, goes a lad of about 22 with one wooden-leg with a good-legged comrade:

> They go north along the densely crowded inland side of the Prom and both are staggeringly drunk. They fall down twice in a hundred yards, the second time crash into a weighing machine. The wooden-legged man reels about and clearly has great effort getting about on one leg. . . . When he falls, his pal grins and helps him up. No one else helps him. Many stop and look. Three chaps, walking behind wait, when he falls down, [and] play on a mouth-organ, 'When the Poppies Bloom Again', which pal croons softly. . . . Then they go on towards Talbot Square turning off the promenade there and heading inland. They have six falls in the twenty minutes that this journey takes them. Near the end, one man, aged 30, and working class, helps by supporting one leg on the other side. No one else. There is plenty of comment:
> Man: 'His crutch slipped.'
> Woman: 'Not with one leg like that – uh.'
> Man in bowler stops observer to say: 'It's a shame you know to let a one-legged man to get drunk like that. It's a shame. They ought to have more sense.'
> Woman: 'Serves him right, too.'

Finally we observe an isolated action by the police:

> I was attracted by a crowd in front of oyster stall. Found policeman holding a man's right arm twisted up behind man's back. Man of seedy Horatio Bottomly type, squat, sturdy, and elderly with red, square, unabashed face, a workman in dress and appearance. He made no attempt to escape but faced and harangued crowd. Policeman seemed a little uncomfortable and kept looking over heads of crowd as if for assistance. Man repeated several times, 'There's no praise in twisting a man's arm when. . . .' and then but only once, 'I'm an old soldier. I fought in the Boer War and in the last one, too,' and 'A bird can't fly with a broken wing.' He spoke loudly and appeared a little drunk. A man said, 'The policeman gave him every chance to get away, but he wouldn't.'

PEOPLE

At no time between nine in the morning and eleven at night from the end of June to October are the streets anything but packed. And the crowd follows the tide of the sea (and of landladies). Even at Easter weekend (1938), before the season really begins, 70,421 vehicles came into town, including 10,000 bikes and 5,000 charas. In an August weekend, there were 700 crowded trains. In the year, 7,000,000 people come here. No other place in England can show a comparable scene. And Blackpool uses its crush photos for publicity. The appeal of people to come and do it – because millions of others already do it – was perhaps first exploited in a big way in this country by Blackpool.

The crowd has an automatic tendency towards release from the constraints of time. This is worthy of immediate study by all competent revolutionaries, but little has been done beyond the rubbish written by theorists like Le Bon – whose book is widely accepted as a standard. It is better to theorise no more till much field work has been done. Instead, take a Worktown millworker describing a day of his holidays:

'Blackpool – City of Laughter and Tears':
I stood on the promenade near the Central Pier and surveyed the scene around me. As far as the eye could see, north to south, was an animated mass of bustling, laughing colour. Young folks, old folks, all out for anything – and the sky's the limit. I reviewed for a few minutes my own position. Here I was at the end of fifty-two weeks of hard pinch and scrape – of answering alarm clocks and not answering bosses. And now I was my own boss with . . .

In many minds this feeling is most clearly expressed in the special Blackpool headgear, extensively worn by young folk of both sexes. In 1937, it was a light cap with alternating blocks of red and white or blue and white, with tassel and peak on which was a written slogan, like:
COME UP AND SEE ME SOME TIME
and
UP THE OLD NARKOVIANS.
Narkover is the 'college for crooks' made famous by film and stage comedian, Will Hay, a Lancastrian, born and bred near Worktown. Hay started the Old Narkovians, which now has 300,000 members; it is the same sort of social group as the earlier A.O.F.B. (the Frothblowers) and W.L.O.G. (Gugnuncs). The Western Brothers have also recently started Cads College with similar immoral and anti-snob satire. The Littlewood's Loyalist Circle and the Mustard Club tighten the link in a vast expanding 'public' between customer and producer of a 'luxury commodity'. If anything, they demand merely a small initial subscription (most of it going to charity). All share amusing rules, badges, or word formulas.

When Hay came to Blackpool's Palace Varieties, the Old Narkovians turned out in force, organised by local 'Junior Master', Reginald Titchener. High spot was the presentation of a four foot red piece of Blackpool rock, with the words UP NARKOVER worked through it. This was immediately taken off to Victoria Hospital. The finale of the show was the Anthem:

We are the boys for fun and noise
Hark at the way we take our joys
Up the Old Narkovians!

Late in the season of 1937, long 'chains' of young men held up traffic at Belisha crossings, went right through Noah's Ark in formation, and silted up the entrance to Pleasure Arcades. This crowd phenomenon, not noted by resident observers before 1937, was attributed by a waitress to a scene in Will Hay's film, shown during the summer. Sometimes these groups were of mixed sexes (with women, for example, riding on men's shoulders), always below the age of 25, and numbering 8 to 22. Others would join who clearly did not know any of those participating:

A 'Crocodile' of 21 youths, each with right hand on shoulder of [the person] preceding. Wheeling round and round prom. Those in rear were singing. Leader shouts, 'Right wheel'. Someone passing by says: 'Let's join in, boy.'

In general, however, groups keep their identities, especially groups of people over about 25 years old. We have recorded many temporary whirlpools of people. In thirty seconds, a crowd will gather and gaze at a man shying at beacons, a little boy lost, splashing waves, a tame pigeon, or a man rolling up his sleeves. But they are temporary. Only the Social Mixer, inside the Fun House, hurls and swirls strangers together. In fact, there is some need to stimulate clowning. Several middle-class observers were surprised by how little laughter there was in Blackpool crowds. One kept a 15 second strip of pavement [i.e. the distance it took passers-by 15 seconds to traverse] in the main amusement zone under observation for a quarter of an hour without recording a laugh. The couples whom we followed all day hardly laughed except in the cinema. They were too engrossed in pennies, resting, reading, gazing, and gaping.

[DRINK]

[The common lubricant of the crowd, of course, is drink. Whirlpools appear in the pubs and along the promenade after they close.]

Off to the seaside, not taking a care and little to wear. Eat, drink, and be merry.
How I want to spend my holidays. Mix fresh air and rest with an occasional 'Draught Bass'.

Thus write Worktowners thinking of holidays. Still current in Worktown is the out-of-date story that chaps arriving in Blackpool do a ritual tour of pubs from the station onwards. Like so many stories, this one proves to represent the pub-goer's image of Blackpool rather than his actual behaviour.

Probably more drink is drunk in Blackpool than any other town of comparable size in the country, but it is drunk on a more random principle. In the last ten years the number of pubs has doubled. The earliest known pub is the 'Eagle's Nest' and most famous is 'Uncle Tom's Cabin' and 'Foxhall'. Foxhall is the alleged site of the original 'Blacke Pulle'; Uncle Tom's Cabin was the original centre of the gypsies who, about 1820, settled on the northern cliffs and developed Blackpool's fortune-telling industry. Uncle Tom's was on the cliff top, now eroded by the sea; the new version keeps the name-value of the old, and a visit to that particular pub is part of the thorough Blackpool holiday. It is also the only Magees Marshall Brewery pub in Blackpool and sells draught Bass.

Magees is a popular Worktown beer. The Worktowner likes, if possible, to drink the same beer on holiday, just as he likes to read the *Worktown Evening News*. Still he welcomes different pubs. In Blackpool he stays in a house larger than he enters at home, with a bath, a waitress, and an upstairs lavatory. In the pub, comforts are similarly extended and expected to be so. In Worktown, the pub is divided into the austere Taproom with places for standing or sitting on simple wooden seats, and the more comfortable 'Vault' (see *The Pub and the People*). In Blackpool, the 'Vault' is usually replaced with a 'Gentlemen's Room' approached through the hall (unknown in Worktown). The upholstery, soft seats, vividly coloured plastered walls with ship or wave effects, distinguish Blackpool from Worktown pubs. What struck observers, who had been studying Worktown pubs for a year, was that Blackpool pubs had people in them at all hours and that more drinking was done before 12:30 than from 12:45 to 2:30. This early-hour drinking is a complete reversal of the Worktown habit. But old routines died hard. As in Worktown, the heavy drinking is done in the evening.

During 1937, there were 196 convictions for drunkenness, 85 'with aggravations'; this is more than in Worktown, but slight in relation to the drinking population. In fact, these figures hardly reflect the reality of breezy Blackpool at closing time. On a typical Saturday night during the season, observers attempted to count the numbers of drunks on the promenade at 11:00 p.m. It proved impracticable; but their estimates of persons undoubtedly 'under the influence' varied from 25 per cent to 35 per cent. It is commonplace to see persons fall into the gutter or vomit on the road.

Nothing could be more in keeping with the pent-up life of the Worktown fifty-one weeks. In Worktown, if you are a respectable citizen, you dare not get blind-drunk. The consequences to job and prestige are too great. In Blackpool, you dare and do. We have seen chaps staggering tight in Blackpool who are known to us in Worktown as sober church leaders and local politicians. Here, through drink, the great crowds are fused more than ever into one common mass of work-free humanity. Inside the pub things get lively as the hours accumulate. Take this one, with a straight public bar and a lounge with ten round tables, stools, leather-seated benches, no spittoons, bare mantel:

1:50 p.m. Young man produces large accordion. Barman, very quick, 'Now put that away.' Cries of 'shut your eyes', but the barman says menacingly 'Nah, ah've told thee!' and turns away.

[But note what happens later:] 9:25 p.m. Approximately twenty-five men, fifteen women. At one side of the room are two girls in black coats and skirts, white silk blouses; they are singing loudly a dirty song; being encouraged by groups of men at table in middle. Song is about old King Cole; the following are extracts from the chorus:

> Have it on the block, said the Butcher
> Put it in and out, said the Tailor
> Slap it up and down, said the painter
> Bounce your balls up and down said the –
> something about a fiddler

This seems to be going on indefinitely. A rival female group at the other end of the room starts singing a jazz song, which eventually . . . drowns the dirty girls. They, however, start bawling, 'The music goes around and around', and they score a complete victory as everybody in the room takes it up.

A Salvation Army girl comes in selling the *War Cry*, which two men buy; one looks at it and puts it down; one doesn't look at it, puts it in his pocket. No cracks made to girl.

Man at a middle table keeps shouting, 'order please, order please', for no apparent reason whatever. No one takes any notice. Now independent singing develops; various groups starting up songs, sometimes one group's song is taken up by another group, sometimes several songs are going at once.

In the middle of this uproar are two very old ladies, sitting next to the dirty girls, wearing fur coats and hair-nets; they are impassive, say and do nothing. As far as observer can see, they have nothing to drink. . . . One of the [dirty] girls gets up, goes over to group of men at the table who have been signalling to them for some time. She sits in the middle of them and sings 'Down at the Old Bull and Bush'. . . . People are coming in and going out all the time; there is a constant stream of women up to the lavatory. The dirty girl comes back to her table, but this time sits next to observer. Two men at the same time contact them and buy them drinks.

The two old ladies suddenly start uproariously cackling. The two men, who have contacted the two dirty girls, are an engine-driver and his mate. His mate is small, round-faced; the whole time he is trying to sing in a thin, tenor voice a sad Irish song of which no one takes any notice, except the girl next to him, who turns and laughs at him now and again. Later Irish songs develop generally.

The girl who sat next to observer asks if he is Hannen Swaffer. Observer is deeply pained. She explains that it is because he is writing things down. He says he is a journalist from the *News Chronicle*, and everyone is pleased about this. Girls say they don't like Hannen Swaffer but they read the *Herald* because they belong to the Labour Party. They are from Worktown. They come over to here most Saturdays on a 2/-excursion. They are very Worktown conscious. One makes a diatribe against people who talk about Worktown wakes. Says it makes her flesh creep 'like this' – and caresses observer's back, and makes his flesh creep a bit too.

At 10:00 p.m. the singing has died down for a while. Loud remark is heard suddenly: 'Mae West is the best footballer in England.' A young man stands up, and makes a jiggling movement, and sings 'I Know All the Tricks that a Cowboy Does'. Girl next to observer is now muzzling at him, with her head, and crossing her leg over his thigh. She talks about football – very technically; and observer has to confirm her opinion about chaps he has never heard of. She goes for the Worktown all-in wrestling, and says she knows it's all a put-up job, but she likes it.

Opposite girl (Alice) produces suddenly from her handbag a large photograph of Mannequin pisse. The old lady leans forward excitedly, and says, 'It's in Brussels. I've been there often.' The engine-driver counters by producing a pen drawing on a piece of paper, entitled, 'Necessity is the Mother of Invention', showing a naked man with drooping penis on which is tied a balloon. He is regarding a naked woman in bed who remarks, 'It's a shame to take the money.'

Girl next to observer asks if he is broadminded. He says, quite truly, that he is, and then [she] proceeds to tell a number of really filthy stories, very fast one after the other, occasionally interrupted by the old lady, who joins in with a good one or two. There are no taboo words whatever.

At 10:30 everyone began to go. There was a big exodus to the lavatories. The engine-driver and his mate lurched off upstairs, and Alice said she wished we could get rid of them. So observer suggested that could be done by walking out of the pub. This was done.

Each girl took observer's arm, and walked along with him, steering him. When they got outside, they were suddenly less boisterous, dragging observer between them. They reached the door of a fish-and-chip shop, where the girl, who had been trying to neck with the observer, began to flirt with the doorman, whom she seemed to know very well. . . .

Both girls order a tenpenny fish, chips, bread and butter, and tea. They are friendly with the waiter. They tell observer that they come here regularly. It is the best cafe in Blackpool. Observer asks them why they like Blackpool; they both say it is because 'it's free, you can do what you like, and everybody is friendly'. . . .

This conversation is suddenly interrupted by the advent of the engine-driver and his mate, who laughingly accuse observer of trying to double-cross them. But they are very friendly; and both girls order another tenpenny for them to pay for. . . . During this Alice is stroking observer's thigh and alternately squeezing his hand very hard, while the other one, at the opposite end of the table, is playing footy-footy. Alice . . . then starts telling dirty stories again. At 11:30 we all leave, arms linked, engine-driver trying to massage Alice's breasts as he walks along.

A typical street scene after pubs have closed is shown by the following:

In narrow backstreets, bottle party is taking place on doorsteps, complete with glasses and Magees Crown Ale. Up alleyway at back, four youths piss. Large number carrying rock and beer. Some take it towards station; some start drinking it as they go along. . . . Chaps fall over and their friends pick them up cheerfully. . . . A fight starts among four young men; the crowd simply opens up to give them elbow room as it flows by; one is knocked out cold and others carry him to back of stall and dump him there. No one seems to take any notice.

But plenty of holiday-makers are not in this spirit, and some are actively hostile:

1 Woman speaks to observer as crowd of drunken young men passes. Says, 'it's a sin for these young men what they do these days, it is.'
2 Elderly woman to man, 'It's disgraceful, these young girls drunk.'

The criticism is nearly always that it is wrong for young folk to be blotto. From time to time the chairman of the Magistrate's Court voices that view, as he did in August to three visiting lads: 'I advise you to leave drink alone, and when you come here to behave yourselves in a reasonable manner.'

But if that advice was enforced by law, Blackpool would lose a great many customers. For a part of release, of industrial leisure for non-religious people, is alcoholic drink. Beer has grown to be linked to the whole idea of seasonal climax; the modern calendar includes not only Easter, Christmas, and New Year, but the week-end. Beer is the catalytic agent in any prolonged opportunity for leisure, and in Blackpool you know that nobody cares how you walk.

Moreover, in Blackpool Saturday continues to be just as much the climax as in the Worktown working week, although there are no longer economic or physical reasons why the holiday-maker should not drink to the maximum on any other night of his week. This crescendo towards Saturday is a part of each Worktowner's life and behaviour; and this is one manifestation of the inability, visible all through this book, to get that change from established habit which Worktowners say they want.

Table 30 Conversation in Blackpool

Topic	Males	Females	Mixed	Men in uniform	Mono- logues	Unspe- cified	Incl. children	Total
Place	291	180	372	55	5	92	113	1108
Question	198	190	311	53	2	57	125	936
Time	259	129	350	52	3	75	59	927
Pleasures	202	125	381	47	5	49	85	894
Imperative	102	92	179	36	1	41	157	608
Exclamation	117	145	100	9	8	26	56	461
Money	138	67	88	30	1	44	27	395
Big shot	82	66	60	22	2	97	11	340
Affirmative	91	68	93	31	0	32	24	339
Negative	89	68	95	23	1	20	43	339
Man friend	63	81	111	5	1	39	28	328
Swear	141	14	121	26	1	5	5	323
Food	59	42	115	30	1	19	18	284
Woman friend	51	62	81	5	1	38	31	269
Rapture	45	59	91	11	1	20	26	253
Health	52	46	63	19	0	29	13	222
Weather	63	36	71	10	1	7	6	194
Clothes	21	60	62	4	1	21	20	189
Laugh	28	24	78	7	2	14	24	177
Transport	45	32	52	7	0	19	18	173
Enemy	39	28	43	32	0	11	17	170
Drink	62	9	62	12	1	12	56	214
Job	51	23	50	12	0	9	6	151
News	35	12	35	13	0	24	12	131
Amusements	55	70	129	15	3	12	56	340
Sex	27	28	57	8	0	2	0	122
Sport	42	6	37	0	1	13	15	114
Home	29	22	27	5	1	4	4	92
Religion	53	12	10	0	0	14	3	92
Goodbye	20	8	45	7	2	5	2	89
Sea	13	12	32	1	0	3	12	73
Children	12	8	28	8	0	6	11	73
Lodgings	20	23	29	0	0	5	4	81
Song	24	10	29	0	4	4	8	79
Dancing	13	19	42	1	0	3	0	78
Stranger	17	9	23	12	1	5	6	73
Greeting	18	8	19	5	0	4	10	64
Crowds	8	6	23	10	0	11	2	60
Holidays	15	18	12	3	0	1	4	53
Others	6	10	10	0	0	3	11	40
Sands	1	7	12	0	0	0	20	40
Whistle	8	0	3	1	2	0	2	16
Photos	2	6	3	0	0	1	1	13
Cough	0	1	2	0	0	0	3	6
Sniff	0	1	0	0	2	0	0	3
Total	2707	1942	3636	627	54	907	1154	10809

WORDS

Binding all the thousands together are the common coinage of movement, sea, air, money, and above all words. Table 30 shows the things that holiday-makers speak of during Blackpool summer.

It would need a book to examine all these conversations. Here we shall take them simply as crude indications. Most conspicuous is the number of exclamations, affirmatives, negatives, questions, and imperatives, pointing to short statements; the trend is stronger with women than with men; and question and imperative are high in children groups. On the whole the correspondence between the different types of group was close, although women were ahead in discussing amusements, clothes, dancing, and lodgings. Pleasures come out top among mixed groups. The pronounced emphasis on place and time reminds us again of the question which is raised by the whole of this book, to what extent can the industrial Blackpool holiday provide effective release from the dominance of routine?

Some of the points are topics of conversation, others just exclamations or noises. Their presence as percentages is thus distinctly artificial; at the same time, it is helpful for comparison. The method of getting data for the whole table was verbatim transcription on the spot, unseen by the speakers.[1] By placing a simplified section of these results against comparable material for Worktown, we find some interesting results (Table 31).

Table 31 Conversation and entertainment topics (percentage)

	Blackpool June–Sept.	Worktown May–June	Song images*	Theatre laughs*	Postcard captions*
Pleasures	20	5	31	9	19
Place	17	9	7	12	2
Time	13	4	18	0	3
Friends	10	21	14	6	30
Money and job	7	8	5	12	6
Food	5	1	3	9	1
Famous people	5	0.1	2	9	0
Swear	4	4	0	0	2
Weather	3	4	3	0	0
Health	3	1	7	18	23
Clothes	2	2	2	5	0
Laughter	2	12	—	—	—
Enemies	4	8	2	0	0
News, politics	2	0.3	1	14	0
Sport	2	2	0	4	0
Children	1	1	5	2	14
Whistling	0.1	12	—	—	—
Cough	0.1	4	—	—	—
No. in sample	7,043	3,844	496	413	224

* Last three columns refer to data gathered in Blackpool.

The emphasis in the theatre on news and politics as the stuff of jokes is striking; it is also noticeable that the two largest joke topics are minor talk topics. If we take Worktown talk as the standard, the variation in other items can be clearly shown.

Talk topics

less in Blackpool	more in Blackpool
Friends	Pleasure
Enemies	Place
Laughing	Time
Whistling	Food
Coughing	Famous people
	Health

These results harmonise reasonably well with our findings concerning the routine and holiday thought presented in earlier chapters. Now, taking the same standard of comparison, let's consider, Blackpool song and entertainment:

Topics less in songs	Topics more in songs
Friends	Pleasures
Enemies	Time
Swearing	Health
Laughing	

Topics more in theatre	Topics more on postcards
Pleasures	Pleasures
Food	Friends (sex and family)
Famous People	Health
Health, News and	Children
Politics	

VOCAL SCORE

In Blackpool, talk is often interspersed with song, and this increases from 1 per cent in the afternoon to as much as 20 per cent in the evening:

[A group] all sing 'Limehouse Laundry Blues'; man plays mouth-organ. Screams with laughter in between. Sing 'Big Bad Wolf', 'You Can't Do That There Ere'. Woman singing something about 'I Love You', man and woman make snoring noises. Woman: 'Coee, swim Sydney.' Another woman: 'Play a bit of Schubert.' Man starts singing 'Inside Your Caravan'. All sing 'Who's That Walking Down the Street'. Man says: 'I think we'd better go 'ome now.' Woman: 'I think we better 'ad.'

They sang 'Chinese Laundry Blues', words and music by Jack Cottrell, a

George Formby hit which links east and west, remote and Cockney, oriental and everyday, in the way which is a major part of Formby's success:

> There's Mister Wu and his Chinese girl,
> With a pipe and a bottle of wine,
> While the laundry's getting soaking wet
> Hanging out on the backyard line.
> Oh, Mister Wu – what shall I do?
> I've got those kind of Limehouse Chinese Laundry Blues.
> This funny feeling – keeps round me stealing,
> Why don't you throw your sweetheart over, do.
> My vest's so short – that it won't fit my little brother,
> And my new Sunday shirt has got a perforated rudder.
> Mister Wu – I'm telling you –
> I've got those kind of Limehouse Chinese Laundry Blues.

The clearing house for songs in Blackpool are the booths for community singing run by rival companies: Lawrence Wright, big London agent, a manager of Blackpool's pier shows, has a booth on Central Beach; so does Mr Feldman, with a great Shaftesbury Avenue business; he has his own arcade on the promenade just south of Talbot Square. A leader of a small orchestra gathers the audience by his patter and gets them to join in the singing of a song. The words are printed in bold, black type on an easel. When one song is finished, he turns over to the next sheet on the easel. Listen to his pitch:

> Ladies and Gentlemen, if you want a bargain in Blackpool, and there aren't many, then get the bargain parcel; they are sixpence each; there are four songs, two shillings the lot; they are the bargain. They are being played with enormous success with Harry Roy and his band on the air, in the halls, and in your own dance-halls. Everybody will soon be singing them; don't be the ones who don't know them. They are sung by people like Jack Buchanan, and last, but not least, by our own Lancashire comedian George Formby. Now let's have 'I'm as Happy as a Sandboy'.

Sellers thread among the crowd with the songs. The leader brings on song after song, pressing people to buy sheet music and records, cracking 'Come on now, you're not singing so well, do you want some bird seed.' Each session lasts about 26 minutes. About 200 people gather, with women predominant, especially age 18 to 22. All, or nearly all, join in the singing; young girls put their arms round the shoulders or waists of friends:

> Many years ago when Grandma was a girl of sweet sixteen
> She began to make the sweetest patchwork quilt you've ever seen.
> All the years that followed after

Saw her pretty pattern grow
Ev'ry piece of silken lace recalling days of long ago.

In the patchwork quilt that Grandma made
There's velvet, silk, and rich brocade.
Ev'ry night on the bed it's laid
THE PRETTY LITTLE PATCHWORK QUILT.
There's a patch of red, a patch of blue,
A touch of black for Grandpa too,
Souvenirs of a love so true
In THE PRETTY LITTLE PATCHWORK QUILT.

But the *Express* reported (19 April 1938): 'It used to be fun to stand bawling out your pet ditty, now they find it more fun to go to the ballroom and dance round Reggie Dixon playing the same tune better.' [And so crowds change and so we should follow them into the ballrooms.]

NOTES

1 All sorts of alternative methods and classifications are possible and desirable, but, surprisingly, we can find only one other system employed, equally limited, devised, by Henry J. Moore, who recorded overheard conversations in Broadway, New York – see the *Journal of the American Psychological Society*, XVII, 1922, p. 210.

16

DANCING

Dancing is a popular evening pastime, for many people as much a part of the day's routine as breakfast at 8:30 and dinner at 12:00. Look at these extracts from a Lancashire girl's holiday diary. She arrived in Blackpool on Friday evening:

> Friday night. Visit the Tower, met two young men from Sheffield, went into the bar and had a few drinks, afterwards danced, then on the promenade, strolled on the sands, had supper at cafe (chips and coffee). Arrived back at digs at 12 o'clock. . . . Saturday evening . . . went to the Tower dancing, from there to the [Winter] Gardens and then back to the Tower, which we like best. . . . Monday, strolled on the prom with friends and met four Scotch boys, went dancing on the pier and drinks in the bar. . . . Tuesday, went on the pier dancing, came off at 11:30, went up the prom. . . . Afternoon, we went to the Tower dancing till 4:00, also had a walk in the aquarium and zoo. . . . Night went to Palace dancing, then to Variety. . . . Thursday. . . . After tea went to Tower dancing with lady friend. . . . Friday. . . . Night went to Winter Gardens. Picked up sailor from New Zealand. Went and had a look round the amusements 1d. machines, he won me two bracelets and a powder box. We danced and then home.

She stayed eight days, and on six of these days she went dancing at least once, on Tuesday three times. We found that her drinking as an accompaniment of dancing, picking-up in the ballroom, and dancing with a girl friend were common. She mentions also dancing in the afternoon. But when the sun is shining, the beach and promenade are more attractive.

Afternoon dancing is catered for in only two public ballrooms, the Tower from 2:30, and the Central Pier where 'DENYS and his IDEAL DANCE BAND' play. On the Pier, the Stratosphere Girl, walking a suspended wire, tempts people to stretch their necks to look up at her before stretching their legs to the season's dance tunes. The total impression is one of desultoriness, not many people under 30 dancing. The true atmosphere of the ballroom, conducive to gaiety, cannot be captured during the daytime in a ballroom illuminated by daylight. The Tower is more popular, even in the afternoon, than the Central Pier. But in the Tower the visitor never dances in natural light. The windows are thickly screened by curtains and the sliding roof, which is occasionally opened to admit fresh air, is too high up to throw any light on the floor. With the Tower Company's customary thoroughness in achieving any atmosphere but an ordinary one, they make good use of the glamour of electric lighting.

At night, the focus of interest switches from the open air of the promenade to the interior of the ballroom. Sometimes the transition is made through the medium of the theatre and cinema. When the shows at the Tower Company's entertainment centres are finished, the audience is not obliged to go straight out, for other diversions are provided. Admission to the Opera House or Winter Gardens cinema buys access also to the Empress Ballroom. The same thing happens at the Palace. There is dancing on Central Pier, too, at night, and in private hotels and large licensed hotels and Hydros as well as the Squire's Gate Holiday Camp.

But the Tower, the best known spot in Blackpool, seems to be the supreme social centre. It has no cinema or theatre and is unusual in its menagerie and aquarium. The Tower's attraction is largely social, yet every night during the summer finds it too crowded to be comfortable. An attraction at the Tower Ballroom is Reginald Dixon, of organ and radio fame. The evening programme starts at 7:30 with the Children's Ballet and dancing begins immediately afterwards. Long before this time, however, visitors are beginning to arrive. At nine o'clock they are still coming in large numbers. Inside the ballroom, an observer reported, 'The place is crowded. . . . About 5,000 people. Two tiers of spectators above, crowds sitting and standing round floor, dances packed' (4 September 1937).

We tried to find out why so many people came to the Tower, why they danced or watched the dancing. Observers got to work, guiding casually picked-up partners around the floor and getting from them the information we wanted. If the observer was female, she stood on the edge of the dance floor and looked as attractive and lonely as she could. Getting a partner, they discovered, was not very difficult.

Nearly forty dancing partners were asked why they came to the Tower and why they danced. Almost all replied that they thought the Tower was the best place in Blackpool, though they did not explain why. They did not know that they were performing an ancient ritual when religion was a magic ceremonial designed to promote life. The primitive dance was performed to a rising crescendo and increasing tempo of music with a corresponding increase in intensity and abandon until it culminated finally in the act of copulation. With the growth of new social habits and customs, the Bacchic dance has been modified in form. The ballroom dance has brought with it new conventions, chiefly that of breaking the music at frequent intervals, each time introducing a new mood and tempo, and with that the habit of changing one's partner. The old element of sexual approach still exists in the dance, but the new form gives dancing a new meaning. The dance is a partial substitute for more intimate sex relations.

A middle-class spectator's opinion: 'My impression is that dancers are mostly adolescents, going to meet the opposite sex, but quite innocently. Young men want to get confidence by dancing with a lot of girls, perhaps wanting love, but very vaguely.' The dancer is aware of the social value of dancing, and he knows that in the ballroom he has an opportunity of getting to know people which is lacking on the promenade during the daytime. So the boys and girls who have failed to 'get off' in the course of the day make another attempt in the Tower and other ballrooms at night. It makes little difference whether they are able to dance or not. The ballroom sanctions the approach without introduction: 'picking-up' and 'getting-off' are accepted as normal behaviour. A female observer who was picked up in this way reports:

> 9:35. Young man about 23. Ruddy, clean-shaven, very nice. Skilled working-class type. Asks me to go for a drink. I say I don't drink, doesn't he dance? 'Not a step', he says, 'that's why I asked you.' 'Come on, just a grapefruit squash.' We go. 'Will an ice do just as well,' I assert. 'Go and sit over there and I'll get it.' I sit at table, and he brings two nice ices.

There is none of the preliminary manoeuvring seen on the promenade. The method of approach is more confident, since it is prescribed by convention, and the chances of success are greater.

Here are a few samples of picking-up taken in several of the large ballrooms during the evening.

> Tower. Evening. Man of 30 goes up to girl of 21 and says, 'May I have the pleasure?' Girl goes on with him and they dance, badly. Two girls behind; one says, 'I bet those two have never danced before.'
>
> Tower. Man of 22 goes up to girl of 18 and says, 'Do you mind please?' The girl: 'Thank you.' The man's pal goes to the girl's pal and says, 'Do you mind?' All four go on floor.
>
> Central Pier. Boy asks girl for dance. 'No thanks.' 'Oh.' Boy stands five seconds near girl deliberating, then walks away.
>
> Central Pier. Walks right across dance floor to girl. Girl gets up to dance. No words spoken.
>
> Man, age 31, smiles at girl and goes 'Whisssssst', pointing to dancers. She smiles back and both walk to ballroom floor and meet there.
>
> Palace. Two men, age 25, standing next to observer. One says, 'Ask her for a sweet.' Pause. 'They'll all be gone soon if you don't buck up.' Man doesn't buck up and observer moves on.

In only one case is the man refused, and in two cases dancing partners came together without a word being spoken. There is an example here of the preliminary skirmishing which takes place when the man lacks sufficient confidence to make a direct approach. As the dancing progresses, however, this feeling fades. People get warmed up.

In fact, much of the secret of the popularity of summer dancing in Blackpool lies in the lack of formality in public ballroom behaviour. The only signs of it are the five uniformed attendants standing around the edge of the ballroom floor. Their authority is well respected by sober people:

On the left of the ground floor at the end opposite to the band, a man (age 61) in navy blue suit; [he] does a sort of hornpipe to the tune of the band. A commissionaire comes up and wags his finger at him. He stops [and] . . . goes to the edge of the floor.

But attendants make no attempt to deal with pleasantly drunk people:

Two men, about 35, come out of the bar and push their way through a small group of people standing on the edge of the floor. One of them stepping out from the side says, 'Come on, lesh go for a drink.' He makes a move to cross the floor through the dancing groups but his friend holds him back. . . . An attendant . . . stands with his back to a pillar but pays no attention. The drunk says, 'Come on, pal', but he does not cross the floor.

Unusual behaviour among the dancers, which would be censured at a private dance, often passes unchecked and only occasionally does the MC stop a couple to warn them to keep away from the centre of the floor. Every large ballroom has its MC in evening dress who rules the dance floor, and no observer records any occasion on which he was challenged:

Man in white tie and tail coat stands under the microphone on the floor, lifts both hands, quivering fingers, says 'clear the floor' – lifts both hands again quivering fingers – 'please'. Men in uniform shepherd people off the floor.

Nearly every dance observer records the large number of girls dancing together. 67 per cent of the 222 people sitting around the ballroom floor at a late night dance at the Winter Gardens were women. Dancing couples

Table 32 Female couples dancing

Dance	No. female couples	%	No. mixed couples	%
Quickstep	32	14	195	86
Rumba	16	57	12	43
Waltz	41	19	175	81
Quickstep	44	24	139	76
Veleta	49	13	324	87
Average	37	18	169	82

counted at the Tower Ballroom (2 April 1938) are noted in Table 32.

In half of the dances, more than 20 per cent of the couples on the floor were female. 'I think', one observer commented, 'girls dancing with girls keep near the outside (of the floor), couples to centre.' He found that 23 of 31 couples dancing on the edge were female. Another noticed that 'during the next dance, two boys separate two dancing girls, and go off each with a partner'. This dancing around the edge of the floor under the eyes of those standing around is a form of exhibitionism:

> Two girls, 18, with chic little hats dancing near edge of floor, break while one of them does a brief step dance. She grins, looking at people standing at edge. They then continue dancing.

Three observers report, too, a tendency on the part of some of these dancing couples to wear identical clothes: 'Two girls dancing together have silk handkerchiefs over their heads.' This implies a previous understanding, a sense of permanency in the choice of a partner.

The percentage of female couples varies considerably with the type of dance. The rumba produces the highest percentage of female couples while the waltz and veleta show lowest percentages. In the waltz and the veleta, with its tender romantic music as a background, the girl prefers to dance with a man. But in the rumba, which is characterised by a more deliberately active step and a purer sex significance, female couples take the floor in greater numbers. In the case of one rumba, the first six couples on the floor were female. After eight minutes, the ratio was sixteen to twelve in favour of female couples.

Each evening during the summer, some 5,000 people go to the Tower Ballroom not to dance but to watch other people dancing. They go as early as 5:30 to get seats in the balconies and on the ballroom floor to watch the Children's Ballet which begins two hours later. When the performance is over, the majority of them stay in their seats simply to watch the dancers and to hear Reginald Dixon.

The audience is composed of middle-aged people and family groups. They have little to say, but sit watching the floor below them just as they sit on the promenade or the beach watching the sea in front of them. Observers asked them why they watch the dancing. Like the dancers themselves, they usually did not know. Only one man tried to explain:

> Observer was standing at the back of the top balcony watching a Military Two Step in progress. A small man, aged about 50, stood near. . . . Observer approached him and asked what he thought of looking down on the dance from such a height. He said, 'It's interesting to watch up here. You get them all going one way, then they stop and twirl round. Then they go the other way. There's like a—' (He hesitates trying to think of a word.) Observer: 'Pattern'. Man: 'Yes it looks

grand. Not like the others where they just go round and round. Look at that couple hopping.'

When Reginald Dixon is playing, the lights are subdued and coloured lights are switched on, with a white floodlight on Dixon and his Wurlitzer. Attention is diverted from the dance floor to the stage. His appearance is popular, applause good, and people seem to like dancing to his music.

In all the public ballrooms there is a bar conveniently near to the ballroom floor. Several of the women observers have been invited to go for a drink, even before being asked to dance. Drinking is an essential part of the evening. Dancing in a crowded ballroom is hot work, and to stand wedged among tightly packed ranks of people between dances is hotter work than ever. This is a scene recorded in the Winter Gardens:

Ballroom crowded. Man gives partner push on coming off floor.
Girl says, 'Don't do that.'
'Man: 'I'm going anyway,' and leaves girl.

Tempers begin to fray after an evening's dancing, and people begin to go out.

From about nine o'clock there is a steady flow of people going in or out of the ballroom. The Tower has the most attractive places of any for sitting out, including the roof gardens and the aquarium as well as cafes and bars. At various times during the evening, observers left their work in the ballroom to make systematic surveys of the other parts of the building. One observer made a rapid survey of the Tower bars:

The long bar adjoining zoo and ballroom is completely packed. People are standing three or four deep at bar . . .; then there are tables by the wall. Nearly as many women as men. Girls sitting on men's knees. The crowded conditions are a bit too much even for this good-humoured lot: 'Isn't it awful', 'What a crush', 'Steady boys'. On the stairs sits a middle-aged woman with 4 month old baby.

In the Palm Lounge there is a quite different atmosphere. It is pretty crowded with people all silent:

Love birds twittering, water trickling, subdued lighting. Two embraced couples as the observer enters. Soulful music by orange-lit gypsy women. Spooning in corners, even on the auditorium seats, listening to music.

Aquarium. Same thing but more so. Opposite the roach and perch is a sequence of eight necking couples; violent necking. One man with bowed head in hands, girl says, 'Come on, now.' Solitary girls in dance frocks.

Behaviour in the bars is rather free: conversations have a personal note, even between strangers. In the cafes, groups talk only among themselves, and sometimes about other groups:

A young man and woman from the same town but they had not come to Blackpool together. They are eating ices. She: 'Are——'s here again this time?' He: 'No. I saw him last night and he said he wasn't coming.'. . . . She: 'Did you know Jack——got married last week?'

As the evening passes, the gaiety of the crowd, losing the first glamorous effects of the Tower atmosphere, changes to fretfulness. The crowd itself becomes spread throughout the building, seeking refreshment, diversion, coolness, and a quiet corner. The audience, having heard Reginald Dixon, leaves its seats to be occupied later by necking couples. These couples, too, are found in every part of the Tower, even at the top of the Tower itself:

Couples go up from the ballroom. There are four spooning couples on the first stage (open-air), one in thin dance dress being hugged passionately, saying laughingly, 'It's cold.'

The tendency throughout the evening has been for the sexes to mix. The first gallery is occupied almost exclusively by young couples sitting on the long comfortable settees around the back of it, with arms round each other and heads close together. Conversation on the floor is less frequent and quieter. Finally the last dance is announced:

At end of dance man in tails, who is in centre of floor, cries out, 'Clear the floor please.' He has hands out above head and quivers fingers as he says this . . .
Suddenly the band, in mid-dance, breaks into 'God Save the King'. All stand for the King. One man (29) turns round to a woman by the wall and, grinning, salutes stiffly.

Under the guidance of uniformed attendants, the clearing of the building begins immediately. The ballroom crowd is ushered out down the large staircases which lead from the top floor right down to the front entrances.

Going downstairs as the crowd pours out at closing time (11:30), the commissionaires divide the men and the women on either side of a rail down the stairs, calling the direction of the lavatories for either sex.

Even during the clearing process, the necking couples are not easily disturbed: 'Aquarium. Still five hectic necking couples when attendant calls "Time, please" about 11:25.'
The evening's dancing is over and the crowd leaves the electric light and warmth of the ballroom for the darkness and cool freshness of the promenade. But an observer finds proof that the new relations made during the evening do not end here. Necking goes on and leads in some cases to what?

Outside one young girl being dragged along between two lads, having passed out with too much drink. Fifty-nine necking couples on way home from Tower [along] about one mile of promenade. One comment: 'You want a tight fuckin' tonight.'

17

SEX[1]

The couple is the preponderant Blackpool unit. [And sex is a dominant theme of the holiday-maker. But we must again separate the image from the reality.] We have seen how the holiday-maker copes with the workless, payless week regulated only by the call to be punctual at meals. [Throughout this book we have considered] how much the Worktowner willingly changes his own life pattern. With sex, it is easier to test exactly the role of habit and change, routine and escape. Sex in Blackpool is especially good for study because here it is bound to be more overt, for there is little opportunity for secrecy or home privacy in the supervised setting of the boarding house. [The study of the image and the reality of sex in Blackpool was the task of 23 observers, 10 females and 13 males.]

Blackpool has its sexual legend. The Squire's Gate Camp and Hydro south of the 'Golden Sands' are misrepresented as sexual Blackspots [by holiday-makers who have never been there]. The same is true of Blackpool as a whole, which in the South widely has the reputation of being an immoral town. In Worktown, this image prevails among people who have never been there. When an observer from Worcester told people there that he was coming up to Blackpool, he was told that 'in Blackpool hotels and boarding-houses, all bedrooms communicate with each other by door.'

The people who know Blackpool admit Blackpool's sex appeal but regard it as something rather romantic. An observer encountered an example of this attitude in a Worktown pub: 'Wife . . . thought that a large number of people went because it revived past memories, love affairs, etc. And by usage it became a habit that they could not rid themselves of.' Blackpool figures again as a matchmaker in a letter from a young man of Worktown. He writes: 'In my opinion, the best way I can possibly spend my next holiday will be to go to the home town of my sweetheart who I met last holidays at Blackpool.'

But Blackpool is more than a place for honeymooners and shy lovers. As Archdeacon Fosbrook noted at a meeting of the Fylde House of Help, in Blackpool 'there must be very many pitfalls and temptations for the girls who naturally visit it from all parts of the British Isles'. Because Blackpool is organised for pleasure, most believe that it is more vicious and dangerous than elsewhere.

[SEX IN BLACKPOOL AND WORKTOWN]

In its publicity, the resort makes an appeal to the sex instincts of the holiday-maker through the medium of the bathing girl. In the Blackpool holiday pamphlet, unlike that of Brighton, sport, entertainment, and environment are subordinated to the charms of the girl in the bathing dress. Seven of the fifty photographs published in the 1937 pamphlet feature specially posed groups of girls shown playing leap-frog, picnicking, riding donkeys and playing ball on the beach. Their sex appeal is in their frankness and healthiness, reminiscent of the photographs of film stars published in fan magazines. Whatever they are doing, they display more vitality and personality than one would find in a hundred Worktown girls. They wear the latest bathing suits, chiefly the brassiere and shorts type which is rarely seen in Blackpool. This Blackpool is created by men who know how to interpret the ordinary man's ideas of perfection without losing the semblance of reality. But sex is no more idyllic in this resort than it is in Worktown itself. The reality is shown in photographs of groups and crowds not artificially created. In these photographs, the sex motif is less pointed and is lost in the complicated pattern of crowd behaviour.

Having aroused expectations of film-star glamour among holiday-makers, Blackpool authorities allow the environment to be pepped up with another false frontage of sex. Along South Shore is a four and a half foot sandstone pillar with a ring near the tip which narrows to a blunt point. At the base of this object are two smaller shapes pushing up from the side, lumpy and roughly oval. In our work, we try to avoid using the facile jargon of psychology. But in this case, all observers called the South Shore column phallic. Little boys, especially, were noticed climbing about on it and fingering it. Even more obviously the town is dominated by the Tower's 520 feet of steel which has been likened to a factory chimney but which is none the less a phallic symbol. It obtrudes itself on the sight of the visitor just as the photographs of the bathing girls obtruded themselves on the sight of the prospective visitor.

Blackpool's sex appeal is firmly based on the body. In the sugar sweets, like 'Mae's Vest' and 'Sally's Whatnots', the body is presented as half a body with no limbs. Otherwise, it is a whole body and too many clothes. Reduction in the number of clothes worn always provokes audience excitement, and this, or its promise or illusion, is a regular feature in the town's shows:

Man and woman imitate Ginger Rogers and Fred Astaire. But keep losing their balance and trip each other up. They lose some article of

181

apparel each time and the woman's dress is pulled down at the shoulder, her thighs become prominent, etc.

Or:

Men and women in rich costumes of eighteenth-century France. Behind, the wrought-iron gates of a manor house. Gauze rises to show a fountain-well. . . . Another curtain rises. Red suns are glowing; chandeliers descend from the ceiling, on which stand lovely girls, breasts naked, nipples upstanding and red.

In this second example from Formby's show in 1939, you can see, for the first time, the breast of a living female fully exposed in Blackpool. Formby's show is at the Opera House, so it is the dominant Tower Company that must be thanked for this contribution to Blackpool's scene. The stress is on the female; she undresses. In the town's classy photographer's window (Capstack's), photos of females predominate, seven to one.

Wherever the Worktowner turns, some new appeal to his sex instinct or his appreciation of dirty jokes appears. Picture postcards run the whole range of sex humour from the seduced innocent to the henpecked husband; slot-machines offer the holiday-maker peeps at intimate scenes for the price of 1d. Such peepshows are scattered in every amusement area, on pier and on land; and a female in lingerie is always placarded on the outside. The machines are generally bioscopes with a series of photos on stiff paper turning over one after another to give a film effect; some are automatic, some turned by hand. They are unmistakably pre-war, but some seem to have been made recently in pre-war style. Some would envy the police who, according to the Chief Constable's report for 1937, inspected 11,704 of these pictures.

The sex environment of Blackpool encourages the 'forbidden fruit' attitude to sex. But there is always an element of anticlimax in the ultimate revelation. The slot machine rarely fulfils the promise of its title. 'First Night' only reveals the irrelevance of the picture of a girl in undies, legs open, reading a book, which is displayed on the framework to attract the visitors' coppers. Seeing the undies of ordinary live girls is possible in one place, in the Fun House, where air-currents blow up skirts – but it costs a bob.

So much depends on clothes. For wherever you have your love, unless it be in a safe bedroom, there will be clothes separating bodies, and thus a frustration from full knowledge. Of course, certain working-class groups have special chances of entering inconspicuously into houses containing naked women, and many are featured in our collections of postcards: a plumber has to apologise for hurrying a nude woman through her bath ('But I'll wash yer back if that'll help'). But naked men appear only in nudist camps, popular sources of jokes: two girls, breasts showing, look at a huge fat man with beard and curved nose in foreground (his lower third covered by green bush). The caption reads:

The girls all took him for a Jew;
This saucy old Barbarian.
But since he joined the Nudist Club,
They see that he's an 'Airy'un.

The women dominate the men more directly in another sex context. A large group of postcards shows husbands being attracted by bathing belles while wives, larger than the husbands, prevent them. One miserable husband in blazer and grey trousers points to his wife in red brassiered bathing dress, talking to young man: 'I don't hide anything from my wife – and she don't hide much from anybody.' These postcards show a sex interest, focused on the female figure, with the unmarried man more 'male' than his married counterpart.

These two contrasting attitudes to sex [the idyllic and the burlesque] are both equally remote from reality. It is more profitable to promise glamour than to reveal the ordinary nature of Blackpool's environment. For the showman, a little 'dirt' draws the crowd on the spot more successfully than a clean show. Normal matrimonial conditions must be parodied to be attractive. The unwritten laws of sex must be presented to appeal to the onlooker's sense of humour.

At a glance, sex scenes are everywhere in Blackpool. In Worktown, we must walk along the backstreets at night, after 11:15, when all lights are put out. There, at scattered intervals along the walls, will be closely linked couples, standing, one or two in each backstreet. Sexual intercourse enjoyed in this way (as common in winter as summer) is generally known as 'having a knee-trembler'. It is the pre-marital or extramarital method of all those Worktowners who have only the darkened backstreets and who often cannot marry for simple economic reasons. It is easy to get a girlfriend in Worktown, if you can show yourself sensible, have some money, and like cinemas or dancing or (less often) drinking. But it takes some time to do anything you like with the girls.

This type of sex, back wall and knee-tremble, is only a fraction of the indoor married intercourse. In both types, there is a marked tendency to concentrate on the weekend, on Saturday night and Sunday early afternoon. The Saturday night out at cinema or central pub (see *The Pub and the People*) is partially preparation for this. Again, on Sunday afternoon, when the children are sent out to Sunday school and you have time to 'forget about work', sex can be fully enjoyed. Intercourse is often downstairs on the sofa, called a 'soffey ender', and such afternoon intercourse is termed a 'mattinay'. Shop assistants, who have Thursday afternoon off, often have their 'mattinays' then. And, if a chap wants a 'shot' during the week, it's OK 'if the wife is willing'. But decent men 'won't take advantage' of their wives.

The unemployed are widely supposed to have intercourse more frequently, and our data indicate that this is true, as it is that they go to bed later and sleep longer. In Blackpool, where a position parallel to that of unemployment is created, we may expect a wide range of sexuality. Certainly the Blackpool background is strongly sexual. [But in reality does this happen?]

PROSTITUTION

In addition to looking at 11,704 peep-show pictures, the police inspect 9,000 postcards and 2,360 books at over 150 premises per year so that the holiday-makers morals are adequately cared for. Interviewed at the police station, a senior officer told us there wasn't 'too much immorality. Of course, we gets one or two prostitutes, but then they're from outside.'

Prostitutes mostly asked observers for a pound. They stand along the front, north of the Tower and in adjacent side streets; they are mainly middle-aged and some are present in winter:

In F. Avenue a mother and two daughters are prostitutes. They have lived there for over one year. One night—'s friend was walking down the road when the mother accosted him; she was rather drunk. She asked him to go home with her for 10/-; when he refused she asked him to go home with her for 5/-. He said, 'Piss off home; you're old enough to be my mother.' They are at the . . . Hotel almost every night from 8:00 till 10:00.

As in many other aspects of the Blackpool holiday, class enters the field of prostitution. The preferred type inhabit hotels whereas the less eligible prostitutes frequent the pubs and cafes. In 1937 there were 39 convictions for prostitution and 20 for frequenting in the Blackpool courts (four times the rate for Worktown). In the same year, there were no arrests for brothel-keeping, suggesting that prostitution is not carried on to any large extent.

Miss Boden, the probation officer, carefully avoided discussing the subject at any length when interviewed by an observer:

She admitted that when girls had been prostitutes long enough to discover what their earnings could be, they were difficult 'to take off the streets'. A woman was sent here by the police yesterday who said she earned £7 a week by prostitution and asked if she could ever earn that honestly. She was one whose family had 'brought her up unwisely, not teaching her the meaning of the word no'. Observer suggested ignorance as a reason for a fall [but Miss Boden] said, 'No, it is lack of self control, and the parents ought to be educated too, so that they can bring up their children properly.'

In 1936 authorities in Blackpool recorded seventy-six illegitimate births. This is the highest rate in England [and represents 6 per cent of legitimate births]. But if you take the six month summer season from April to October, we find that there were four fewer illegitimate conceptions than during the off-season. Blackpool's record illegitimacy rate cannot be saddled on to the holiday-maker as visitor; he may be responsible, however, as disorganiser of the home life with a consequent dislocation of morals throughout the year. The statistics are illuminated by one of several reports:

> Plump girl, 18, ginger hair, from Sheffield. Strong built. Answered advertisement in paper – like thousands of girls each year. Met at station by agency woman, who [took her] to large boarding house. Landlord soon interested in her. Unlimited hours of work, generally 6:00 a.m. to 11:00 p.m., 10/-a week and keep. Landlord kept on handling her, finally got her into bed and 'seduced' her. Then knocked her downstairs into basement where she sleeps. When girl accidentally broke the apartment's sign, landlady claimed two weeks' wages and refused notice. So girl told about landlord, of which previously she was ashamed. Landlady livid, said defamation of character. Girl sacked and forfeited wages. . . . Girl is taken by friend to police, where she makes statement, has medical examination, etc., and police say serious matter. Girl goes home to mother. No consequences otherwise.

HOLIDAY SEX

It is now possible to examine holiday sex in its own right. Now we can go out on to the dunes and into the alleyways. As people come out of the Tower and ballrooms, many were in mixed couples, having met for the first time that evening. The mechanism of contact and pick-up is the essential start. Its simplicity is best illustrated from the holiday diary of a mill girl [see 'Dancing' for extended excerpts]. Her diary reveals that finding a boyfriend is intimately linked with such amusements as dancing, drinking, and car riding, but not with going to shows. She went to the Tower, Winter Gardens, and Pleasure Beach and was picked up in each place; she was also picked up twice on the promenade. She went drinking three times but only after being picked up. For the young Worktowner, a drink is the accepted method of improving social relations after contact has been made (most often at a dance hall).

But whatever the development of relations between the sexes, their behaviour is regarded with disapproval by their elders:

> Unemployed man, Worktown. . . . had not been in Blackpool since 1921. . . . Believed that Blackpool was no good for young people since they were unused to that sort of freedom for fifty-one weeks of the year, and went wild in their one week in Blackpool.

But a police-sergeant gave a different opinion:

> 'Young girls are not so easily led up the garden path. They're hard boiled nowadays. Of course, some comes and keeps taking a glass of this and that and mixing their drinks and of course they're brought

in drunk . . .' 'Fair number of drunks', he added, but 'no cases of rape'.

Although the males are supposed to do the picking-up, the females make their opinion sufficiently clear by their behaviour:

Two girls walking towards the Manchester Hotel, about 18 years old. Both smile luringly at three boys passing in the opposite direction. No effect. Two more boys come up. They smile again. All stop and talk. After about ten minutes of talk, they walk on in the opposite direction. Running across the road out of the way of a bus, the girls bump into four boys whom apparently they know. They all stop, talking and laughing, for two minutes. They then walk on again, still laughing, the boys once more going in the opposite direction. They occasionally glance at busy stalls but never stop to buy anything.

George Formby is not wrong when he gives Beryl the part of a forceful young lady who vainly tries to pick him up when he plays a shy boy. In 65 per cent of recorded cases, the girls took the initiative.

Here are the impressions of a young local male, August Bank Holiday night:

One line of girls walking along, with two separate groups of men following them. The [girls] walked very slowly and turned around at every provocation. Both groups of men following were evidently wanting to pick them up. . . . One group was more or less reserved and comparatively well dressed; the other, a crowd of complete toughs, very poorly dressed, shouted to the girls and made loud jokes among themselves. It was this group that had most success with the girls.

But unaccompanied females will have difficulty in saying no, as a female observer, blonde, 35, wife of an Oxford don and Labour Party activist, found as she stood outside the Tower and received five invitations in rapid succession. Here are excerpts:

Middle-aged man in bowler and mackintosh: 'Will yer come to bed with me love? Ave yer done it before?' Very tall middle-aged man fairly well dressed: 'Are you all alone sweetie? Come along with me and I'll give you a real good time. Come on, now, don't be shy. You don't want to be alone tonight, do you?' Man, 30, wearing mackintosh and cap. 'Come to show with me lass? I'll pay for you but you'll have to give me a cuddle. What about it lass, come on.'

This simple contact *en passant* is replaced at the expensive hotels by a more elaborate system. Paying more than 15/-a day, you are in a place large enough to enable bedroom manoeuvres free of landlady censorship. In one of the most expensive and supposedly 'loosest' hotels, with stories of a bell being rung at 8:00 a.m. so that people can get back to their own rooms, an observer stayed for a week in September 1937:

> At dinner on Monday, man at table to girl: 'I'm sure I've met you before here.' Girl does not recognise him but says that his face did seem familiar. . . . Observer heard this form of introduction used six times, and . . . in no case were names exchanged. . . .
>
> Woman writing in hall, time 12:30. Young man approaches.
>
> Man: 'Good morning.'
>
> Girl: 'You've said that before.'
>
> Man: 'Have I? Well it's afternoon now.'
>
> Girl: 'Well, if it's afternoon, why do you say good morning?' Both laugh loudly at this.
>
> Girl: 'This is the place I was staying at.'
>
> Man: (looking at postcard) 'Why did you leave it for Blackpool?'
>
> Girl: 'We were driven here by the weather.' Man and girl continue to talk about Scotland, Ireland, weather.
>
> He: 'Well, I must be going. Be good.'
>
> She: 'I always am.'
>
> He: 'No. Really?'
>
> She: 'Well, my only fault is smoking too much.'. . . . He smiles knowingly and goes away. She continues to write, humming 'In September'.

Here, in one of Blackpool's largest and more exclusive hotels, one might expect sex relations to be endowed with a little of the easy glamour seen at the cinema. Instead observers discovered that boy meets girl on the middle-class sophisticated back-chat plane, and that intimacy during the daytime and in public is discouraged by the fatuous and conventional riposte. Flirting, which is taboo under such conditions between social equals, prompts men, largely middle-aged, to transfer their attentions to the hotel employees: 'Man in cafe blows cigarette smoke straight into the waitress's face. She smiles and flirts with him.'

At night, after dancing, and when the public is remote, sex activity is more apparent. The dancing makes it easier:

> Middle-aged man leading young girl, about 18, upstairs to bachelor's quarters at about 10:30.
>
> Two couples on dark sofas in lounge at midnight on Monday. One woman and two men coming downstairs at 1:00 a.m. See two people sitting on stairs. Woman: 'What a place to choose. Use your imagination.'

The loose reputation of the large middle-class hotel arises out of legends which are reminiscent of the orgies of the early cinema's wealthy capitalists.

But let's go back along a small strip of promenade and sand at 11:30 where the workers are less inclined to be roundabout:

> Man leaning against bathing van. Girl in white swagger coat up against him, embracing. Lying on ground, man trying to get hand up girl's dress. She has left leg pointing into air balanced on right knee, as if trying to prevent him. Couple sitting above hulkings. Two couples in shelter, embracing. Man feeling girl under hulkings. Couple kissing in a shelter. Two men leaning over hulkings to peer at couple, who get up, girl arranging her dress. Then watchers go away, grinning.

Watchers are not youths only. For older men of scoptophilic tendencies, the sands at night are a happy hunting ground. Whenever a couple get down on the sands in the dark shadows of the Central Pier, they very quickly have a ring of silent, staring individuals around them less than two yards away, apparently immune from rebuke.

This tolerance naturally helped observers in their study. We have already said that the backstreet is the *locus classicus* of unmarried love in Worktown; here are the results of turning car headlights on backstreets in the central Blackpool area:

> In the backstreet behind Vance Road, seven couples necking against the wall and in the corners of doorways. In the other backstreet, on the other side of Vance road, are five couples. . . . One of the couples emerges behind us: 'Ooh, come on now, it's five to twelve.'

There is none of the vigorous activity that Worktown backstreets show at the same hour. Sample counts of couples under 50 during daylight gave 49 per cent with no contact between them, 1 per cent in a handclasp, 47 per cent arm in arm, 3 per cent arm around waist. A different sample of couples from 11:30 p.m. to midnight show very different results (Table 33).

Table 33 Couples on the beach

Embracing sitting down	120
Embracing lying on sands	46
Embracing standing up	42
Kissing sitting down	25
Necking in cars	9
Girl sitting on man's knee	7
Kissing standing up	3
Total	252

There are only 25 cases recorded of kissing as against 208 cases of embracing; and of these, 162 couples are described as sitting down or standing up, a sentimental response, while only only 46 are recorded as lying down on the sands, which is a much more serious business at night. When we began work in Blackpool, we expected to see copulation everywhere. What we found was petting and feeling.

Observer units combed the sands at all hours, crawled around under the piers and hulkings, pretended to be drunk and fell in heaps on couples to feel what they were doing exactly; others hung over the sea wall and railings for hours watching couples in their hollowed-up sandpits below. With wild cries observers set out, fortified by a meat-pie supper, speeding through the night in a car to the extreme southern boundary of the town. Here is traditional sex area Number One, the sandhills, famous locally as the scene of alleged seductions and assaults. Little more than 200 yards wide, the dunes from fifteen to thirty feet high are ideal for the intimate scenes they are said to conceal. This is what observers found:

Heavy wind this night. Sand blowing. Along a strip of sandhills quarter of a mile, [observer] came across only one sign of life, a squawk, perhaps of assent; could not find the girl who had uttered it because of the dimness and the wind. Later [another observer] reported that he almost stepped on a couple in the same spot, heard girl's voice sobbing, 'Oh, Ted, Ted. Oh, what are you doing?'

All the alleged sex areas were covered in this way, including four miles of promenade, two miles of artificial cliff, six miles of sand, acres of dune and park. Typical of the difference between truth and legend was an incident at 1:00 a.m., when a band of weary observers stopped for coffee at an all-night stall on the promenade. The stall holder, an old hand in Blackpool, said that it was disgusting the way some of the young people went on, that right now there were thousands on the sands, and the large part of them stay there right through the night. In fact, there were three couples.

Altogether, as a result of exhaustive research and many pick-ups by observers themselves, we scored only four records of copulation [in 1937?]. One of these was by an observer:

Observer gets talking to group of five people, three women and two men. One of the women said her name was. . . . and resided at Leeds but used to live at Worktown, been married eight years and had a girl, aged 8. I asked her was her husband with her; she replied, 'No'. Observer bought her a drink (gin) and she told me that her hubby was a neurasthenic and she had come to Blackpool for some fun. . . . I asked her if it would be alright if I took her home and she agreed. So after closing time we came out, and with her being a married woman, the arrangement was that I should follow behind her. . . . We dived down several poorly lit streets until we came to Back Charnley Road. Observer got her to lean against a wall so that he would not dirty his clothes. She is about 5 feet 8 inches in height, well developed, brunette dressed in blue costume, white tammy and sandal type of shoes with no stockings on. She was quite gushing when I kissed her and, after several more, observer began to play near the thighs and felt a pair of artificial knickers, pulling these down, at the same time kissing her.

Observer proceeded in a normal fashion but was not allowed full sexual satisfaction; she said, 'Oh, don't, Jack, you might get me in trouble' and 'No, no more, Jack, I'm afraid'.

It is our considered opinion that the amount of extramarital intercourse is negligible, less than on a Saturday night in Worktown. When we told reporters that 'Blackpool was the most moral town in England', this seemed positively to annoy the municipal authorities. The sexual myth apparently must be preserved. Although the imputations of brassiered belle on postcard and publicity brochure bear little relation to the real thing, they are nevertheless true in the minds of innumerable Worktowners.

SEX TAKES A HOLIDAY

Dreaming of physical distances, why shouldn't holiday-makers go the whole physical distance? An important reason is that the girl does not want that. She is seldom prepared to let a man have his way unless she knows him, his background, his earnings, his health, where he can be found again, and whether he will be ready to take her out and love her some more. To most mill girls, sex is still definitely linked to the idea of marriage. The girl who will go with any man on first acquaintance is 'bad' in the Worktown moral code. On holiday, when you don't know who the man is, it is all the more reason to be careful. But this defence would obviously break down more often if there was real pressure from the males, especially as many girls are more or less drunk by closing time. Evidently the males are also careful or merely flirtatious. We think that this is so because, for the average young Worktowner, Blackpool does not offer a special outlet for sex. This he can generally satisfy as well in Worktown. Both men and women go to Blackpool for the things they cannot get at home – oysters, sleep, sea air, the Big Dipper, Formby in person, a first-rate dance band, variety, and no factory. The tension of sex, often as severe as the tensions of time, money, and work, is a thing from which for one week you try to get away. The random pick-up, a new one each day, and the surface satisfaction that it provides, apparently keep the tension under control.

Another factor contributes to inhibit sex pleasures, as well as other joys. Through these pages, constantly reappearing as the symbol of the Worktown routine, is the landlady. She is the matriarch, the time clock, and the booking clerk. In the large hotels and hydros such restrictions, if they exist at all, are rarely enforced. In this way, Blackpool's largest hotels have acquired reputations which are apparently without foundation.

190

But the Worktown holiday-maker does not normally have the opportunity of intimacy with middle-class girls on the settees in the lounge of large hotels at midnight, and the millworker is not seduced into paying a prostitute a quarter of a normal week's wage for her professional attentions. In fact, the youth of Worktown does not even bother to think such things might be happening. He takes his pleasure in a different way with the Worktown girl. He is driven to developing his relations with the other sex outside his lodgings. In this again, he is frustrated by his lodging-house keeper. He must be in at 12:00 p.m. or be locked out. In the majority of the cases, he chooses the more pleasant of the two inevitabilities. Thus the less well-off once more have their pleasures restricted. There cannot be sex, apparently, until the crowds have mostly gone indoors and the lights are low. And then there is little time to go through the inevitable preliminaries which 'any decent girl' (as one put it to an observer) expects.

Merriment and noise, not sex, are what people seek. On the promenade any summer evening about 10:45, it will be like this:

> Two men arm in arms singing 'Pennies from Heaven'. Two men refer loudly to two women: 'Oh, look at that.' Two couples are necking on the front outside the big pub on the corner. They are standing a few yards from the main pavement. . . . In the background you can hear a voice saying loudly, 'Colonel Barker on left, Bride on right.'

NOTE

1 Portions of this text appear also in Angus Calder and Dorothy Sheridan, eds, *Speak For Yourself: A Mass-Observation Anthology, 1937–1949* (Jonathan Cape, 1984; Oxford University Press, 1985), pp. 48–62.

18

INTERSEX AND THE MORAL LAW

[This chapter explores the fringes of morality – the allure and control of sexual ambiguity, a theme often noted by historians of festivals.]

> Saturday night. 12:00. Fine and cold after rain. A fat woman (40) to another: ' 'Ere's Colonel Barker, your old friend. You'd better go and see how she's getting along.' Shrieks of laughter.
>
> Old woman (60): 'Ee, isn't it sensation.'
>
> Young girl with gang of girls: 'Ay, I'm not going in there – make me blush it would.' She goes in.

In Colonel Barker we have the most famous intersexual character of our time. And holiday sex and its inhibitions are associated with a persistent interest in intersexual states.

The leading impresario of intersexuality is the famed showman, Luke Gannon. He lives in a semidetached house on South Shore. His wife is the noted Palmist and clairvoyant, Madame Kusharney. Gannon talked to an observer for three hours: of how he was born in Burnley in 1879, sold everything but his Rejuvenation tablets, went into the tipster business with Madame but did poorly, and switched to a stall on the promenade. He took to showing people in barrels. He became a topnotcher with his presentation of the Rector of Stiffkey. Always he has been a leader for enterprise and has a special insight into the Blackpool crowd and the Worktown holiday desire. It was Gannon who cabled in August 1935:

Her Majesty
The Queen of Abyssinia.
As a Pioneer of Peace, who last year suggested that Blackpool should stage a Pageant of World's Peace, having just seen that you have completed a sixteen days religious fast, as a protest on the eve of a threatened war, I suggest you come immediately to carry out a fast at Blackpool, which for the next eight weeks is a visiting centre for tourists from all over the world.

His purpose was revealed in a later letter to Her Majesty:

[A fast] would accomplish what the much vaunted League [of Nations] has failed to do, namely, cement by sympathetic understanding of the simple-minded, sincere people of good will, which forms the great bulk of the population of every country,[1] that universal spirit of brotherhood, by which alone can any lasting peace be secured.

Gannon has submitted (vainly) to the Town Council a plan for 'A Grand Spectacular Pageant having for its primary object the earlier commencement of the Seasons. . . . One of the most stupendous and magnificent events ever produced in the Entertainment World' would require 'at least one hundred performers . . . in each section to obtain the necessary realistic effects.'

Still Gannon has put his ideas into practice. All Blackpool is his canvas. Let's look at Luke Gannon's corner of Central Beach, set back fifty feet from the promenade, with a steady line of people always going in or coming out. One of the oldest properties now standing on the Central Promenade, it is not very impressive, but it houses Blackpool's most notorious and profitable sideshow.

ON A STRANGE HONEYMOON
LOVE CALLING
COLONEL BARKER
ADMISSION TWOPENCE.
COLONEL BARKER AND HIS OR HER BRIDE
HOW LONG CAN A LOVING COUPLE REMAIN
UNDER THESE CONDITIONS?

Smaller posters say, 'He's the secret hero in many women's lives'; 'A woman marrying a woman! Incredible! Yet it is true'; and 'From a woman to a man'. Other signs inform us: 'Served in the Army and was not discovered to be a woman. Married a man and now on a honeymoon.' And 'I am taking this step for the woman I love.' On this now famous royal remark, Gannon commented:

I suppose you think I took it from King Edward. . . . But I wrote those words three years ago [1935?]. I was able to show the police a receipt for my order for those words to be printed by the Gazette office. . . . Now don't you think it is the king who should be apologising to me for using my words.

INSIDE THE BOOTH

You pay at a circular pen-desk to a middle-aged female. Ticket, 2d., yellow. Up two steps, then anticlockwise between wooden walls decorated with cardboard cupids and Richard Coeur de Lion in red war-suit who is blessing the bride and bridegroom. Through glass, you look down on the couple in pit below. Two beds, and beside each a Belisha Beacon; between the beds is a broad track marked out with metal traffic studs on the floor. Traffic lights at red. A table and stand are beside the beds, covered with papers and novelettes, Craven A cigarettes, comb, etc. In each bed is an alive woman.

Holiday-makers pass in an almost continuous line queuing during peak periods, staring down, kept on the move by attendants. Stream of remarks:

Woman: 'That's Belisha stopping 'em.'
Man: 'Well, is he a man or a woman?'
Woman: 'He looks like a man.'
Man: 'Anyone who mistook him for a man would be crackers.'

This problem of sex, presented by the his or her bride poster outside, is overlooked by the man who keeps up the patter:

'Colonel Barker is on the left. Keep moving please. The first person in the world to have the now famous operation changing her sex from that of a man to a women [sic]. He's six weeks and three days to go down there. The condition of the wager is they don't cross to each other for the twenty-one weeks. They are watched night and day. He's come here for a wager, to win I believe it's two hundred and fifty pound.'
A lad says: 'The silly bugger.'
Man: 'I call it a frost.'
Attendant: 'They won't believe before they come in, so they won't have it.'
The man: 'He never were a colonel.'
Attendant: 'I don't care whether he was a corporal myself.'
A woman: 'He doesn't look so bad off it.' . . .
The man: 'He's getting some bloody easy money.'
Attendant: 'I wish I could get it as easy.' . . . Attendant does seem . . . to have gotten up genuine dislike for the Colonel.

In October, as the Illuminations come to a close [and the season is about to end], there are some changes in the pit:

Colonel wearing red pajamas with dark large epaulets. Bride has dalmatian puppy in bed. . . . Bottle under Colonel's bed. The Belisha beacon marks on the floor between beds are considerably worn since last seen. Observer asks attendant whether the Colonel ever comes out. He says, 'Never comes out. We keep watch day and night. All as they 'ave, we takes down to them.'

We too, snoopers all, kept watch night and day. Soon we located the Colonel's lodgings in a Larkhill Street house; But the Colonel had shifted by the time our observer arrived. The landlady said:

He left us last week and never paid us the last week's rent for himself and his woman. He was a dirty sod, and that's what he called us. . . .

That woman, Colonel Barker, is living with the wife of another man, her husband comes from Manchester, but she ran away to Blackpool.

The bride in the other bed is Eva. She came to Blackpool with Spud Murphy to do a 'Starving Bride' act, then went into the Barker show. Barker is 6 feet 2 inches, 18 stone. During the 21 weeks of her ordeal in the pit, watched day and night, never allowed to cross, etc., she and Eva never failed to occupy their room at the lodgings.

Here we have Blackpool from the front and back view. Sexual inhibition linked to sexual mystery, linked to a wholly different private life. Sometimes several thousand people an hour paid to walk around the pit for an average of one minute each and look down on the bedroom scene below, at the Beacons and the beds and two ordinary, pleasant looking people in bed, in no way exhibiting their bodies or making any sort of sex appeal.

The Colonel herself hates a great deal of it. This is the best way she can make a decent living. In a series of articles in the *Leader*, she has documented her life history. As a child at Bramley, she dressed often as a boy, and 'literally grew up with animals'. In the war, she served as a nurse and in the Women's Royal Air Force:

> Three times one year, men proposed marriage to me. I refused them all until Major Stewart (as I shall call him) appeared on the scene. He was eighteen years older than I. He had a strange appeal for me. One night in a quiet lane, the trees rustling and whispering soft music in the summer breeze, he told me that he worshipped me.

But Stewart was imprisoned by Germans and his love waned. She married a young Australian officer. With him, she was not happy, and later lived with another Australian:

> I still longed, as any normal girl would, for real romance to come to me, and I saw in him an ideal. So that when at last the moment came, and he offered himself to me, I was ready. By every moral code, it was wrong. I know it. I knew it then. But I felt the penalty for the mistake of my marriage was too terribly harsh if it should transform the rest of my life into long years of lonesome suffering.

She had two children before she left her husband. Then 'a new project':

> For months I had been turning it over in my mind – in brief, to change my sex, to embark on my masquerade as a man. I had to kill every gentle thought and passion, every feminine feeling, the very power and desire to love. For me, there was to be an Eleventh Commandment, 'Thy Shalt Not Love.'
>
> Do it big! That was the advice I gave myself. . . . And it was in the name of Sir Victor Barker that a room was booked for me at the Grand Hotel, Brighton. For there, my new life was to start.

This story, and sideshow, is a vital cog in the Blackpool scene. We asked Gannon about the beacons that guard the path between the beds: 'The Belisha beacons are a sign of futuristic love. People go so fast now in their courting, and the beacon is a sign for them to pull up and go a bit slower.' The Gannon-Barker complex leads to the Museum of Anatomy's exhibits and the Ruxton furniture, with Belisha beacons and traffic lights encouraging you to go in.

On the way, we had better try to size up what the beacon means in contemporary culture. An instant joke, the Belisha beacon, with its black and white bands, orange knob, has steadily increased in popularity. Note the advertisement for the ' "New" Card Game, BELISHA without possible question the most attractive card game ever produced'. Numerous postcards hinge on it: a card shows a girl perspiring great beads from boyfriend's kisses on sofa, her legs over his; black cat with red protruding tongue close by grinning, and, through the window, a big traffic standard with only a red light shining at STOP. Caption: 'George! Quick! look at the traffic light.'

Equal with the Belisha, the motor car learner's 'L' is a joke in our culture, especially in Blackpool. In 1938, it got into the exclusive group of sugar-sweet jokes, the new design being a simple 'L'. These are new symbols of restriction, but apply only to persons well enough off to have cars. We may learn a little more from the way holiday-makers behave at beacon crossings. An *Evening Standard* reporter (12 April 1938) overheard in a pub: 'Bang it and blarm it! If us can't cross the road where us likes, us might as well be Germans.' In fact in observations of 500 people at a Belisha crossing on the promenade, we found only about a quarter use it. A minority, therefore, can legitimately be pedantic about the movements of Colonel Barker and his bride.

Late in the 1937 season a traffic crossing was placed on the pavement on the inland side of the promenade outside Tussaud's Waxworks. People were noticeably intrigued; more entered the waxworks. Early in 1938 the central window was filled by an automatically giggling policeman and a miniature traffic light on a high stand, with the coloured lights reading:

STOP
THINK
GO

Notices beside it:

AN INTERESTING COLLECTION!
AN INTELLECTUAL STUDY!!
AND A PUBLIC ADVANTAGE!!!

PERMUTATIONS ON A THEME FROM BETHLEHEM

On the top floor are the special attractions in Tussaud's Waxworks, the Chamber of Horrors and the Museum of Anatomy. There are 292 exhibits in the museum (transferred from Liverpool in 1937) whose walls are plastered with notices like the following: 'How Very True he that Knoweth his Master's Will and Doeth it not Shall be Beaten with many Stripes.' These comment on many portions of human anatomy (See Table 34).

Table 34 Exhibits at the Museum of Anatomy

Type of exhibit	No. of exhibits
Human body under normal conditions	160
Effects of venereal disease	52
Effects of other disease	2
Childbirth and stages of pregnancy	51
Miracles	9
Animal skeletons, etc.	8
Masturbation and its effects	6
Circumcision	3
Operations (other than childbirth)	1
Total	292

The central position of the museum is occupied by two large shallow glass cases with a full-size human figure model lying in each. On the left we have Louise Lateau who, according to the catalogue,

was born in January 1850 at a place called Bois d' Haine. . . . in Belgium, and until she was 17 years of age enjoyed robust health. However, from the beginning of 1867, till the 16th of April in the following year, she suffered intensely from neuralgic pains in the head; . . . on the 16th of April she was so exhausted that her friends thought she was dying and, in consequence, she received the sacrament. From that day she rapidly improved. . . . This may be regarded as the turning point from a girl to a woman. Three days [later] the 'Stigmata' first appeared, and thirteen weeks later, July 17th, she began to exhibit the phenomena of Ecstasy of Trances. On Friday, the 24th April, 1868, blood began to issue from her left side, between the 5th and 6th ribs. On Friday, May 8th, blood began to flow from both her feet, from the upper surface as well as the soles, and, by nine o'clock, it also flowed from the palms and backs of both hands. . . . The fits terminate in the most appalling manner; the arms fall; the head drops on the side of the chest; the eyes are closed; the nose becomes pinched. . . .

Louise lies naked in the case on a silken cloth, chaplet on head, blood on temple, feet, hands, cloth. Long black hair, youthful breast, and a tiny artificial leaf over mons veneris. The catalogue describes Louise Lateau as a religious mystic; but she is more than that: she is a female Christ. She lies like a picture of the dead Christ in an Italian old master. In her, there is an intersex symbol more potent than Colonel Barker because it has the weight of 2000 years of Christianity behind it. The blurb particularly stresses the fact of regular bleeding, and the cycle is not merely a monthly one. It has been speeded up four times and comes weekly. Menstruation has relevance to religion in so far as it is expressive of the cycle of life and the seasons.

Opposite is another marvel of science, the Pregnant Male, which, though lacking the religious force, is no less a miracle, and a more horrifying one. A waxen man lying naked, his belly open with four flaps of flesh cut back, showing about a square foot of entrails, in which there is a sort of window, three inches square, of transparent tissues through which a small lump is seen. The catalogue describes: 'EXTRAORDINARY FREAK OF NATURE OF A MAN BEING DISCOVERED IN THE "FAMILY WAY" ':

> So like the serpent in the egg shell . . . these living rudiments lay quiet for a few years – within the body of the brother, the impregnated egg lay, and then, formation commencing, the wonder and the catastrophe (death) ensued! The young man became pregnant with his twin sister. . . . [When] the youth was 8 or 10 years of age, . . . after much enlargement from his 'Pregnancy', and much pain and flooding, the youth died.

Here we have a Colonel Barker, but a Barker who is fertile, and, as the catalogue says, it meant death for him. These female males naturally resolve into a hermaphrodite. Three exhibits present the sexual parts of a hermaphrodite to the eyes of Blackpool:

> He was devoid of a scrotum, and a testicle was found on either side of the entrance, enveloped with the external labia. The clitoris was the size of the first joint of a finger and the mouth of the vagina was very small.

If the hermaphrodite is the prevailing idea in this museum, what about the normal sex organs? The female organ is always concealed by a fig leaf unless repulsively distorted by childbirth; and the only male organs shown are invariably not in a normal state, and all equally repulsive. The majority illustrate the effects of venereal disease:

> A model of the head and neck, showing the awful and degraded state into which women come when they disobey the laws of God. 'The wages of sin is death.'

And:

A model of the head of a child suffering under a similar disease. In this model the visitor sees the awful effects of men leading a depraved life! 'Visiting the iniquity of the fathers upon the children and upon the children's children and to the fourth generation.'

The Museum of Anatomy's miracles and monstrosities have the sin of sexual indulgence as their moral. It is a product of another century, daringly original, and defiant against a moral code which forbade the exhibiting of table legs. In the environment of the seaside resort, the abnormalities exhibited are doubly stressed, and its sensationalism is only legalised by the attempt to justify it on educational grounds. Inside, the pornographic interest of the exhibits is suppressed by the repulsive character of the exhibits. There are 51 exhibits representing various stages of pregnancy and childbirth, and 22 of these are abnormal; of 54 exhibits dealing with disease, 52 are venereal. The moral pointed by all is 'Thou shalt not copulate.'

Deprived of sexual intercourse, the visitor finds that the alternative, masturbation, is even more of a taboo. The effects of this 'pernicious habit' are second only to the ravages of VD, and are illustrated in a vivid guidebook which threatens damnation in order to shock even the most habitual masturbator into superhuman self-control:

Exhibit 106. Face of an old bachelor; a confirmed onanist. He became idiotic and rapidly sank into second childhood. (What a fearful account he will have to give of himself at the Judgement Day.)

The Museum of Anatomy is the successor to Luke Gannon's show, with hermaphroditism as a common feature. In both, the primary idea is that of repression. The Friday cycle of stigmata and the longer cycle of awful death through sin impressed observers. The venereal exhibit for every week of the year now clarifies the use of the traffic lights and the policeman in the Tussaud window. Neither Barker nor the lad on holiday must cross, even within the stud marks. The Museum of Anatomy warns the visitor with physical disgust and moral proverbs that he must pay a terrible price for his sexual indulgence. So we find that there is repression as well as ozone in the Blackpool air. The Belisha beacon and the traffic light, ignored by the holiday-maker as to their ordinary meaning, are employed to warn him of a worse fate.

A related theme is displayed in the Rector of Stiffkey. After his trial and dismissal from the Church in 1932 for alleged behaviour with girls contacted during rescue work, he appeared in Blackpool. According to an article published after his death by Mrs Davidson (*Leader*, 11 September 1937), Gannon begged Stiffkey 'to go to Blackpool and put in an appearance, in any capacity, and he offered a salary of £100 a week'. Stiffkey agreed and went to Blackpool. Mrs Davidson continued:

To his horror he found he had been billed to sleep publicly in a barrel whilst a girl named Barbara Cockayne was doing a fortnight's fast in the same show. And posters had been put up outside announcing that 'The Rector would watch over Barbara.'

His dislike of appearing in such a show did not prevent him appearing on two subsequent occasions at Gannon's place on Central Beach, once fasting in a glass case and on the next occasion lying amid the flames of an artificial hell where he was being prodded with forks.

On each occasion, the show was presented to the public as punishment, self-inflicted or otherwise, for his behaviour in the past, culminating finally in the flames of hell. This was his goodbye in Blackpool. His private reason for staying so long was that he wanted money to appeal against the judgement found against him. After leaving Blackpool, his technique changed. There was no penance or punishment in his Skegness performance in a lion's cage. In Skegness he appeared as a saintly man like the prophet Daniel; in Blackpool he was kept in a barrel or a glass case, framed as a living illustration of the price of sexual misbehaviour.

The Rector was mauled by lions in his new show at Skegness and died towards the end of August [1938]. Outside the booth in Blackpool, resting on the top of the barrel where he lived the previous year, a plank was laid. A sheet was thrown over this, and there was a lump resembling a body underneath. There was no notice or any indication of what this might be, but several people were drawn away from the promenade to see it. One remarked, 'Look Bill, the body's in the bag.'

EVE AND ADAM IN EVENING DRESS

[Despite these repressive themes] it is possible and popular for holiday-makers of either sex to make a change of sex on the spot in Blackpool. In photographers' booths there are human designs painted on canvas with a hole at the face through which you put your head, thus seeming to be part of the figure. You can appear to be a Cossack or an airman, or even Eve and Adam in evening dress.

One of the few photographic and non-scenic postcards on sale in town is of a child with distinctly girlish features and chest, bobbed black hair, a penis (close examination suggested that this was made of rubber and had been tied on to the child for the photograph) and a handful of cherries. Caption: 'For Sweet Remembrance'. Imbued with a similar interest, the Tower Company's programme announced the film of 'Wings of the Morning' at the Winter Gardens: 'To escape from revolutionary Spain, [Annabella] masqueraded as a boy, and [her] impersonation is amazingly successful and more convincing than any yet seen on the screen.'

On the live stage, intersexuality, homosexuality, and transvestism are seldom omitted, whether it is the comedian with brassiere slipping or the 'Royal Follies' with the gag: 'Fat man postures up to porter, railway scene. Porter makes extravagant feminine gestures in imitation. Says, "Well you can't have me, I'm spoken for. . . . " ' The Palace comedian gag: 'My name was Cissie three days before I was born.' This pre-conception conception finds mature form in Formby's 'King Cheer', where two American wise-crackers put the case:

> Woman says, 'Sex-changing is taking place a lot these days. The only way to tell the difference between the sexes is to tell a rude story. If the person blushes, it's a boy. That's one of mother's jokes.'
> Man: 'What are you? One of father's?'
> Woman goes on to tell of her honeymoon and how the first night her husband took off dummy arms, legs, teeth, etc., and put them on the top of dresser.
> Man: 'What did you do?'
> Woman: 'I climbed on top of the dresser and slept there, because there was more of him there than in bed.'

Fundamental to all these jokes, exhibits, and actions is the holiday function of liberation from mill and boss routine, neighbour and time restriction, into a place where the law will not worry you if you are sick in the gutter or blocking the pavement or shouting at 11:15 p.m. For a week you change the routine, the restrictions, the laws of everyday, and even the laws of nature.

In such an environment, Colonel Barker and the Hermaphrodite became the supreme symbols in Blackpool. [They fascinate, but they also] symbolise repression, not impotence and infertility, because of the fate which follows freedom of sexual contact. The popular interpretation of this unwritten bye-law is found in a story, circulated in both Worktown and Blackpool, about a man who got so stuck into a little girl on the sands at Blackpool that they had to have an operation to be separated. Observers found that less than 1 in every 10,000 Blackpool visitors takes this risk.

NOTES

1 Gannon said to an observer: 'I always say that you can divide the public like this – 50 per cent certifiable, 30 per cent, on the brink, and the other 20 per cent living on the others.'

Part 5

19

[BLACKPOOL PEOPLE]

[Many of these chapters have obliquely addressed the intentions and behaviour of the impresarios and stall holders of Blackpool. But the Mass-Observers studied more directly the makers of the Blackpool holiday, the entrepreneurs, the publicists, and the workers.]

BIG BUSINESS

In 1769, the whole hamlet contained only 28 houses, 4 of which had slate roofs, but 3 inns had been built. Of these, Bonny's (originally known as Old Marjory's) charged 10*d*. a day, and the Old Gynn, 8*d*. a day. The third, a small inn on the site of the present Clifton Hotel, was the first in Blackpool.

(W. I. Curnow, British Association Survey, citing Richard Pocoke)

Today Blackpool, with its £1,500,000 promenade and its 7,000,000 summer visitors, stands carved out of these individual efforts. But in tune with world trends, it now has a different view of the individual. Private persons, like the Davidsons of Utility Airways or the sideshow impresario, Luke Gannon, can still survive the pressure of the Corporation. Nevertheless the Corporation, and the interests it represents, are increasingly making Blackpool fit their pattern; with their new airport, they will have proper control of the Davidsons; with their new million-pound scheme for replanning the town centre, they will abolish the historic Gannon booths.

[This trend was long in the making.] Blackpool's 50 houses in 1790 had become 421 in 1849, with the boom after the extension of the Preston–Fleetwood railway to Blackpool in 1846. The train brought in a new type of visitor, the cotton worker, the Worktowner. Not rich but very numerous, his needs were met by the Blackpool Pier Company, capital £12,000 in 1861, whose North Pier was opened in 1863. A rival company built the Central Pier to the south of it in 1867, to be followed 25 years later with the South Pier. With £14,000 in 1871, a syndicate bought a Catholic Convent, Raikes Hall, and its 48 acre park half a mile from the sea. This became the Royal Palace Gardens:

Nobody came to Blackpool without visiting Raikes Hall. That once immensely popular gardens was delighting thousands of Blackpool visitors with its classic double-arched entrance gateway for carriages, its grand statuary avenue, its skating rink and conservatory, monkey-house, boating pool, pavilion theatre (and concert hall), open-air dancing platform, and its magnificent fireworks displays.

(Allen Clarke, *The Story of Blackpool*, 1923)

The venture failed, however, because of competition nearer the sea, and in 1896 the 14 acres remaining from the original estate were sold for £80,000.

The first competitor on the promenade was Dr Cocker, first Mayor of Blackpool (1876), who bought the seashore residence of Sir Reginald Heywood for £16,000 and opened it as an aquarium. In 1880 he turned the business, with the Beach Hotel, into the Blackpool Central Property Company, and in 1884 sold out his interest in the concern for £44,000. With mayoral foresight, he started the Winter Gardens and Pavilion Company in 1875. The Winter Gardens prospered under his direction.

Meanwhile, in 1891, a London syndicate, the Standard Debenture Corporation, bought Blackpool Central Property for £65,000. They wanted a site for the English Eiffel Tower. The aquarium, aviary, and menagerie were grouped around the base of the 520-foot Tower, with the addition of a ballroom and circus. The young company grew to be the biggest in the town; its first secretary and general manager, George H. Harrap (1894–1926), was appointed to the job from a post in the Town Hall. In forty years, Tower Company gained control of three serious rivals in the entertainment business and helped to force the Raikes Hall Company out of business. The Alhambra Variety Theatre, Circus, Ballroom, and Cafe had opened in 1899 but were taken over by the Tower Company in 1902. Under John Bickerstaff's guidance, it bought the Grand Theatre in 1907 for £47,000, thirteen years after it had opened; and the Company's last competitor, the Winter Gardens, was absorbed in 1928.

At a council meeting in January 1938, councillor Smith declared: 'If there is a councillor who has no Tower shares, he is either unlucky or unwise.' Tower dividends are high, yet not exceptional for Blackpool (see Table 35). Lowest dividends are paid by the oldest companies, the piers. At the other end of the scale is Waller and Hartley, sweet manufacturer, who employs 700 girls (earning 14/-to 25/-per week), and has good connections with Woolworth.

The C. and S. Brewery owns the Grand Hotel and the Carlton, and is closely linked with the County and Palatine Hotels through an alderman and two councillors. Councillors' connections with licensed concerns inspired Mayor Quayle's crusade early in 1938 against use of municipal standing to benefit these companies. Now entertainments are no longer run by the town councillors. There are still two Bickerstaffs on the board of the Tower

Table 35 Blackpool big business

Company	Founded	Dividends (1936–7)
		%
Blackpool Tower Company	1891	22.5
Waller and Hartley	1927	60 (1935–6)
Palatine Hotel	1896	27.5
County Hotel	1896	25
Blackpool Winter Gardens	1875	22.5
Catterall and Swarericks Brewery Co.	1894	20
Blackpool Pier (North)	1861	17.5
S. Blackpool Jetty	1864	16
Imperial Hydro Hotel	1897	12.5 (1935)
Blackpool S.S. Pier	1890	6.5
Savoy Hydro	1925	6.5
Blackpool Entertainments	1920	0

Company, but none on the council. Nevertheless the council still includes four hotel owners and seven company directors (five from hotels) as well as eleven professional men and five builders.

In fact, the town Corporation is the largest business organisation of all. As a result, until recently Blackpool boasted the lowest rate in the country, 8/6 in the pound. The Corporation owns and operates its own gas and electricity works, its own tramways, buses, public baths, and markets as well as airport, cemetery, slaughterhouses, housing schemes, and salt water works. The Corporation's earliest and most profitable deal was the purchase of 2,068 acres of foreshore for £960, from which the rent of the stalls yielded £4,466 in 1935–6. The biggest turnover is in transport with trams taking £68,000 and buses £19,000 in August [1938].

The Central Beach Clearance scheme is the climax to Blackpool's progress in the last few years. It involves building a new railway station and municipal centre by clearing sixty acres of the town centre. Although 78 per cent of the eligible electorate did not vote on this scheme, it passed with a majority. Representing owners of properties to be demolished, William Parkinson, JP, observed that in 1891 the 'rock sellers, phrenologists, ice-cream vendors, Punch and Judy Shows' were prohibited 'from using the sands for their wares. . . . Why not let this class of business be carried on the sands? If not, the vendors will have premises in some part of town. . . . They will never be driven out as they are part of the town.'

There will be an attempt, however, to limit those which the Corporation considers undesirable. Phrenology, yogi, five-leggedness and intersexuality, as such, are not threatened, for all thrive at present in the big or Corporation-linked concerns. The threat is against the little independent man, he who carries on guerrilla warfare with the police about selling postcards on the sands or displaying a Rector in a barrel. Moreover, the new scheme will surely give a new emphasis to the section inland from the promenade, nudging on that movement away from the sea. When the scheme is completed, the Corporation will have an associated dictatorship over all the major amusement areas. Wise from our experience of 'Sheikh', 'Hand-Impressionist', and 'Robot King', we will venture no predictions as to the result.

IN BRIMMING MEASURE

In Blackpool's only paper, triumphant editorials are commonplace:

> Like Blackpool, Southport claims to have eclipsed all its previous Bank Holiday Records.
> But while Blackpool's visitors easily top the half-million mark . . . Southport estimates its holiday crowds to have been at least 150,000 or less than one-third the number of visitors who came to Blackpool. . . . Happily, the crowds continue to grow in size, and they come from a much wider field every year.

In the depths of December, when the visitors are gone away, the star local gossip columnist, 'Sirius', tells us, through his column 'Beneath the Stars', how it's done (*Gazette*, 4 March 1938):

> Publicity, Publicity, Publicity!
> Every day and in every way we get it in brimming measure.
> As I have said before, it doesn't just happen. These sensations . . . in the Blackpool Council Chamber . . . are all part of a plan – a plan so cleverly conceived and so cunningly concealed, that the outside public do never guess it.
> Why, it's so brilliantly managed that it takes in those men who think they're the smartest guys on earth – the news editors of the daily papers. And for every penny we spend in the advertisement pages we get a pound's worth of value in the news columns.
> The biggest marvel is how we keep it up, year after year, winter and summer alike.
> But we do!

That is true. The Corporation's publicity department sends out eighty-nine tons of propaganda a year, but the best stuff is indirect, never weighed.

To propagate the notion of Blackpool and progress, in 1879 the town secured through the Third Blackpool Improvement Act what no other town has managed to do: it got parliamentary sanction to levy a rate of 2*d*. consecrated to municipal advertising. Blackpool's publicity is all over the world. As barber Jeff Hart, shampooing an observer, observed:

In the war period, when we were pushing Jerry back, we were at the
Battle of Waterloo Fields; and there was a place there called Brown's
Hotel; and what did I see written up on the gable-end but 'GO TO
BRIGHT BREEZY BLACKPOOL'.

The *Blackpool Holiday Journal* (1938) has for its cover a door with the
coat of arms and motto of Progress, and scarlet lettering reading 'OPEN THE
DOOR TO HOLIDAY HAPPINESS'. Within, under the title, 'Blackpool for
Health', and above a picture of two women in bathing dresses with legs widespread jumping over two women in bathing dresses, is the text:

> Blowing directly across more than 700 square miles of the Irish Sea,
> Blackpool's prevailing breezes arrive clean, pure, and dustless, laden
> with fresh oxygen and bringing with them that appetising 'tang' of the
> sea.

Compared to the publicity of Brighton and Bournemouth, the Blackpool
guide of 1938 heavily stresses bathing belles: twenty-two of these pictures
show them compared to none in Brighton and seven in Bournemouth (and
none of the latter show brassieres). Cars are scarce in Blackpool photos
compared to the middle-class resorts; and Blackpool's is the only brochure
showing a railway train, superimposed oversize on to the Central Pier and
the sea.

But as the local gossip columnist observed, the poster, leaflet, and
brochure advertising is only a penny in the pound of publicity. Blackpool
goes all out to get all sorts of conferences held there. That brings trade,
publicity, and well-to-do visitors, who may come back for more. Thus 1938
included the Rotary International's official delegate list of 3,000; the Trades
Union Congress; the National Association of Local Government Officers,
attendance 2,000; the National Federation of Textile Workers' Associations
with delegates from all over the world; Sons of Temperance Friendly
Society, 500 delegates; and the United Council of Disabled Servicemen's
Associations.

Blackpool has learned that bringing important people to Blackpool brings
important publicity. Back in 1878 financier and Mayor, Dr Cocker,
organised a state visit of the Lord Mayor of London, the Sheriff of
Middlesex, and the Lord Mayors of fifty cities and towns of the North and
Midlands, 'together with their ladies', for the opening of the Winter Gardens.
He entertained them for a week at the posh Hotel Metropole and the bill was
met by public subscription. Commenting to the British Association meeting
at Blackpool in 1936, a local schoolmaster and Marxist writes: 'This was a
most effective piece of publicity and set the high standard in the art of
advertising which Blackpool has ever since been obliged to maintain in a
world of ever-increasing competition.'

In 1904 the Publicity Bureau celebrated Blackpool's incorporation as a

County Borough by turning the promenade into a motor-racing track, with success. The place went sky-high in 1909 when it followed a hint dropped by Lord Northcliffe and initiated aviation week, expecting to be the first one in England. Despite elaborate publicity, bad weather and high wind spoiled the week. And very much to Blackpool's annoyance, Doncaster, without elaborate publicity or preparation, held an aviation week a week earlier. The Publicity Bureau now has a network of Blackpool agents, who promote or organise in workshops, clubs, Sunday Schools, and savings societies for a Blackpool holiday. There are 200 such societies in the industrial North. Perhaps the most effective of all indirect methods is the music hall.

Observers go frequently to report on Worktown's single music hall, with a different road-show each week. Of these, during twelve months, three had single scenes of jokes about Blackpool (10 July, 13 August, and 12 November) and two dealt wholly with Blackpool (28 May and 15 July). Here is an excerpt from a scene in 'Sammy in Variety', observed 12 November 1937:

> Scene against Blackpool backset, with Illuminations trappings, painted on normal backcloth looking to Tower from North Cafe and Union Jack on housewall. Toni Rigoletto plays piano accordion solo on stage, orchestra below. Gradually gets audience humming 'Cherry Blossom Time' and singing softly. Then lights out and the backset gives actual Illuminations effect; backcloth is left dark with Illuminations shown by shining lights through at suitable places, e.g. Tower tip. Applause at this. Plays 'Just a Song at Twilight'. Many sing now.

'Lights out at Eleven', 'the Latest Uproarious Comedy-Success', has 'the entire action in the Lounge of a Blackpool boarding house' known as 'Seaview'. It's 'lights out at eleven' because it is respectable.

Finally, four weeks before the holidays, appeared 'Blackpool Breezes', with Mona Vivian and her Blackpool Wavelets, Etienne, the Continental Danseuse, the Eight Little Burglars, and Roy Barbour and his beastly dog. The special number is 'Let Blackpool Breezes Blow Your Troubles Away'. Scenes include 'Blackpool Station', 'Walking on the Pier', 'Illuminations', 'Pleasure Beach', and 'Moonlight Fantasy'.

In the 'Moonlight Fantasy', two men on roller skates come on as Adam and Eve. Eve's breast coverings keep on falling down, the biggest audience laughter of the evening. The female star is Mona Vivian, who in a circus song tells how she left half her tights on the flying trapeze; imitating Mae West, swaying hips to loud laughter, she says, 'Say, don't anybody recognise the motions', and then she tells one of the orchestra his name must be Nero, 'because I'm burning up – while he's fiddling'.

The male star was Roy Barbour. His yellow card was distributed all over Worktown, heavy capitals asking:

WHO HAS THE UGLIEST DOG IN WORKTOWN?

Roy Barbour wants an ugly dog . . . to appear with him in a sketch for one week. . . . For the purpose of the sketch, [it] has got to be the kind of Dog that Blackpool Landladies would refuse to have in their boarding houses. The uglier your dog, the better its chance of obtaining a part in this record-breaking show. And Mr Barbour will personally select the Least Choice Specimen.

Smart Alderman Ashton, JP, 'immediate ex-Mayor' of 1938, is an elected Chairman of the Publicity Committee of the Corporation. Ashton welcomes all sorts of publicity (spending about £40,000 of the ratepayers' money for this purpose) and has travelled widely to see other sorts. On Coney Island, they called him Lord Ashton. The only sort of publicity he never welcomes is Mass-Observation reports. Ashton's son, Eric, when asked about Blackpool's publicity manager, said, 'He has absolutely no imagination. That's probably why he's so good at his job.'

WORKERS

[Publicity and the close linkage between the Corporation and big business are the key to Blackpool's notions of progress.] But if the profits of the C. and S. Brewery are particularly high, the wages of pub workers are particularly low. We collected much wage information, and Table 36 is adequately repre-

Table 36 Wages in holiday jobs

Women		Men	
Sweet-maker	30/-	Rock-moulder	70/-
Toffee-maker	25/-	Rock-seller	45/C
Woolworth assistant	30/-	Chef, Tripe-shop	60/-
R.H.O. assistant	35/-	Chef, cafe	40/F
Cafeteria girl	25/F	Chef, Winter Gardens	140/-
Waitress, S. Pier	25/-	Chef, big hotel	160–240/-
Waitress, Lockhars	23/F	Waiter, big hotel	20/-
Waitress, big hotel	20/F	Barman	20/-
Waitress, small cafe	25/C	Shop lad (age 14)	12/6
Pub cleaner	17/6	Tripe-shop attendant	30/-
Boarding-house		Plateman, hotel	25/-
cleaner	15/F	Attendant, cinema	15–50/-
Chambermaid, big		Attendant, Winter	
hotel	25/F	Gardens	60/-
Baths attendant	30/-	Baths, foreman	60/-
Slot-machine tender	25/-	G. boy, decoy	25/C
Girl decoy for		Slot-machine tender	50/-
slot-machine	50/-	Skee Ball tender	70/-
Mannequin	120/-	Penny games tender	60/-
Prostitute	140/-	Barker, Fairyland	60/-

sentative of the main holiday jobs; they are figured in shillings per week; 'F' means food provided; 'C' is commission; tips additional in the usual type of tip job.

Hours of work are particularly difficult to ascertain in Blackpool: in the majority of summer jobs, they are undefined or unlimited. Bus conductors and drivers, working on an hourly rate, reach ninety hours a week at the season's peaks and Waller and Hartley toffee girls constantly work overtime. Boarding-house girls, drafted in from all over the country largely through agencies which take a pound per head commission, seldom get more than one night off a week, and during the rest of the time they are working almost incessantly. Barkers and attendants generally have a seven-day week. No union or overtime rules cover the thousands of slot-machine and Central Beach workers. Shortest hours are those worked by the highest earning group of females, Blackpool's handful of prostitutes.

Two days before Good Friday, 1938, the *Evening Gazette* published this caption: 'S O S for Easter Workers. BLACKPOOL SHORTAGE. Catering Trade Calls' and the following note, 'Employment Exchange officials, though still making every effort to engage women from inland towns, confess that the position is "grave", and point out that it will be even more complex when the season proper arrives.' Of 3,500 women on the unemployment register, about 2,500 had already been engaged for Easter.

An observer met one of the imported waitresses who worked on South Pier in summer and at Lews' in Birmingham in winter. She earns 27/6 a week for a twelve-hour day from 9:30 a.m. As for waiters:

> The chaps who come here for the waiter's jobs . . . get about £1 a week and have to depend on what they can make in tips and what they can fiddle. . . . I know of a case in which a party of four went to an hotel and had champagne; when they had finished, the waiter gave them a bill for £5 too much. He had put empty bottles at the side of the table to prove it. Luckily one of them was a very light drinker. . . . He sent for the manager who saw that he would have trouble . . . and sacked the waiter. But he knew that the game was always carried on.

Another time an observer heard an employer refuse to hire a chap who claimed to be honest:

> My experience is that them as says they're honest is that they won't work. I want somebody who will fiddle for himself a bit, no more than a £ a day; then they will work hard for me as well.

['Fiddling' included robbing:]

> the couples lying out on the sands; they are too bloody keen on what they are doing; you . . . see their handbags an snaffle em; they never tell the police 'cause they don't like their folks knowing where they were at that time.

Or, selling 'rock that's made a bit thinner, so they can offer more bars to the bob'. Fiddling might also mean simply taking a job at the football matches in winter while on the dole.

Still, not all are driven to such extremes. A Tower Company clerk, one of its 1,500 summer staff, said of his wage, 'It's not much and they're not satisfied. Still, nobody's satisfied. We get just enough to live. In Blackpool, it's a good job – a twelve months' job if you're on the staff. In other places, it'd only be a three months' job.' A driver of a Streamline Taxi found his job

O.K. in summer, take £3–4 a day. In winter, average three to five shillings. Has to save in summer for winter. Plenty go on dole rather than carry on. He gets a bit above dole in winter most weeks, but not all. Just depends on fares. . . . He has sixteen hours on the job and sixteen off.

From all over England, girls and men come into Blackpool for the summer and take jobs. An unemployed waiter said to an observer:

Anyone who can get a dress suit is a waiter here. No good catering here. People don't know the meaning of tipping. The waiters: riff-raff. They talk and drink with the customers.

The head waiter at the County [Hotel] rings up the Labour Exchange for extra waiters if he wants them for a meal. He pays extras 7/6 for the day or 6/6 with a dinner and he gets them the same day, even though you get 4/10 a day on the dole.

In an attempt to remedy their circumstances, the floating population of waiters tried a strike – with pickets and union approval – immediately before Easter in 1937. It was defeated in two days. The head waiter at the County Hotel commented.

We had no trouble with the regular staff; only the floating population of waiters were troublesome and they soon gave up the idea when they began to lose money. If another strike is organised, the leader will be run out of town.

Wages are often inferior even to that in Worktown. With workers drawn in from all over the place and the town's strong Conservative traditions (with only one Labour councillor in its history), union organisation is negligible.

REMEMBERED BITTERLY

The end of the season in Blackpool is as much an event to be anticipated or feared by the inhabitant as the holiday week is for the Worktowner. Blackpool is a gold mine for the shareholders [and the off-season is a time to enjoy it]. But the end of the season means six months of unemployment for 10,000 Blackpool seasonal workers and the end of twenty weeks of hard work at long hours. Thus, as the season draws to a close, the nice division is indicated in two articles on 21 September in the local newspaper. First, 'On the Threshold of the Social Season. Winter Months are Months of Gaiety':

> In the trail of the Illuminations there will come Blackpool's own nights of joy, the start of the social season, as we ourselves call it.
>
> Those who have been engaged in a busy summer welcome the season with its nights of gladness.
>
> They find the winter gaiety so complete a change that, in pursuing the pleasure that it offers, they derive both mental and physical rest from it.

Second, 'The Work of Social Service. Winter will Mean more Calls for Help':

> Appeals for help for the Blackpool Social Service Council are daily growing in number – a sign that the season is drawing to a close and that winter will soon be upon us.
>
> For many people, the end of the Autumn Illuminations will mean a return to hardship, and for these it will be a constant struggle throughout the winter months to make ends meet.

Within a few days, the town of Progress and Prosperity becomes a Depressed Area. The position is well, if over emphatically, put by F. G. Poulton, writing to the *Spectator*, following an article on Blackpool by an observer:

> What is Blackpool like in the 'Off-season', the winter season in the months after the 'lights are out', till Easter comes again? A perusal of the local press will reveal the fact that there are more charitable societies than in any inland town. The live register of the Labour Exchange shows some 10,000 unemployed during the winter months, with the addition of several thousands of poor-law relief and unemployed assistance, many of them being boarding-house keepers. At Stanley Park and the Aerodrome, many hundreds are doing task work either for a few shillings poor-law relief for sixteen or twenty-four hours or, in some cases, even for 'food vouchers'. One church not far from where I live gives fifty-four gallons of skimmed milk away daily, besides stale bread, to the unfortunate people who are now out of work, now the season is over. The social service council and the Ladies Sick and Poor also give milk, eggs, and food parcels to the needy, and so also does the ex-service men's society and many other agencies.

At the Employment Exchange, in an old school one minute from the prom, just south of the Central Pier, we see:

> Out in the alley, on the wall opposite the gate, . . . there is a board-window with the notices of the Blackpool branch of the NUWM [National Unemployed Workers' Movement]. It gives the bulletin of

the state of the 'Slave Camps', and gives the warning that, . . . if, while [workers] are there, they are injured, there is no redress. . . . [The bulletin] gives an instance of a man with his eye knocked out, another with neck broken, and the 'victim has no remedy'.

Also a bill with the cost of living, and on the board is a note, 'We are going to stop all outside labour re[garding] steel erection.' Chalked up on the wall nearer the road, in the same alley, . . . is a notice, 'The Wages of Sin is Death.' Then another larger [notice], 'Let us all join Sir Oswald Mosley's Blackshirts for Peace and Money.'

There is a special job in Blackpool, worth special mention:

[T]he unemployed of Blackpool can always be found when the tide has gone out at . . . different places along the sands. Men work in pairs, one with a spade, the other with a riddle. They wade into the water that has remained in the pools around the pipe outlets, and get as near to the wall as they possibly can. The spade is dug well into the sand and then placed into the sieve, and while the observer was watching a penny, a halfpenny, and a small pearl were the results of fifteen minutes' work. This is known as 'Klondyke'.

At the end of the season, when the firms who appealed for waitresses at Easter are 'standing them down' until the following Easter, information like this appears in the local newspapers:

The shareholders of the South Blackpool Jetty Company Ltd, which owns the Central Pier, were well pleased with the past year's working. . . . The reason was that the Company paid a record dividend of sixteen per cent less tax, which is one per cent more than has ever been paid in the history of the company.

(*Gazette*, 13 November 1937)

Meanwhile the winter unemployment figures goes up to its usual 10,000.

20

LIGHTS IN AUTUMN

[Reflecting both Blackpool's commercial orchestrations and Worktown's mentality is the following impression of that attempt to extend the magic of the summer holiday into the darkening days of autumn, the Illuminations.]

In Worktown the millworker's day is planned by the mill owner, and even in Blackpool, where he is on holiday, the landlady orders his time. But Blackpool gives him full opportunity to make a change, if only by lengthening his day. In Worktown the day's entertainment comes to an end at 10:30 when the pubs have closed and the cinemas are emptying, but at the same time in Blackpool there is still another ninety minutes to spare for pleasure. This is one of the things which the resort's caterers encourage.

In the same way, the Blackpool authorities make plans to extend the normal four-month season. Not content with lengthening the day's pleasure, they have found it possible to start the holiday season a few weeks before other resorts. In 1938 there are reduced rates for many activities for the early holiday-maker. Whether it will satisfy the hopes of its sponsors is still doubtful.

But there is no doubt that the autumn Illuminations succeed in extending the holiday season. In September and October Blackpool defies early darkness with a blaze of electric light for a month after the last industrial town has its second holiday. Yet this means of extending the summer season into autumn is not a new idea. It began in 1912. Since that time the original scheme has been elaborated continually to accord with Blackpool's ideas of progress. The few days at the end of September have grown to six weeks, and Blackpoolians are still demanding that the Illuminations should be longer. A letter to the local newspaper suggested this:

Sir . . . At Southport . . . they make the very best of the shopping centre with fairy lights, illuminated fountains, and floodlit buildings etc., thus drawing crowds of people for Christmas shopping and amusements.

May I suggest that a few Christmas tableaux be placed in prominent

positions during the month of December? It would not only feel brighter but would be profitable for transport and business, etc.
(Correspondence column, *Blackpool Gazette*, 3 December 1937)

In 1937, as early as August, 100 men were already erecting the 650 flagpoles necessary to carry the 27 miles of festoons and 300,000 bulbs which were to stretch in a zig-zag pattern down the 5 mile length of promenade covered by the scheme. In addition 66 pylons of modernist design were erected and lit up by concealed lamps, 42 promenade shelters were fitted with strip lighting in various colours, and 800 electric street lamps were masked with shades of coloured glass. This was the work of the Illuminations Department. Private enterprise joined in the scheme too, and large hotels, cafes, piers, and entertainment halls were lit with 700 floodlights. Searchlights in the turret of Olympia amusement centre and in the 'crow's nest' of the Tower were brought into operation; from Central Pier a battery of smaller searchlights swept the promenade and the sea. The addition of about fifty illuminated tableaux made the seafront a spectacle which the *News Chronicle* described as 'FIVE MILES OF LIQUID FIRE'. Darkness was defied at a cost of £18,000 for six weeks, which capital expenditure brought up to nearly £100,000.

But these costs seem unimportant when compared with the influx of visitors attracted by the Illuminations. On the third day of the 'lights', *Evening Gazette* headlines shouted:

500,000 VISITORS

ALL TRAFFIC RECORDS BROKEN

QUEUES EVERYWHERE

In the town there were queues 300 yards long waiting for trams on the promenade, the Pleasure Beach and Talbot Square. Each of the four elements in the Blackpool holiday background discussed earlier in this book finds a place in the Illuminations design – orientalism, magic, progress, and time.

ORIENTALISM AND MAGIC

'In the neighbourhood of Central Station a new type of pylon and illuminated features will be seen in 1938, and from this point to North Pier an avenue of coloured pylons, each surmounted with a floodlight Union Jack, will give an oriental effect' (*Gazette*, 1 February 1938). But orientalism is already evident. The ornamental roofs of the promenade shelters, outlined in coloured lamps and silhouetted against the sea beyond, are like small pagodas. The South Pier pavilion has more domes, some Moorish in appearance with voluptuous curves. During the Illuminations this building is

217

bathed in intense white floodlighting, startling and foreign looking even for Blackpool, as it rises apparently from the sea.

Blackpool propaganda presents the whole display as an accomplishment not of technical skill but of magic. In the *Gazette*'s 'Illuminations Supplement' of 1937, the phrase, 'Fairyland of Lights', is repeated three times. In fact, more than half of the tableaux on the cliffs at North Shore have fairy tales and nursery rhymes as their subject. These tableaux are composed of figures cut out in coloured wood which are set against a trellis frame and outlined with coloured lamps. Some parts of the figures are duplicated and are illuminated separately in quick rotation to give the appearance of movement.

The first tableau, a popular nursery rhyme, was introduced in 1930 and was a great success. In seven years the legendary subject has dominated this medium of display: and the North Shore scheme now includes such nursery rhymes as Hickory Dickory Dock, the Cat and the Fiddle, and Mary, Mary Quite Contrary. In the first tableau, the clock has a beaming face whose expression turns to one of squinting misery as the mouse runs up the side and enters the works, presumably tickling him. No less miraculous is the story of Cinderella which is presented in a series of four tableaux. The transformation of Cinderella from a kitchen-maid to a Princess, and the rats and pumpkin to a coach and horses, is the best trick of the evening. At South Shore the story of the Babes in the Wood is presented in the same way.

Not only the accepted legendary figures are used, however. A new one, with a topical significance, has been created. This is Fylde Ferdie. He is seen playing darts with which he manages to knock off an old gentleman's hat, tying a boot on the rod of a sleeping angler, putting his mongrel terrier through its tricks, and riding an old penny farthing bicycle with the dog following on a scooter. Fylde Ferdie, with his unusual behaviour, may represent the holiday spirit, but it is difficult to explain why he is in evening dress.

PROGRESS AND TIME

At South Shore a tableau presented 'Progress in Transport, 1864–1937', from the stagecoach to the modern streamlined car. Here seventy-three years of road traffic were presented in about as many feet. Further north, as if by a miracle, the four seasons of the year appear side by side, symbolising Blackpool's defiance of the late seasons.

In these tableaux, nature and the countryside appear for the first time on the Blackpool promenade. Unsuccessful attempts have been made in the past to grow flowers in the promenade gardens. But the Corporation can, at least, create gardens of electric light. Along the full length of the promenade, illuminated floral arches are erected with bluebirds in flight suspended over the road at intervals on a wire network. The long narrow garden on the promenade at Gynn Square is decorated with a coloured waterfall over which is perched a parrot. North of this at the cliffs are the seasons' tableaux where Blackpool's made-to-order countryside is seen at its best. For example, the spring tableau is framed at each end by a tree, on which sit on owl with blinking eyes and two birds feeding four fledglings in a nest. Under the tree are two mating rabbits with tails bobbing and ears flapping; a cupid fires arrows at a couple of country lovers who are framed in a heart in the centre of the set piece. In 'Holiday Dream' we found few wanted to go to the country and even fewer went. But some people criticised Blackpool because it has no natural background. It is this failing that the Corporation remedies in the Illuminations.

[THE AUTUMN FESTIVAL]

The Mayor, opening the Illuminations, assumed that the 2,000,000 people who were expected during the following weeks were coming to look at the Illuminations. But were they? Observers first concentrated on the vantage points from which the lights could be seen. Two observers took samples of thirty-six remarks made by people at the top of the Tower (Table 37). At the highest point in Blackpool, where probably the best view of the Illuminations is to be found, only 11 per cent of the remarks recorded were about the lights. The same result was found on Central Pier:

> Observer remarked that he wondered why more people didn't come on to the pier to see the Illuminations, as . . . one got a much better impression than when on the promenade itself. Attendant said that at night very few people did come on to the pier and then only 'for a bit of hugging and kissing' . . . [P]eople come and ask isn't there any dancing and isn't there a cafe. They don't come to look at the lights, which is the only attraction we can offer them.

Observers' reports tend to prove that it is not the whole scheme which excites people's interest, but only those parts of it which they can understand. The Illuminations visitor dislikes abstract designs, but he likes the

Table 37 Tower talk

Subject of conversation	Number
Illuminations	4
View	5
Sea	1
People below	4
Jumping off Tower	5
Miscellaneous	17
Total	36

219

tableaux which present things familiar to him. An observer spent an evening recording remarks made by people watching the tableaux at North Shore, and two samples from this report will show that here the visitor finds something which he can recognise and appreciate. Take, for example, the Football Tableau celebrating Blackpool's rise to First Division: two forwards are standing in front of goal. One shoots, goalkeeper jumps for ball, misses and falls on his face. This is scene every Worktowner can appreciate:

> Woman: 'Ha, has First Division.'
> Woman: 'Oh, First Division Blackpool.'
> Man: 'Hoo hoo he missed it. Look where he's landed.' (laughs)
> Crowd on passing bus cheer as goal is scored.

It is clear that these tableaux are more appreciated than the view from the top of the Tower.

What happens on the Central Promenade where the Illuminations do not have the potential interest of familiar things? The percentage of conversations concerning the Illuminations during three evenings on the Central Promenade were only 4 per cent, 26 per cent, and 8 per cent, while they reached 84 per cent on the cliffs where the tableaux represented familiar themes. In one case, the most popular subject of conversation among the crowds between Central Pier and North Pier was their acquaintances, which constituted 13 per cent of 160 remarks analysed. Next in popularity was discussion of where to go next (12 per cent); third place went to the Illuminations (4 per cent). In one report, Illuminations visitors preferred to look at two boys on roller skates than the electric serpent that continually climbs up the side of the Tower.

People enjoy donkey riding or just walking on the sands in the glow from the Illuminations. Attracted by the coloured flare of searchlights on the waves and the antics of people riding donkeys in semi-darkness, many people leaned against the promenade railings, just as they did during the summer. They turned their backs to the Illuminations.

A large part of the thousands of people in Blackpool each evening during the Illuminations came for a good time. Observers' reports indicate plenty of high spirits, and some bad language and drunkenness. Conversations on street on the last evening of the Illuminations:

Girl: 'I've had four drinks and I'm not goin' to 'ave no more.'

Woman (40): 'These lights don't make your face look very nice. I prefer those old-fashioned flares.'

A middle-aged woman to her husband as she sees some drunk women coming along: 'Ee, they've had 'nough to drink!'

Man talking to two elderly women: 'She'll have to change 'er name alright, or 'e'll have to change his. Anyway they've got to get married and that's the only way you can do it if you're a Catholic.'

Only one postcard in our collection of 224 expresses the visitor's attitude to the Illuminations. This shows a young couple walking along the promenade. In the girl's right hand is a red, white, and blue firework which sends out coloured sprays of light. Both are grinning happily – but they are not looking at the Illuminations or the sea which are show in the background. They seem to be enjoying some private joke.

21

RELICS FROM HOLY BLACKPOOL

[Working] Blackpoolians recollect Blackpool's summer with feelings of anta-
gonism. There are good reasons why the opposite should be true of Worktowners. Blackpool has meant to them a break away from Worktown and its
scheme of morals. They are returning from a shrine of magic. They bring
back with them relics to remember it by. A present or souvenir brought
home from Blackpool is, at once, a proof to others that they have made the
pilgrimage and an aid to vivid memory of it.

SOMETHING TO REMEMBER US BY

To supply and exploit this need is the souvenir racket, one of some antiquity;
it came with the amusements and the tradesmen to Blackpool. A cheap and
simple way of obtaining a relic would be to wrap up a portion of the Blackpool soil and take it back home. Once we saw that happening, when a child
packed up a bag of sand, the typical Blackpool earth, and carried it to his
father to take home. But sand is neither sufficiently displayable nor identifi-
able to be very satisfactory. The manufactured souvenir is called for, and it
must be made convincing by a Blackpool symbol. The Tower, which
proclaims 'This is Blackpool' in every photograph, is the prevailing token.
Crude china replicas of the Tower buildings are sold at Woolworth's. On
bags, penknives, brooches, rubber balls, handkerchiefs, and even suspenders, the Tower symbol occurs. As a woman said to an observer regarding the suspenders, 'It makes a nice present, doesn't it, though.' The Tower
stamp, said the proprietor of this shop, makes a difference 'definitely' even of
objects of no apparent utility.

Other symbols, endowed with lesser power, can be detected in a brief
catalogue of some of the things that lie on Woolworth's souvenir counter
(September 1937). 'Artistic Figures – 6d. each' of china include donkeys,
Eskimos, different sorts of crockery ornamented either with Dutch men or
women in costumes, or pearly gypsies. The Dutch people are on the sewage
windmill and at Feldman's Theatre; the gypsies are ancestors of the palmists
and the Telepathic Robot; the donkeys are on the sands, never dying; the

Eskimos arrived at Olympia in 1938 and were hailed on the South Pier as 'God's frozen people' in 1937. Then comes a man in costume riding a hobby horse. The hobby horses recall the old travelling fair. Sea references follow: a seagull, and, with a hint of the Grotto, a white rabbit on skis. Among these souvenirs there is nothing representing machines or modern costume. All these are labelled FROM BLACKPOOL, thus providing verbal as well as pictorial proof of authenticity.

Souvenirs acquire visible kinship with Blackpool [and carry away some of its magic. But souvenirs also offer a way of bringing the personal into the mystique of the pleasure shrine. For example, souvenir counters offer gift hints for those left behind.] Leather goods like purses are often marked with a tag: FOR DAD, FOR SONNY. A large cup, on sale in another big store, is tagged FOR MY OLD MAN, and the caption raised a big laugh in a group of women under observation. [More to the point] is the stall in Woolworth's which advertises: 'Have your name or motto written in gold.' This operation is carried out on your cigarette-case, purse, or compact-case. Similar is the Name-Plate Machine to be found in most amusement arcades. On this machine the letters of the alphabet are arranged in a circle clockwise, with a pointer in the middle like a clock finger. You put a penny in the machine, and then move the pointer round the dial to the letters of the alphabet that spell your name. A small metal plaque, two inches long, one inch broad, drops out, with your name roughly hammered in. At this point the utility value of the souvenir practically vanishes. There is no use to which these crude strips of metal can be put. The point is in seeing your own name, and has analogies with the mirror amusements in which you see yourself, and the dark tunnels in which you are left alone with yourself.

There is another class of object which is neither useful nor decorative, but is generally sold as a souvenir. In its milder form it is a joke, like the thing described in this observer note:

> In chemist's shop on south front. Small cup with two handles, mounted on a black wooden base, bearing inscription BEERSHIFTERS CHAMPIONSHIP CUP. On card behind it is . . . 'Present one to your friends.'

Other cups of the same sort include one 'For Story-Telling,' another 'For Valour at Darts'. On Woolworth's counter, the same crack, with its basis in pub behaviour, appears not on cups but medals.

From jokes of this sort we go on to 'Jokes, Tricks, Wigs, Novelties and Puzzles', as the first page of a catalogue describes them. Part of the Blackpool insult theme, they are sold in all the crowded areas from Central Beach to the piers. Usually these trick gadgets are based on the everyday acts of Work-towners, lighting a cigarette, handling a knife and fork, and shaking hands. Look at no. 1 in the catalogue, for instance:

PLATELIFTER. We place this first on the list of Table Jokes knowing it to be one of the finest jokes, in any category, ever in existence. You may know of it, but have you tried it? The effect is that, during a meal, someone's plate moves up and down, it wobbles from side to side, it heaves at them while they are actually cutting the food on the plate. The plate will tilt slowly, very slowly, then suddenly fall back with a flop. The whole gadget (a long rubber tubing) is completely hidden from view, being under the tablecloth. 6d.

Trick shop men name various items as the most popular of their sales. One said that his was the matchbox. Several tricks come into the matchbox category. One box of matches is apparently full, then becomes empty as soon as you touch one of the matches. Another ejects a shower of sparks. Another sends the matches shooting out at you in one string. There is a fourth, described as 'a boon to every housewife', where the safety matches will not let light in any circumstances. They 'never light, but they last for ever.' A different stall holder said that his best line was the whoopee cushion. You sit on it and the air goes out with a suggestively rude noise. Clergymen, he said, buy this. Another trick said to be popular with clergymen is the joke jam pot from which a green snake jumps. Another joke, seen in most shops and linking up with Blackpool sewage problems, is the brown lump of papier mâché, remarkably realistic.

The photograph is a major twentieth-century form of souvenir. Two of our Worktown correspondents, discussed in the 'Holiday Dream', wished for a holiday with cameras. One writes:

My idea of spending September holidays is to visit some of the old historical castles and Abbey ruins. Taking with me a camera, as they always look so grand as a photograph.

In Blackpool, however, observers' impressions are that Worktowners with cameras are comparatively rare. In a survey of what holiday-makers carry when they came out of Worktown station, only 1 of 201 articles was a camera (3 July 1937). If few Worktowners have cameras, Blackpool amusement centres are full of ways of getting your photograph taken. First, there is the photographic booth. The Blackpool photographic booth is equipped with backsets and build-ups to frame you in almost any comic postcard or romantic scene [see 'Intersex and the Moral Law'.]. You may be photographed as an actor in one of these dramas. In the Pleasure Beach one can be photographed as a Cossack or even Adam and Eve in evening dress.

But before you reach any photographer's booth, you will have been snapped several times as you walked. With their large tripods and cameras stationed in crowded parts of the streets are the Walkie Snap men or the Kine-Snap men, who train their camera on passers-by and then step forward and hand their subject a card which invites them to see their photograph at, for example, the 'Joytown Kiosk in five hours, without obligation to Purchase. True to Life 'Action' Snaps that will always bring back happy memories of your holiday.' There are other amusement places where photographs are thrown in with something else. On Central Beach, for example, a weighing machine presents you with your photograph as well as your weight. The marksmanship game at the Pleasure Beach presents you with your photograph if you are crack shot enough to hit the bulls-eye. The photograph business is booming in Blackpool, and one of the reasons why it thrives is that Worktowners have not got, or don't bring, many cameras.

[The souvenir also has a religious aura.] While up-to-date chromium crucifixes for the mantel are sold, a religious token more in harmony with other features of Blackpool is the lucky mascot, the little brown Buddha, Tiki. At Easter 1938 it came to Blackpool with a shop-window display in the centre of the town. Tiki is a brown, roughly shaped and hideous-featured image of the grinning Buddha, less than an inch long, with a white printed card attached: 'THE BUDDHA THAT BRINGS YOU LUCK 1/-'. The Tiki shop is plastered with photographs and testimonials. Pictures of celebrities, especially the ones who have some connection with Blackpool, are all over the window. Included are Sandy Powell, Hal Swain, Billy Merson, Will Hay, Albert Sandler, Max Miller, Will Fyfe, George Formby, Kitty Masters, Jack Hylton, Gracie Fields (one in each window), Les Allen, Sid Mandall and band, Roy Fox and Princess Pearl, and Bertini. One letter reads:

> Dear Sir, All my band have got one of your mascots and we find they have a tremendous influence on us. You can use this letter any time or display where you please.
> Yours etc.
for the band
Hal Swain.

Interspersed among these are photographs from the East, one of an elephant and one of a huge Burmese temple with a cross-legged Buddha dominating the view. On Easter Sunday, of 44 people who looked at the window in ten minutes, 31 were women and 13 men. One conversation overheard was

> Woman (35): 'I think I'll buy one.'
> Husband (30): 'It's a waste of money and it's nothing but a fraud.'

Inside the shop:

> Observer walked in shop and was served by a girl about 19. [She] sat inside a kiosk . . . reading *Woman* and a 2d weekly book. She said, 'Follow carefully all the instructions but above all don't show it to anyone.'

So that for 1/-you can buy here a souvenir that will take Blackpool's magical virtues back to Worktown with you, and the face of Gracie Fields in both windows stands guarantee for its efficacy.

THE LAST SIP OF BLACKPOOL

[Gathering souvenirs eases the transition back to Worktown. But, finally, the holiday week ends.] Friday, the slack night in amusement places, means preparations for departure. Next day sees the trek to the station. Massed around both Blackpool stations are public houses. They are there to catch people on their way into the station, and they succeed. A study of thirty groups leaving the sands showed that twenty-seven of them called in a pub between the Central Pier and the New Inn. These were mostly day-trippers, but the habit is not peculiar to them. The pub is the last bit of Blackpool holiday-makers make contact with. The account that follows could be duplicated any Saturday evening in the season:

> Group of three women, four children followed from Central Pier to New Inn . . . [meet with fathers inside.] Discussion . . . on crowds going and chances of getting seat without struggling. Women . . . decide that it is alright coming but they always wish they were back when evening arrives, 'don't like the train journey home, too tiring'. All watch clock and at intervals comment on shortness of time – 'It will soon be over now' was said four times by different individuals in the six. (15 April 1938)

As the pleasure-seekers go towards the station, there is haste, confusion, and anxiety about getting away. The time of departure of a train becomes the central interest in the rush to secure seats. The only other major interest is in the lavatory. It is the calling place for most people between the entrance to the station and their platform. In five surveys only one middle-aged couple, wealthy enough to have booked a reserved compartment, was indifferent to time, and the man's visit to the lavatory demonstrated his independence:

> For five minutes before the train leaves, no one arrives. . . . Just as it is about to start, a middle-aged couple appears at the entrance to the station walking quite slowly. Everyone shouts 'Hurry up, Come on, Get through', but the man goes quietly into the gentleman's lavatory. The woman waits by the barrier and is somewhat embarrassed. Finally a porter with a broom is sent into the lavatory to fetch the man, and when he reappears some of the people round the barrier clap; others laugh. They walk very slowly through and he can't find the tickets. They are shown into the reserved compartment and, as the train draws out, the collector hangs on to the window for some way till [the man] has found his ticket. (8 September 1937)

226

Compare this with the bustle in a large, more typical, family on the same day:

> The Worktown train left at 9:30 from the excursion platform. At five to nine already everyone was hurrying down the road as if it were going the very next minute. Observer followed one large and particularly flustered party of five fat women and at least six small children. They kept dividing up, stopping for things, getting lost, shouting, and, in spite of their haste, only moved at a speed of about one mile an hour.

Nearly everybody is afraid of being left behind in Blackpool. [This anxiety is the pervading mood. There is no singing or loud talking in the waiting crowd. According to one observer,] 'The main contrast between arrivers and departers appears to be that arrivers make loud noises, departers don't.'

Several women overheard on the departure platform weren't feeling good about the prospects of travelling back in the same carriage as men who had come from a long stay in the pub: 'Most departing males are drunk, have bags of rock and pockets full of beer bottles. Some sleep on steps or seats in station nursing bottles.' Drink will out, and if it doesn't come out in drunkenness, it does so in another way. A Worktown observer, an ex-policeman over 40, travelling back to Worktown after a long visit to a Blackpool pub, had this common experience:

> The conversation was mostly about the good time they had and the good it had done them. . . . Observer was bursting to pee and would have done it through the window, but for the fact of putting fear into the children, so that I had to bend my body. . . . and gradually relieve myself into my trousers and hope for the best. . . . By the time I arrived at Worktown, 12:40 a.m., I was wet through and nearly double. I made my way to the urinal to have silent meditation for ten minutes. Several men were grumbling about the train taking the time it did and remarks were passed about laws that ought to be made to compel the Railway Comp. to have urinals on trains travelling over a certain distance. After a great relief, I made my way to the barrier, at the same time searching for my ticket and, to my surprise, found it in my trousers pocket wet through and in a little ball, only two numbers being discernible. I handed it to the collector and told him that I was sorry but I had to piss in my pants and he had quite a laugh about it much to my discomfort owing to wet pants. . . .

And so Worktowners get back to Worktown, with some discomfort and one soaked ticket, and among those leaving the station between nine and ten one evening:

83 heavy cases
48 light cases

39 paper shopping bags
10 rucksacks, and canvas bags
9 fish rods, baskets
6 bunches of flowers
2 dogs
2 golf bags
1 china bowl
1 camera

and the accumulated effects of the fifty-second week in Holy Blackpool.

AFTERWORD:
MASS-OBSERVATION'S
BLACKPOOL AND SOME
ALTERNATIVES

John K. Walton

The leading lights of Mass-Observation understandably found Blackpool irresistible. Its sheer scale, its cultural novelty, and above all the illustrations it seemed to provide of the juxtaposition and interpenetration of the 'modern' and the 'primitive' in working-class culture, were well calculated to attract and retain the interest of Tom Harrisson and his acolytes. But their assemblage of vivid evidence, valuable and compelling though it is, views Blackpool as if through one of the distorting mirrors in which so many of the sideshows specialise. Mass-Observation's Blackpool needs to be set in context.

Blackpool had ample time to establish the identity which Mass-Observation found so seductive. It was the world's first specialised working-class seaside resort, and its economy had been shifting inexorably in that direction since at least the 1870s.[1] By the late 1930s, at Easter and Whitsuntide, throughout July and August and even on into October, its central stretch of shoreline had long been a seething mass of cheerful and unpretentious humanity. Its publicists claimed 7,000,000 visitors a year in the 1930s, far in excess of any other British resort.[2] Even according to the 1931 Census (a source which always understates the numbers employed in the holiday trades), Blackpool contained nearly 4,000 lodging-and boarding-house keepers, and over 1000 'persons professionally engaged in entertainment and sport'.[3] These were the off-season figures generated in a spring census, and at the same time over 15 per cent of the town's population was said to be living in 'hotels, boarding houses, lodging houses, etc.'[4] At the August Bank Holiday week end of 1937 Blackpool played host to 425 special trains, and one forecast suggested a likely influx of 31,800 motor cars, 5,300 motor coaches, and 6,360 motorcycles.[5] Not surprisingly, the local newspaper claimed a record, and although it notoriously did this with such regularity as to take some of the gloss from the achievement, it was nevertheless entirely plausible.

The unique scale of this activity was quite enough, in itself, to arrest the attention of aspiring social investigators. And, of course, the Mass-Observation team was enticed to Blackpool anyway by the discovery that most of the population of 'Worktown' (or so it seemed) fled thither during the local holidays to celebrate the magic 'fifty-second week' of escape from the regular workaday grind. Once drawn to Blackpool, the Mass-Observers took root there for the summer, and maintained a presence of some sort for more than a year; they did not leave *en masse* when the Bolton holiday-makers did. What kept them was not just the sheer enormity of the place: it was the richness and strangeness (to the outsider) of the holiday culture which flourished there. They were overwhelmed not only by the vitality of the great late Victorian pleasure palaces, the Tower and Winter Gardens, or the sophisticated amusement technology of the Pleasure Beach. These had counterparts of a sort elsewhere. So did the promenades and piers, and even the municipal bathing pool, although Blackpool made its brash claims of superior size and excellence in these spheres as well. It was the exuberance, the released energy of a pent-up labour force, the atmosphere of carnival and the bizarre artefacts and practices which flourished in this conducive climate that fascinated the observers. They were drawn especially to the sideshows and stalls, the pubs and crowded promenade, in their efforts to record the behaviour of people whose actions and motives seemed every bit as problematic – and, it was tempting to suggest, primitive – as those of Polynesians.[6]

As with the rest of Mass-Observation's work, their Blackpool material oscillated between the revealing, the suggestive, the best kind of 'thick description', and the banal. But enough enthusiasm was harnessed and disciplined to offer really valuable insights into the holiday culture, and at points the wider life experience of the working classes of Northern and Midland England. But Mass-Observation's view of Blackpool is only part of the story and it is highly coloured by the leading observers' own predilections.

In the first place, Mass-Observation Blackpool is a snapshot sequence, taken during two seasons, at a time when Blackpool and its holiday industry were at a transitional stage in their development. So it would be dangerous to present Mass-Observation's Blackpool as representative of 'traditional' or even inter-war holiday-making even if we accept that it offers a plausible picture of the Blackpool of 1937–8. Second, it should be stressed that Mass-Observation reveals largely one face of Blackpool: that of the working-class holiday-maker in the central area at the height of the summer season. We hear a lot less (despite the efforts of some of the more plebeian members of the team) about the *local* working class, their problems and privations; we hear very little from the point of view of landladies or trades people, apart from a few interviews with heroic plebeian entrepreneurs like Luke Gannon or James Pablo; and we hear even less about Blackpool's civic governors, or of its growing residential population of commuters and the retired. Except for those staying at the Norbreck Hydro and private hotels, the observers tell us little about the better-off visitors who were very much in evidence at either end of the promenade, and especially at North Shore. Finally, Mass-Observation's images of Blackpool need to be juxtaposed with other powerful images which were put out at the time by the Corporation, the press, contemporary novelists, and social observers of a more conventional kind. We should be aware that there are alternative versions of Blackpool and that Mass-Observation had its own preconceptions and ground its own axes.[7] In developing these three themes, which should put the Mass-Observation study in perspective, I begin with the place of the summers of 1937–8 in the longer-term development of Blackpool.

I

The Blackpool of the late 1930s was undergoing rapid change in several respects. The visitor catchment area was widening and their spending power was increasing. A building boom was bringing new residents and the resort's social structure was changing in significant ways. Within the holiday district, palatial new buildings in the distinctive streamlined style of the time were proliferating, and grandiose plans for redevelopment were being mooted. New kinds of traffic problems were developing, and some feared that new threats to social order were emerging among a rising generation of holiday-makers. Changes were taking place in the accommodation and entertainment industries. So Mass-Observation depicted Blackpool at perhaps an especially dynamic point in its history.

Blackpool had long been extending its visitor catchment area. Already in the 1880s it was spreading its tentacles beyond its original heartland of cotton Lancashire and the West Riding of Yorkshire, and beginning to attract visitors from Birmingham and the Black Country. But efforts to extend the range beyond the English Midlands to the London area, the South-West, the North-East, and Glasgow bore limited fruit before the First World War.[8] But by the late 1930s not only had the prospering West Midlands around Birmingham and Coventry become very important indeed to Blackpool's economy, as the lists of excursion train arrivals made abundantly clear, but the accents of London, Northampton, Glasgow, and even Plymouth were in evidence on the promenade. A municipal attractions and publicity budget which ran at well over £40,000 per year in the late 1930s, and which concentrated particularly on developing the 'Blackpool habit' in new areas, was now really making an impact.[9] The Lancashire Wakes and the Yorkshire Tides and Feasts were still indispensable to the resort's economy, but Blackpool was far more than just Bolton or Oldham by sea. This geographical diversity was not stressed by the Mass-Observers. But it was of growing importance.

The Blackpool building boom drew forth much self-congratulatory local comment during 1937. At the end of August it was reported that the town's housing stock had more than trebled since 1906, and more than doubled since 1921. A further 1,391 houses had been added in the past year.[10] There was an enormous backlog of unmade streets, but a columnist could also expatiate on the 'romance of bricks and mortar that is being woven round us, obliterating all the traces of our youth', to accommodate 4,000 new residents a year in 'modern and pleasant' houses.[11] These were houses for private residents rather than seaside landladies, and the growth of the commuter traffic to Lancashire's inland towns was stretching the railway facilities to breaking point.[12] Some of the new households were not above taking in a few visitors at the height of the season, to the annoyance of their heavily rated rivals in the town centre, but incipient tensions of a more direct kind between holiday and residential interests were also beginning to surface. Thus in mid-August the local newspaper denounced a sequence of complaints that the interests of rowdy working-class visitors were being elevated above those of residents and ratepayers. Without Blackpool's 7,000,000 visitors, came the magisterial warning, 'we should all be in a sorry plight'.[13]

The new residential building was taking place on Blackpool's periphery, away from the older centres of the holiday industry, but change was also in the air around the stations and between the piers. New landmarks included a six-storey Woolworth's and a four-storey Lockhart's cafe, a new Ice Palace on the Pleasure Beach and sun lounge on the North Pier, and the Lion Hotel at South Shore. Plans were afoot to set back Central Station for a quarter of a mile with new boulevards, a major replanning scheme, and the demolition of a lot of the old property in which Mass-Observation's favourite activities were concentrated. A major drainage improvement scheme was getting under way, threatening to transform another aspect of Blackpool which fascinated the more scatological of the Mass-Observers. The town was visibly changing in important ways which the Mass-Observation material hardly mentions.[14] Only the re-development scheme, and its potential for further increasing the already considerable power of the Corporation, receive the attention of the observers.

Most people still went to Blackpool by train; but the importance of road transport was increasing rapidly, and this was posing problems in the town. Not only were congestion and parking generating nuisance and controversy, and much discussed in the local press: the growing popularity of the charabanc trip was thought by some to be promoting disorder. The police were complaining of 'bottle parties by road', with day-trippers taking crates of beer on the coach and charabancs disgorging passengers who were already drunk on arrival at Blackpool. As one of the extracts graphically illustrates, such behaviour was less practicable on the non-corridor trains which still predominated. This conviviality on the journey was particulary prevalent during the autumn Illuminations season, whose astonishing success set

AFTERWORD

Blackpool apart from other resorts with shorter seasons. It seems to have
been more of a saturnalia than the summer Wakes season (as suggested in the
chapter, 'Lights in autumn'), and the Corporation lavished a great deal of
ingenuity and expense upon the decorations.[15]

The Illuminations were not new: indeed, they had originated in 1912. But
the later 1930s saw an impressive growth in their scale and sophistication.
And the entertainment industry more generally was changing in step: more
mechanisation, more national and international (or at least American)
influences, less local idiosyncrasy and regional distinctiveness. This is easier
to assert than to prove, but it does chime in with J.B. Priestley's comments in
English Journey:

> [Blackpool] lacks something of its old genuine gaiety. Its amusements
> are becoming too mechanised and Americanised. Talkies have
> replaced the old roaring variety turns. Gangs of carefully drilled young
> men and women (with nasal accents), employed by the music
> publishers to plug their 'Hot Broadway Hits', have largely replaced the
> pierrots and nigger minstrels. The entertainers are more calculating,
> their shows more standardised, and the audiences more passive. It has
> developed a pitiful sophistication – machine-made and not really
> English – that is worse than the old hearty vulgarity.

This could be dismissed as ill-informed nostalgia and empty rhetoric, and
Mass-Observation provides a useful corrective in its eager celebration of the
oddities of stall holders and bawdy comedians and its *emphasis* on the
persistence of the heartiest of vulgarity. Even so, it is likely that the trends
Priestley identifies were working their way through in the Blackpool of the
1930s: they had just not advanced so far as he supposed.[16]

The accommodation business was certainly changing sharply, however,
and contemporaries were well aware of this. Small establishments remained
the norm, despite the continuing development of impressive-looking (but
often financially shaky) new private hotels at either end of the promenade. In
1931 only 868 of Blackpool's 23,904 houses had more than 8 rooms.[17] But the
old apartments system, whereby visitors bought their own food and the
landlady cooked it, imposing small charges for cooking, 'attendance', and
use of cruet, was in sharp decline. Ever-growing numbers of visitors opted
for full board, which was more expensive but saved time and trouble. As
such, its popularity reflected the rising living standards enjoyed by those in
work in the late 1930s, a time of rising wages, falling unemployment, and the
extension of the availability of holidays with pay.[18] The Hotel and Apartments Association tried to expedite the transition by imposing full board on
its members' visitors at the height of the season, pointing out that its adop-
tion would make the difference between £1 and £3 profit per week on each
couple. The Association's spokesman also pointed out that more and more
landladies were now keeping proper books, a practice which had been a

233

great rarity until recently. More generally, the local newspaper suggested that, 'the old-fashioned landlady is dying out. They are not the motherly persons of the old company-house. They are alert business women, up-to-date and efficient in their methods. Times have changed indeed.'[19] This was pushing it a bit, and a more casual approach survived in some of the back streets as well as in some of the small unofficial cut-price establishments on the outskirts, which Mass-Observation referred to as 'Kippaxes'. But again this argument merely exaggerates the speed and impact of a genuine and accelerating transition.

These changes in Blackpool are important, and for all its attempts to provide a historical perspective on Blackpool, Mass-Observation tells only part of the story. It also largely ignored the many facets of Blackpool which lay beyond the experience of the Worktowners.

II

The Mass-Observers were, of course, aware that Blackpool had severe problems of seasonal unemployment and deprivation. They made an attempt to collect details of wages and exploitation, and to signpost the extent of winter poverty. But this was not a major emphasis, and the wage figures are only for holiday trade occupations. Workers in the building trades, which were so important to the town, or in transport remain invisible. For a fuller picture of working-class life in Blackpool itself, we need to go to a different kind of source: oral history or personal reminiscence, for example. An indication of the possibilities comes from Harold Palmer's auto-biography, which tells us a great deal about the problems and possibilities of life in Blackpool. Mr Palmer arrived in Blackpool from the Potteries in 1930, at the age of 13, when his father's health broke down and he lost his job as an insurance agent. From the standpoint of a holiday-maker, Blackpool looked like Eldorado and place of refuge; and it sucked this family, like so many others, into the maw of its off-season poverty. The Palmers spent a wretched winter with neither heating nor furniture, and practically lived on pilchards and tinned fruit. For a long time their family economy was sustained by mother's laundry work and children's hawking of toffee from door to door or (illicitly) on the beach. The Chief Constable's charity supplied children's clothing of a humiliatingly conspicuous kind. Eventually, as the children moved into regular employment and father was rehabilitated as a commercial traveller, the Palmers went up in the world again, and managed to move ever closer to the town centre and the opportunity to make useful money from the visitor trade. Harold himself gained further insights into the exploited labour of Blackpool's underworld through the experiences of the orphaned teenager who came to work as a maid-of-all-work for his mother, and whom he eventually married. This kind of material is a necessary supplement to Mass-Observation's cursory glances from outside the culture.[20]

At the other end of the scale, Mass-Observation only briefly notes Blackpool high society and the civic elite. The study mentions in passing the sort of people who participated in the social round of parties and amateur dramatics which followed the end of the Illuminations, and by February might have taken refuge 'at the winter sports, or on the Riviera'.[21] Invisible are the kind of visitors who were photographed in fancy dress at the 'gay New Year's Eve balls' at the big hotels, or paid fancy prices at the Imperial in August: all we get is a little prurient speculation about their sex lives. The importance of the Corporation is recognised, and some hints are given about the social composition and business interests of its members; but the observers ignore the revealing ambiguities of popular attitudes to the municipality, whose towering importance as employer, property-owner, publicist, image maker, and custodian of morality was at least ironical in a town so dedicated to the free market principles of ruthless competitive individualism.[22] The tone of public comment – in editorials, at public meetings and in letters to the press – suggests intense pride in the general influence and past endeavours of the Corporation, along with fierce criticism of councillors and officials on specific issues. The characteristic tone of self-congratulation, which fused the Corporation with 'the town' personified as a whole, is caught by rhetoric like this: 'The courage and enterprise of the past ten or fifteen years have enabled Blackpool to withstand much of the depression which has assailed Lancashire and the North.'[23] But the image of the Corporation – and the realities of who held power and how they used it – would repay extended study beyond the impressions offered by the Mass-Observers.

This seductive material from Mass-Observation might lead the reader to believe that it captures the quintessential Blackpool. Of course I am not suggesting that the Mass-Observers should have undertaken a full historical or sociological study of all aspects of Blackpool life. After all, they intended to study only *Worktowners* at Blackpool. But the picture is incomplete, and its entertaining asides and historical vignettes on unresearched themes are sometimes misleading. There are other images of Blackpool, which may not be as attractive but, it might be argued, have validities of their own.

III

Mass-Observation's was not the only way of seeing the Blackpool holiday crowds. Here is another version, from the *Blackpool Gazette and Herald*, whose correspondent went to look at the early arrivals on the August Bank Holiday Monday, 1937:

Those pale-faced people who strolled along the promenade at 3:30 on Bank Holiday morning had travelled long distances for the wholesome joy of getting here, of taking deep draughts of the air of the open sea, of being part of the crowd, of mixing with their fellows. . . . Oh the pleasure, the keen delight, the ecstasy reflected on the beaming faces of those mothers and fathers, many carrying parcels of food; on the faces of chattering little lads and lasses with their buckets and spades; on the faces of the young lovers; of the silver-haired, the aged and infirm, the cripples even, who had journeyed through the stuffy night to be with us on Bank Holiday.

Some told me they had entrained soon after 11 the night before, and would be returning at 1:40 a.m. Some wore mackintoshes, some were stripped to the waist. They were all people we could not help but like. They were people of the order who have made us what we are. They have raised our resort into the unchallenged Playground of the People.[24]

This is sentimental, arch, and superficial where Mass-Observation is knowing, acute, and prurient. It is difficult to recognise this as the same holiday crowd as Mass-Observation, with its bias to the other end of the day, depicts in full pleasure-seeking spate. It is, in some sense, an official view: Blackpool as, in some contexts, it might like to see and present itself. It chimes in, for example, with the complacency with which Blackpool's annual drunkenness statistics were regularly received. In 1937, 188 convictions were reported for the previous year, and the Chief Constable was full of praise for the way in which the pubs were managed, while the conduct of the patrons was 'satisfactory throughout the year'.[25] This might be hard to believe from Mass-Observation's portrayals of the inner life of pubs, and at very least, a generous definition of drunkenness was clearly operating. But Mass-Observation, too, celebrates at times an ultimate innocence and harmlessness in the behaviour of those whose excesses it chronicles; and a balanced view might take on board the admittedly self-congratulatory offerings of press and civic orthodoxy, weighing them alongside Mass-Observation rather than rejecting them out of hand.

This point of view is reinforced by the way in which the press itself sometimes offers seemingly deadpan chronicles of events so surreal that they slot into aspects of the Mass-Observation canon with disturbing ease. Thus the report on the Bishop of Burnley's presence at the 'annual service for employees and concessionaires' at the Pleasure Beach:

On his right he saw a company of coffee-coloured Indians, romantic figures in their gaudy, picturesque robes of the Orient. Sitting close to them was a Member of Parliament, and behind him the white uniformed Beach attendants. Flanking the centre gangway was a swarthy 'devil dancer', magician, fire-eater, and an Indian who twice a day 'defies death on wheels'. The remainder of the seats were occupied by men in overalls, women in fashionable dress, and a native girl who has danced before most of the European princes.[26]

Here in the *Gazette and Herald* is official Blackpool celebrating its exoticism and its ability to bring together classes and races in an ultimately safe and controlled setting. 1,000 people attended this service, and the symbolic significance of this collective act of submission to convention on the part of Blackpool's biggest fairground was reflected in the prominent place it occupied in the newspaper. The Pleasure Beach was proclaiming its integration into an idealised wider community of supposedly shared Christian values.

Here was a threat defused, and so were others. Just before Mass-Observation appeared on the Blackpool scene J. L. Hodson's novel, *Carnival at Blackport*, was published. There was no doubt that it was set in Blackpool, and the *Gazette and Herald* gave it an extended review, praising its documentary and imaginative qualities and its picaresque attributes. Hodson should indeed be read alongside Mass-Observation; it is compelling on the inner life of boarding houses, and gives an interesting perspective on the people of the Pleasure Beach (who all have hearts of gold, however) and the seedier aspects of Blackpool high life. The novel does tend to echo other sources in stressing the unpretentious friendliness, likeable eccentricity, and propensity to mutal aid of its main characters. But its main plot-line is darkly sexual, and one of the high points of the plot is a hasty, eager coupling in one of the enclosed cabins of the recently defunct Gigantic Wheel, about which there must have been many salacious legends in Blackpool. This episode gives added point to the tragic demise of two of the central characters at the end. Here is a permissive Blackpool which Mass-Observation failed to find, and which the *Gazette and Herald* review preferred not to discuss. Should we regard it as simply a convenient piece of dramatic and commercial invention by a popular novelist, or should we regard it as an additional angle of vision on inter-war Blackpool, with a possible validity of its own? This is far from being a straightforward issue, as is the question of how we should treat the Blackpool passages in Priestley's *English Journey*. And we can also recover a visual rendering of the Blackpool of the mid-1930s, for prints survive of the Gracie Fields film *Sing as We Go*, which chronicles the ups and downs of a mill girl turned seasonal worker in the holiday trades, and was shot on location in Blackpool. We should not ignore these sources, and we should particularly bear in mind the way in which Hodson's book was received in the local press, with a telling combination of praise and quiet censorship.[27]

Mass-Observation itself was treated with bland tolerance. Herbert Howarth, who was introduced as 'Christ Church, Oxford, and an old boy of Blackpool Grammar School', was given space in early August for a rather dull account of Mass-Observation's aims and a plea for recruits; and in September, Ralph Parker contributed a longer and more circumstantial piece. Tom Harrisson's *Spectator* article on Blackpool was described as 'A Writer's Tribute', and his phrase that Blackpool was 'one of the most moral of towns' was quoted in the headline.[28] Whatever the Town Hall and its publicity department may have thought of Mass-Observation's attempts to demythologise sex in Blackpool, the *Gazette and Herald* was quite happy to accept the praise which was offered, without going into too much detail about the surrounding descriptions. One of the Blackpools which Mass-Observation failed (or rather did not try) to penetrate was the sedate, Church-and-Chapel-going residential public which was numerous and influential enough to make an impact on the tone and agenda of the local press. From Mass-Observation (as from other outside commentators), this and other Blackpools took what suited them and discarded or ignored the rest.

But Mass-Observation had its own selectivities, and we should not privilege its discourse and agenda above all others. There were several Blackpools, and there are several overlapping ways of seeing the Blackpool that Mass-Observation made its own. This book, very usefully, makes available to a wide audience a wonderful array of material. But in this essay I have tried to point out that there are other perspectives. I invite readers to use Mass-Observation's evidence critically and to compare it with a range of sources.

NOTES

1 On this theme see J. K. Walton, *The Blackpool Landlady: A Social History*, Manchester, 1978, and 'The Social Development of Blackpool, 1788–1914,' Ph.D. thesis University of Lancaster, 1974.
2 W. Dougill, 'The British Coast and its Holiday Resorts', *Town Planning Review*, December 1935, p.265, footnote. No indication is given of how the figures are calculated, and it is difficult to believe that Rhyl or Redcar attracted (as claimed) anywhere near one-third of Blackpool's visitors. A pinch of salt is indicated.
3 *Census of England and Wales*, 1931: County Lancaster, occupational tables.
4 *Census*, 1931, as above, table 12.
5 *Blackpool Gazette and Herald* (hereafter *B.G.H.*), 31 July 1937.
6 See Gary Cross's introduction in this volume, and references cited there.
7 See above, note 5.
8 Walton, thesis, Chapters 5 and 7.
9 *B.G.H.*, 17 April 1937.
10 *B.G.H.*, 28 August 1937.
11 *B.G.H.*, 16 January, 13 February 1937.
12 *B.G.H.*, 27 February 1937.
13 *B.G.H.*, 14 August 1937.
14 *B.G.H.*, 2 January, 27 March, 29 May, 17 July, 31 July 1937.
15 *B.G.H.*, 13 February, 11 September 1937.
16 J. B. Priestley, *English Journey*, London, 1934, p.267. This version of inter-war

Blackpool runs counter to Tony Bennett, 'Hegemony, Ideology, Pleasure: Blackpool', in *Popular Culture and Social Relations*, T. Bennett, C. Mercer, and J. Woollacott, eds., Milton Keynes, 1986, which offers contemporary (and earlier) Blackpool as the expression of a distinctively regional, anti-metropolitan alternative popular culture. However tempting this argument might be, it is vitiated in practice by Bennett's cavalier disregard for what his sources are actually saying, and by the complete absence of any serious research of his own.

17 *Census*, 1931, as above, table 10.
18 S. G. Jones. *Workers at Play: A Social and Economic History of Leisure 1918-1939*, London, 1986, pp.20, 27-33; and his 'The Lancashire Cotton Industry and the Development of Paid Holidays in the 1930s', *Historic Society of Lancashire and Cheshire*, no.135 (1986), pp.99-115.
19 *B.G.H.*, 17 July, 26 June 1937. See also Walton, *Landlady*, pp.177-82.
20 H. Palmer, *Not a Sparrow Falls*, Preston, 1988, Chapters 15-20.
21 *B.G.H.*, 13 February 1937.
22 J. K. Walton, 'Municipal Government and the Holiday Industry in Blackpool, 1876-1914', in *Leisure in Britain, 1780-1939*, J. K. Walton and J. Walvin, eds., Manchester, 1983.
23 *B.G.H.*, 20 February 1937.
24 *B.G.H.*, 7 August 1937.
25 *B.G.H.*, 13 February 1937.
26 *B.G.H.*, 15 May 1937.
27 Review in *B.G.H.*, 5 June 1937.
28 *B.G.H.*, 7 August, 4 September 1937.

INDEX

grotto 103, 104, 108, 109
gypsies 117–20, 163; *see also* fortune-
tellers

Harrisson, Tom 1–6, 10, 11, 16, 62,
229, 238; *see also* Mass-Observation
hats 151, 161
Hay, Will 161, 162
health and healers 75–83, 140; *see also*
disease; Blackpool air and breezes
herbalists 78
hermaphrodites 198, 199, 201
Hilton, John 2, 8
Hodson, J. L. 237
holiday camps *see* Butlin's Holiday
Camp; Cunningham's Young Men's
Holiday Camp; Norbreck Hydro
Holiday Fellowship 9
holidays, annual: and families 39, 41;
in Lancashire 40–51, 57–60; with pay
8, 9; and savings 36–40, 42, 51, 233;
views of intellectuals 9, 10
Hood, Walter 6
hotels (private) 64, 66, 67–9, 187, 233;
see also boarding houses; kippax;
landladies
housing (in Worktown): housing estates
32, 33; street dwellings 24, 32, 33
Howarth, Herbert 6, 237

ice cream 70, 71
illegitimacy 184
illuminations: attitudes toward 219–21;
origins of 216, 232; tableau themes
217–19
India and Indians 23, 25, 78, 110, 111,
113, 115; *see also* orientalism;
sideshows
Isle-of-Man 48, 136

jokes: in music halls 116, 129–31, 168,
169; and sex 165, 166; as souvenirs
222–4
Jovial Poems 101

Kamiya, 100–1
Keynes, John Maynard 3
Kingsbury, George 80–1
kippax (family unlicensed lodgings) 64,
68, 69, 138
'Klondyke' 215

Laing, Stuart 5

Lancashire 7, 9, 19, 21, 25, 37, 99, 137,
230
landladies 56, 61, 63–6, 70, 186, 190,
210, 211, 233, 234; *see also* boarding
houses; hotels (private)
Lateau, Louise 197
laughter 107, 116
Lawrence, T. E. 110
Le Bon, Gustav 10, 114
Left Book Club 2
leisure (in Worktown): evening 27, 28;
working-class patterns 7–11; and
weekends 27–33; *see also* children at
leisure; women at leisure
Lent 34, 35; *see also* Easter; religion;
seasonal cycles
Lewis, C. S. 79
Love on the Dole 7
Luna Park 99, 100, 110
Lynd, Robert 4

Madge, Charles 1–4; *see also* Mass-
Observation
magic 112, 116, 217, 222, 225; *see also*
astrology; fortune-tellers; India and
Indians; occult
Malinowski, Bronislaw 4
markets 29; *see also* fairs
Marx Brothers 135
Mass-Observation: at Blackpool 6,
229–31, 235, 237–8; limits 10, 11;
methods 3–7, 10, 11, 142; origins
1–3, 10; *see also* Harrisson, Tom;
Madge, Charles
masturbation 197, 199
May Day 36
May the Twelfth 2
Middletown 6
money: and holiday saving 22, 30, 41,
42; and holiday spending 38, 124–7,
147–9, 151, 152, 158, 162, 190;
scarcity of 22, 20, 142; *see also* class
distinctions; workers; wages
Mosley, Oswald 215
Mumford, Lewis 99
Museum of Human Anatomy 87, 196–9
music halls 70, 128–34, 210, 211; *see
also* jokes; pierrots; songs

National Unemployed Workers'
Movement 214
nature, attitudes toward 34, 45, 46, 75,
89, 90, 219

'Social Mixer' 106
songs: in music halls 129, 132–4, 138,
    168, 210; sold as sheet music 170;
    sung on street and in pubs 159, 160,
    164, 169–70
souvenirs 222–6
Spanish Revolution 115, 200
sports 28, 30, 32, 33, 43, 44; see also
    pools, football; 'slot machines' and
    pinball games
spring 33, 34
Squire's Gate Camp 60, 136–8, 141,
    142, 180
Stiffey, Rector of 192, 199, 200
Story of Blackpool, The 76, 226
Stratosphere Girl 102, 172
Sunday School 32
superstitions 2, 5, 7; see also fortune-
    tellers; magic
Swaffer, Hannen 165
Swain, Hal 225

Taylor, Robert 31
television 122
time: consciousness of 20–2, 68; and
    Blackpool routine, 145, 149–51, 168;
    release from 161; see also seasonal
    cycles; routine; weekend
Tower 59, 60, 61, 72, 87, 89, 100, 102,
    103, 109, 135, 206, 222, 230
trains 58–61, 89, 161, 226, 227, 229
transportation see cars; buses; trains
transvestitism 200, 201
Trevelyan, Julian 6, 11
Tussaud's (Madame) Waxworks 109,
    115, 116, 196

venereal disease 197, 199; see also
    diseases; Museum of Anatomy

Walton, John 11
weekend 29–33
West, Mae 72, 165
Whittaker, James 8
Winter Garden 175, 177, 206, 207, 230
women: at amusement parks 105, 106;
    attitudes toward holidays 40, 42, 45,
    63; and beauty contests 138–9; with
    children 154–7; dancing with each
    other 175, 176; and fatigue 42, 45; at
    home 27; and leisure (Worktown) 28,
    29, 31, 43, 55, 59; magazines 23; and
    savings 37; and sports 43; at work
    20, 23, 27, 55, 211, 212; see also
    couples; landladies; family life; sex
Woolworth's 61, 223
Wordsworth, William 106–7
working class: attitudes toward work
    20, 23, 25; rest, amount of 30, 44,
    149; sociability 21, 22, 23, 26;
    unemployment 20, 22, 26, 214; union
    activities 20, 24, 213; wages 20,
    211–13; working conditions 20–2, 26,
    211–12, 234; see also class
    distinctions; family life; Lancashire;
    leisure; money; women; Worktown
Worktown: and cotton mills 19, 20,
    23–5, 55; and environment 7, 19, 20,
    32, 33; and leisure 27–33; and Mass-
    Observation 1, 3–7, 10, 11, 235; and
    seasons 33–6